Developing
Habits *of* Mind
in Elementary Schools

An ASCD Action Tool

an ASCD
Action*TOOL*

Developing Habits *of* Mind
in Elementary Schools

Karen Boyes
Graham Watts

ASCD

Alexandria, Virginia USA

1703 North Beauregard St. • Alexandria, VA 22311-1714 USAPhone: 1-800-933-2723 or 1-703-578-9600 • Fax: 1-703-575-5400Web site: www.ascd.org • E-mail: member@ascd.org

Author guidelines: www.ascd.org/write

Gene R. Carter, *Executive Director*; Nancy Modrak, *Publisher*; John L. Brown, *Content Development*; Mary Beth Nielsen, *Director, Editorial Services*; Judy Ochse, *Project Manager*; Gary Bloom, *Director, Design and Production Services*; Georgia Park, *Senior Graphic Designer*; Mike Kalyan, *Production Manager*; Valerie Younkin, *Desktop Publishing Specialist*; Sarah plumb, *Production Specialist*

All Web links in this book are correct as of the publication date below but may have become inactive or otherwise modified since that time. If you notice a deactivated or changed link, please e-mail books@ascd.org with the words "Link Update" in the subject line. In your message, please specify the Web link, the book title, and the page number on which the link appears.

PAPERBACK ISBN: 978-1-4166-0887-5 ASCD Product #108015 n09/09

Quantity discounts for the paperback edition only: 10–49 copies, 10%; 50+ copies, 15%; for 1,000 or more copies, call 1-800-933-2723, ext. 5634, or 1-703-575-5634.

Library of Congress Cataloging-in-Publication Data
Boyes, Karen.
    Developing habits of mind in elementary schools : an ASCD action tool / Karen Boyes, Graham Watts.
        p. cm.
    Includes bibliographical references.
    ISBN 978-1-4166-0887-5 (pbk. : alk. paper)   1. Thought and thinking—Study and teaching (Elementary)   2. Cognition in children.   I. Watts, Graham (Graham C.)   II. Association for Supervision and Curriculum Development.   III. Title.
    LB1590.3.B695 2009
    372.1102—dc22
                                                                                                2009026218

16 15 14 13 12 11 10 09   1 2 3 4 5 6 7 8 9 10

Developing
Habits *of* Mind
in Elementary Schools

An ASCD Action Tool

TOOLS FOR EXPANDING CAPACITIES

TOOLS FOR INCREASING ALERTNESS

TOOLS FOR EXTENDING VALUES

TOOLS FOR BUILDING COMMITMENT

RESOURCES AND REFERENCES

Downloads

The tools are available for
download at **www.ascd.org/downloads**.

Enter this unique key code to unlock the files:
G8412-07C62-26A11

If you have difficulty accessing the files,
e-mail webhelp@ascd.org or call 1-800-933-ASCD for assistance.

Acknowledgments

We would like to thank Art Costa and Bena Kallick for giving us the opportunity to work together on this learning journey and for believing in us, even though we were almost strangers at the start. We are eternally grateful for your insight and endless encouragement and hope this work does justice to the legacy you have created.

We also thank the team from ASCD for getting all the details sorted out and making this project a reality.

From Karen Boyes
I'd like to pay tribute to my teachers and colleagues who have inspired me and taught me so much about the Habits of Mind, especially Art Costa, Bena Kallick, Georgette Jensen, Adrian Rennie, Ross Kennedy, and Trudy Francis. A huge thanks goes to the team at Spectrum Education, in particular Jess Woodmass and Jenny Porter, who kept everything running smoothly so I could complete this project. Finally, I wish to acknowledge my family—my parents, Tui and Trevor, for always being there for me; my two gorgeous children, Hamish and Sasha, who embrace the Habits of Mind and grow each day because of them; and my wonderful husband, Denny, who is my rock, my foundation, my love.

From Graham Watts

I want to thank all those who have taught me, worked with me, and helped this work come to fruition. I offer particular thanks to Gill Hubble, Nola Tuckey, and Niki Phillips for their ideas and intellect, and to my parents for their generous support and endless belief in me.

Rationale and Planning

WHAT ARE HABITS OF MIND?

Habits of Mind are thoughtful behaviors—what some have called "intellectual dispositions"—that allow us to cope with a complex and rapidly changing world. They are powerful tools we can use to intelligently navigate the moral, ethical, and spiritual challenges we encounter in our increasingly complex world. Habits of Mind also serve as guiding principles to promote successful lifelong learning both within the classroom and in the world beyond it. Habits of Mind can be used to

- Establish and maintain positive relationships, including appreciation of the unique perspectives and points of view evident in our culturally diverse world.
- Develop and use effective communication techniques and strategies, including active listening, consensus building, and interpersonal awareness.
- Apply flexible thinking strategies to complex situations requiring authentic problem solving and decision making.
- Demonstrate powerful character traits, such as self-reflection and resilience, that have been labeled 21st century skills for our global economy and increasingly interdependent world.

Habits of Mind are as useful for adults as they are for students. When educators internalize these intellectual dispositions, they can better model the behaviors they want to see in their students. In addition, Habits of Mind are relevant to students of all ages and in all subjects. In essence, they can become catalysts for creating and sustaining a whole-school learning culture and promoting true communities of learning.

WHY DEVELOP HABITS OF MIND?

Habits of Mind can help us answer a range of powerful and essential questions: Just what do human beings do when they behave intelligently? What behaviors do efficient, effective problem solvers and decision makers demonstrate? How can we help students become lifelong learners who are increasingly proficient at using intelligent intellectual dispositions to explore their world? Research in effective thinking and intelligent behavior indicates that there are some identifiable characteristics of effective thinkers—characteristics that have been identified in successful people in all walks of life.

The critical attribute of intelligent human beings is not only having information but also knowing how to act on it. Employing Habits of Mind means having a disposition toward behaving intelligently when confronted with problems that have no immediately known answers. It means using a composite of many skills, attitudes, cues, past experiences, and proclivities. It means that for different problems, decisions, or situations, we need to determine the value of one pattern of thinking over another, making choices about which is most appropriate for a specific context. Over time, we learn to reflect on, evaluate, and modify our use of Habits of Mind, and we carry their impact forward to future applications.

UNIVERSAL CHARACTERISTICS OF PRODUCTIVE HABITS OF MIND

This ASCD Action Tool will help you to explore 16 significant Habits of Mind. As you explore and apply each, consider how they share the following characteristics:

Value	Choosing to employ a particular pattern of intellectual behavior (Habit of Mind) rather than other, less productive patterns.
Inclination	Feeling the need to use a pattern of intellectual behavior (Habit of Mind).
Sensitivity	Perceiving opportunities for and appropriateness of using a particular Habit of Mind.
Capability	Having the skills to apply the behaviors associated with key Habits of Mind.
Commitment	Constantly striving to reflect on and improve performance while using a Habit of Mind.

FOCUSING ON 16 IMPORTANT HABITS OF MIND

This ASCD Action Tool looks at 16 significant Habits of Mind. The habits reflect what intelligent people tend to do when they are confronted with problems or decisions about which there may not be a clear answer or preferred pathway for resolution. The habits are not meant to be seen as discrete or mutually exclusive; instead, they should be viewed as "permeable membranes," interacting with one another and mutually supporting the capacity for intelligent behavior as expressed through critical, creative, and self-regulated thinking. The 16 Habits of Mind we investigate are the following:

1. Persisting. Intelligent people stick to a task until it is completed. They don't give up easily. They take a systematic approach to solving problems—knowing how to begin, what steps must be performed, and what data need to be generated or collected. Because they are able to sustain a problem-solving process over time, persistent people are also comfortable with ambiguous or open-ended situations and tasks.

2. Managing Impulsivity. Intelligent, reflective individuals self-regulate and self-monitor, considering alternatives and consequences related to several possible directions prior to taking action. They decrease their need for trial and error by gathering information, taking time to reflect on an answer before giving it, making sure they understand directions, and listening to alternative points of view.

3. Listening to Others with Understanding and Empathy. The ability to listen to another person— to understand and empathize with another point of view or perspective—is one of the highest forms of intelligent behavior. Being able to paraphrase others' ideas, detecting indicators (cues) of their feelings or emotional states in their oral and body language (empathy), and accurately expressing their concepts, emotions, and problems are indicators of active listening and open and accurate communication.

4. Thinking Flexibly. People who think flexibly have the ability to change their mind as they receive additional data or expand their experience base. They can hypothesize multiple and simultaneous outcomes and activities related to a situation, drawing upon a repertoire of problem-solving strategies and practicing style flexibility—for example, knowing when it is appropriate to be broad and global in their thinking and when a situation requires detailed precision. They seek novel approaches and usually have a well-developed sense of humor.

5. Thinking About Thinking (Metacognition). Metacognition is the ability to perceive and analyze both what we know and what we don't know. It is our capacity for planning a strategy to produce the information needed to solve a problem, to be conscious of our own steps and strategies, and to reflect on and evaluate the productiveness of our thinking. The major components of metacognition involve developing a plan of action, keeping that plan in mind over a period of time, and reflecting on and evaluating the plan upon its completion.

6. Striving for Accuracy and Precision. People who value accuracy, precision, and craftsmanship take time to check over their products or performances. They review the rules by which they are to operate, the models and visions they are to follow, and the criteria they are to address. They also confirm that their finished product or performance matches the criteria exactly. Accurate and precise learners take pride in their work. They strive to attain the highest possible standards and pursue ongoing learning to focus their energies to accomplish tasks.

7. Questioning and Posing Problems. Effective problem solvers know how to ask questions to fill in the gaps between what they know and what they don't know. Effective questioners are inclined to ask a range of questions. They also recognize discrepancies and challenging phenomena in their environment, probing into causes and meanings. Successful questioners request data to support the conclusions and assumptions of others, pose questions about alternative points of view, pose questions to establish and confirm causal connections and relationships, and generate hypothetical problems and approaches to investigate them.

8. Applying Past Knowledge to New Situations. Intelligent human beings learn from experience. When confronted with a new and perplexing problem, they draw upon their store of knowledge and experience as sources of data to support ideas, theories to explain, analogies to compare, or processes to solve each new challenge. They are able to abstract meaning from one experience and carry it forth to another. Ultimately, they confirm their understanding of knowledge and skills by being able to apply them creatively and independently to novel, new, and unanticipated tasks, situations, and settings.

9. Thinking and Communicating with Clarity and Precision. Language and thinking are closely entwined. Intelligent people strive to communicate accurately in both written and oral forms. They take care to use precise language, define terms, and use correct names as well as universal labels and analogies. They strive to avoid overgeneralizations, deletions, and distortions. Instead, they support their statements with explanations, comparisons, quantification, and evidence. Clear and precise language plays a critical role in enhancing our cognitive maps and our ability to think critically. Enriching the complexity and specificity of language and how we use it produces more effective thinking.

10. Gathering Data Through All Senses. Intelligent people know that all information gets into the brain through the sensory pathways: gustatory, olfactory, tactile, kinesthetic, auditory, and visual. We derive most of our linguistic, cultural, and physical learning from the environment as we take it in through our senses and subsequently observe and analyze its patterns and processes. Those whose sensory pathways are open, alert, and acute absorb more information from the environment than those whose pathways are withered, immune, and oblivious to sensory stimuli.

11. Creating, Imagining, and Innovating. Creative human beings try to conceive solutions to problems differently from the norm, examining alternative possibilities from many angles. They tend to project themselves into different roles using analogies and visioning strategies. Creative people take risks, pushing the boundaries of perceived limits. They are intrinsically motivated, working on a task because of the aesthetic challenge rather than material rewards. Creative people are also positively responsive to criticism. They hold up their products for others to judge and seek feedback in an ongoing effort to refine their techniques and approaches.

12. Responding with Wonderment and Awe. We want our students to be curious, to commune with the world around them, to reflect on the changing formations of nature, and to experience awe in the face of creative expression. Ideally, they should feel engaged and passionate about learning. Students who respond with wonderment and awe can find beauty in a sunset, intrigue in the geometry of a spider web, and exhilaration at the iridescence of a hummingbird's wings. They continually think outside the boxes of tradition and norm-based perspectives, striving to see the unseen. They approach lifelong learning as a powerful and positive process that sustains and enriches them.

13. Taking Responsible Risks. Intelligent and creative people often seem to have a powerful urge to go beyond established limits, feeling compelled to place themselves in situations where they do not know what the outcome will be. They accept confusion, uncertainty, and higher risks of failure as part of the normal process of learning—and they tend to view setbacks as interesting, challenging, and growth producing. At the same time, they do not behave impulsively or recklessly. They take "educated" risks, drawing on their past knowledge about consequences with a well-trained sense of what is appropriate and inappropriate.

14. Finding Humor. People who engage in the mystery of humor have the ability to perceive situations from an original and often interesting vantage point. They tend to initiate humor more often, place greater value on having a sense of humor, and appreciate and understand others' humor, and they are often verbally playful when interacting with others. Those who have this Habit of Mind can distinguish between situations of human frailty and fallibility that are in need of compassion and those that are truly funny.

15. Thinking Interdependently. Working interdependently requires the ability to justify ideas and to test the feasibility of solution strategies on others. It also requires the development of a willingness and openness to accept feedback from a critical friend. Human beings who think interdependently typically express a range of observable and productive behaviors, including listening, consensus seeking, giving up an idea to work with someone else's, empathy, compassion, group leadership, knowing how to support group efforts, and altruism.

16. Learning Continuously. Intelligent people are in a continuous learning mode—striving for improvement, always growing, always learning, always modifying and improving themselves. They perceive and approach problems, situations, tensions, conflicts, and circumstances as valuable opportunities to learn. Our wish for our students should be that they become creative human beings who are eager to learn. That process includes the humility of knowing what we don't know, which—according to Kallick and Costa—is the highest form of thinking we will ever learn.

ORGANIZATION OF THIS ACTION TOOL

This ASCD Action Tool is arranged to follow five dimensions of growth that move from an initial exploration of each Habit of Mind through a comprehensive internalization of the habits in students and teachers. Designed to scaffold learning, each dimension represents a step students commonly take as they embrace intelligent behaviors during core learning experiences. This action tool guides students through the dimensions and helps both students and teachers create a deep understanding of each Habit of Mind. Students learn to recognize Habits of Mind and appreciate their usefulness in learning and in life. Each dimension is the focus of one section as follows:

- **Exploring Meanings.** This section contains a series of resources designed to help students understand the terminology, concepts, and definitions associated with the 16 Habits of Mind. The tools in this section can reinforce students' understanding of operational language. This language can serve as a cognitive anchor or trigger, allowing students to monitor and describe their own thinking as they acquire and apply each of the Habits of Mind. By using the resources included in this section, educators can help learners build a scaffold or platform from which they can extend and refine their use of the Habits of Mind that follow.

• **Expanding Capacities.** This section builds upon the foundations established in the Exploring Meanings section. As teachers and students become familiar with the 16 Habits of Mind, they can use them to become increasingly fluent in self-assessment and self-regulation. The tools and resources in this section will help educators extend and refine students' understanding and application of the Habits of Mind in their academic lives as well as beyond the classroom.

• **Increasing Alertness.** This section takes the previous two a step further by extending students' work with the habits to see their innate potential and applicability to academic and daily life. Thus, this section marks a shift from teacher-led growth toward student-led growth. It serves as a bridge between external understanding of the habits and true internal and personal understanding. The tools in this section lead educators and students to investigate people that matter to them—for example, famous people, world leaders, and local people they respect—and significant global and local issues. As they identify applications of the habits to the world around them via case studies, interviews, and research projects, they grow in their understanding of how the habits can be extremely beneficial in learning and in life.

• **Extending Values.** This section explores strategies that will help educators and students create a "school as a home for the mind," a theme that is central to Costa and Kallick's belief that the full potential of the 16 Habits of Mind cannot be realized unless this framework is applied schoolwide to all aspects of school culture. The activation model presented in this section is designed to integrate the Habits of Mind into all facets of school improvement planning and organization development. The tools and resources focus on leaders, teachers, students, parents, and the wider learning community.

• **Building Commitment.** The tools and materials presented in this final section are designed to take learners from thinking consciously about using the habits to internalizing them so that they become a regular part of how the learners think, behave, and live. In effect, the habits then become so much a part of the individual's mind, emotions, and consciousness that they unconsciously and automatically guide and inform the person's decision-making and problem-solving processes.

The Resources and References section contains two appendices:

- **Appendix A.** Appendix A offers greater depth and detail on each of the 16 Habits of Mind. It contains useful quotes, explanations, and icons to help broaden teachers' and students' understanding and application. An interesting activity to do with teachers and students is ask them to design an equivalent document with original icons, personal quotes, and new definitions.
- **Appendix B.** The planning, teaching, and assessing tools referred to throughout the action tool can be found in Appendix B. They are provided as black-line masters for easy use in classrooms, but their use is not limited to the form in which they appear. As you become more familiar with the Habits of Mind, you may want to adapt, combine, re-create, or improve these resources to meet your needs and the needs of your students.

STRUCTURE AND PLANNING

The first page of each section includes a summary and a list of contents. The individual tools (which can also be considered lessons) include step-by-step instructions, as well as worksheets, sample completed worksheets, and resource pages as appropriate. Teachers can pick and choose from the available tools. They may use each tool as a lesson plan as given; teachers who prefer to create their own lesson plan may want to use the lesson plan template available in Appendix B.

Teachers may adapt the tools and activities to meet specific age and curriculum goals. The idea is to set a solid foundation by first introducing the Habits of Mind to students and then developing students' understanding, appreciation, and commitment to the habits as they progress through the elementary and secondary grades. Thus, all of the worksheets and related resources in this action tool are intended to be starting points from which teachers can customize to suit the ability level and age range within different classroom environments.

ELECTRONIC TOOLS AND RESOURCES

The tools are available for download. To access these documents, visit www.ascd.org/downloads and enter the key code found on page viii. All files are saved in Adobe Portable Document Format (PDF). The PDF is compatible with both personal computers (PCs) and Macintosh computers. **Note: You must have the Adobe Acrobat Professional software on your machine to save your work.** The main menu will let you navigate through the various sections, and you can print individual tools or sections in their entirety. If you are having difficulties downloading or viewing the files, contact webhelp@ascd.org for assistance, or call 1-800-933-ASCD.

MINIMUM SYSTEM REQUIREMENTS

Program: The most current version of the Adobe Reader software is available for free download at www.adobe.com.

PC: Intel Pentium Processor; Microsoft Windows XP Professional or Home Edition (Service Pack 1 or 2), Windows 2000 (Service Pack 2), Windows XP Tablet PC Edition, Windows Server 2003, or Windows NT (Service Pack 6 or 6a); 128 MB of RAM (256 MB recommended); up to 90 MB of available hard-disk space; Internet Explorer 5.5 (or higher), Netscape 7.1 (or higher), Firefox 1.0, or Mozilla 1.7.

Macintosh: PowerPC G3, G4, or G5 processor, Mac OS X v.10.2.8–10.3; 128 MB of RAM (256 MB recommended); up to 110 MB of available hard-disk space; Safari 1.2.2 browser supported for MAC OS X 10.3 or higher.

GETTING STARTED

Select "Download files." Designate a location on your computer to save the zip file. Choose to open the PDF file with your existing version of Adobe Acrobat Reader, or install the newest version of Adobe Acrobat Reader from www.adobe.com. From the main menu, select a section by clicking on its title. To view a specific tool, open the Bookmarks tab in the left navigation pane and then click on the title of the tool.

PRINTING TOOLS

To print a single tool, select the tool by clicking on its title via the Bookmarks section and the printer icon, or select File then Print. In the Print Range section, select Current Page to print the page on the screen. To print several tools, enter the page range in the "Pages from" field. If you wish to print all of the tools in the section, select All in the Printer Range section and then click OK.

TOOLS FOR TEACHER TRAINING

Who dares to teach must never cease to learn.
—John Cotton Dana
Librarian and museum director

A teacher affects eternity; he can never tell where his influence stops.
—Henry Brooks Adams
Novelist, journalist, historian, and professor

Exposing the Habits of Mind to teachers can greatly enhance students' capacity to learn and apply the habits in multiple ways and can help to build a school culture infused with Habits of Mind. The following pages present lesson plans for two training sessions for colleagues, administrators, and other interested school staff. The materials put the bulk of learning and exploring onto the shoulders of the teachers, so it is not necessary to be an expert to facilitate these training sessions.

The first tool provides an introduction and launching pad for teachers to familiarize themselves with the habits and begin applying them. The second tool allows teachers to work together more extensively to share ideas and expand their capacity to teach these valuable lifelong skills. These tools, or lessons, may be presented at a staff meeting, in an after-school training session, or through work teams. Teachers generally respond well to the model as a viable way to develop intelligent behaviors within their students.

Action Tool 1: Exploring the Meaning of Habits of Mind with Teachers

PURPOSE OF THIS TOOL

A good starting point when introducing Habits of Mind into a school is to first introduce the habits to teachers and staff. The experience will be more powerful for students if teachers develop a deep understanding and appreciation of the habits themselves before they present them to students. They may have numerous initial questions: What do these habits mean? How will they work with my age group or in my subject? How can I put the model into practice? Rather than answering the questions, begin with the Y-Chart activity in this tool.

The resources in this action tool will enable participants to

- Identify the 16 Habits of Mind.
- Explore several Habits of Mind for personal meaning.
- Define each Habit of Mind and identify appropriate uses.
- Prepare to model the 16 Habits of Mind to students.
- Prepare to recognize the habits in students.t

HOW TO USE THIS TOOL

This tool presents a series of resources that can be used to introduce and reinforce for teachers the meaning of the 16 Habits of Mind. The following is the suggested sequence for exploring these habits, as well as a list of resources included to support this process:

- Summary of 16 Habits of Mind handout (Introductory Activity)
- Y-Chart worksheet (Introductory Activity)
- Defining Habits of Mind worksheet (Core Activity)
- Discussion (Reflection Activity)
- Describing16 Habits of Mind (Extension Activity)

The activities and tasks included in this tool should take about 60 minutes to complete. You will need the following materials:

- Summary of 16 Habits of Mind (Appendix B)
- Describing 16 Habits of Mind (Appendix A)

TIPS AND VARIATIONS

1. Introductory Activity

- Distribute the list of the 16 Habits of Mind. Read the names of the habits but do not discuss them yet.
- Have teachers form small groups. Assign the Habits of Mind to each group such that every group has at least one habit to consider, and all of the habits are covered. For instance, if you have four groups, each group will have four habits to consider.
- Give each group one copy of the Y-Chart worksheet (page XX) for each Habit of Mind they are considering; for example, if each group has four habits, they will need four copies of the worksheet. (Alternatively, teachers could write information for each of their Habits of Mind on one sheet.)
- Ask the groups to use the chart to unpack the meaning of their assigned Habits of Mind. For example, for the first habit, Persistence, they might ask themselves questions such as

> What does it look like when someone in class persists? What facial expressions might I see? What body language? What does persistence look like outside the classroom? On the baseball field? In a chess tournament? At the airport? At the beach?
>
> What does it feel like when I persist? Is there just one feeling or emotion, or several? Do my feelings change as I apply persistence? Does everyone experience the same feelings when they persist?
>
> What does it sound like when someone persists? What words might I hear? Other noises? How might I talk to myself? What advice might I offer a friend who needs to persist? How might the sounds change from the classroom to the football field?

- When teachers have finished, have each team discuss their Y-charts with the whole group. It can be very interesting to see the breadth of ideas teachers will produce.

2. Core Activity

- Give teachers a copy of the Defining Habits of Mind worksheet.
- Ask them to work individually to complete it, defining each habit in their own words (column 1) and listing two or three ideal times to use each (column 2) as well as two or three occasions when the habit would not be useful (column 3).

3. Reflection Activity

- Lead a group discussion about the value of Habits of Mind.
- Explain that teachers will really begin to see the benefits as they watch students apply the habits in learning situations.

4. Extension Activity

- Distribute the article "Describing 16 Habits of Mind," found in Appendix A.
- Encourage teachers to take the materials they have received with them to study as they prepare to introduce the Habits of Mind to their students.
- Suggest that teachers review Costa and Kallick's *Learning and Leading with Habits of Mind* (2008, ASCD), if they have not already done so.

Name _____ Class _____ Date _____

Y-Chart

You can use this chart to explore your thoughts about the Habits of Mind.

Topic:

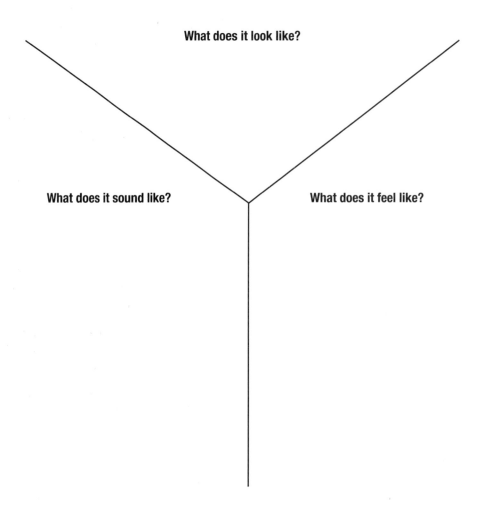

Name _____ Class _____ Date _____

Defining Habits of Mind

Habit of Mind	My Definition	Good Times to Use	Bad Times to Use
Persisting			
Managing Impulsivity			
Listening with Understanding and Empathy			
Thinking Flexibly			
Thinking About Thinking (Metacognition)			
Striving for Accuracy and Precision			
Questioning and Posing Problems			
Applying Past Knowledge to New Situations			

Name _____ Class _____ Date _____

Defining Habits of Mind, *continued*

Habit of Mind	My Definition	Good Times to Use	Bad Times to Use
Thinking and Communicating with Clarity and Precision			
Gathering Data Through All Senses			
Creating, Imagining, and Innovating			
Responding with Wonderment and Awe			
Taking Responsible Risks			
Finding Humor			
Thinking Interdependently			
Learning Continuously			

Action Tool 2: Expanding Capacities with Teachers

PURPOSE OF THIS TOOL

This tool builds on the concepts developed in the previous tool. Teachers should now be familiar with all 16 Habits of Mind and have a working understanding of what they mean. This tool helps teachers gain more in-depth knowledge and understanding of the habits so that they will be better prepared to foster them among their students. The resources in this action tool will enable participants to

- Discuss with colleagues their experiences in applying the Habits of Mind so far.
- Define each Habit of Mind in as many ways as possible.
- Use analogies to gain perspective on each Habit of Mind.
- Describe how they can integrate each Habit of Mind into the classroom.
- Contribute to and build on the ideas of colleagues.

HOW TO USE THIS TOOL

This tool presents a series of resources that can be used to extend and refine teachers' understanding of the 16 Habits of Mind. The following is the suggested sequence for exploring these habits:

- How's It Going? (Introductory Discussion)
- Word Splash, Y-Chart, and Classroom Integration group activity (Core Activity)
- Final Review group activity and discussion (Synthesizing Activity)
- Results folders (Follow-Up)

The activities and tasks included in this tool should take two hours, best divided into two close-proximity days to complete. Note that you will need to complete some advance preparation as well as some follow-up action. You will need the following materials:

- Large roll of butcher paper or a couple of self-stick wall charts
- Package of markers
- A bell, whistle, or other noisemaker (optional)
- Folders (one per teacher)
- Clock or watch

TIPS AND VARIATIONS

1. Advance Preparation

- Set up stations around the room, one for each Habit of Mind. At each station, hang three poster-size pieces of butcher paper specific to one habit. (See the following pages as examples for the habit Persisting.) Have extra butcher paper on hand in case additional space is needed for recording ideas. Place a number of markers at each station.
- On the board, write three sample charts such as those shown on the following pages for the habit Persisting. These samples will serve as guides for the teachers.

2. Introductory Discussion

- Stimulate discussion about experiences teachers have had with the Habits of Mind so far by asking questions such as the following:

  How have you used the Habits of Mind in the classroom?

  What have you learned?

  What problems have you encountered?

  What questions do you have?

- Spend some time sharing your ideas and having other teachers do so as well.

3. Core Activity

- Tell teachers that to further help them think about and share ideas related to the Habits of Mind, you have created stations around the room, each with three charts: a Word Splash, a Y-Chart, and a chart titled Classroom Integration. Direct the teachers' attention to the examples on the board as you explain each type of chart.
- Explain that word splashes are brainstorming activities. Teachers should think of as many ways as they can to rephrase the name of the Habit of Mind. Tell them that by the time all ideas are recorded, everyone should have a thorough definition of the habit.
- Remind teachers of their previous experience with Y-charts. Say that this chart will allow them to draw analogies to express what they think, feel, and hear regarding each habit.
- Explain that the Classroom Integration chart serves as a tool for teachers to share their ideas about how they use or could use the Habits of Mind in the classroom, as well as times to avoid using the habits.

- Instruct teachers to get up and go to any station. Allow five minutes for teachers to add their ideas to each chart at that station, and then blow a whistle, ring a bell, or call "time" and instruct teachers to move to the next station.
- At about halfway through this activity, allow teachers to take a break. Ideally, they would return to the activity fresh the next day.

4. Synthesizing Activity

- When everyone has been through the 16 stations, allow them time to mingle around the room and look at everyone's comments.
- Lead a group discussion about the experience.

5. Follow-Up

- Tell teachers you will type up their collection of ideas. At a later time, give each teacher a folder with all the group's ideas and encourage them to apply the ideas in the days, weeks, and years to come.
- Have teachers add the handouts and materials they received in Action Tool 1 to the folders, so they will have a Habits of Mind resource available at all times.

Rationale and Planning

Word Splash for Persisting

Persisting means ...

Y-Chart for Persisting

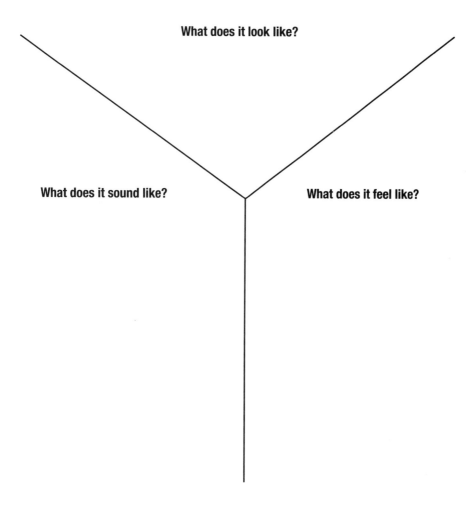

What does it look like?

What does it sound like?

What does it feel like?

Classroom Integration for Persisting

1. It is important to use this Habit of Mind when ...

2. This Habit of Mind is not useful when ...

3. I could introduce this Habit of Mind by ...

Word Splash for Persisting

> The following is an example of what you are asking teachers to record on the appropriate posters at each station. These answers are simplified. Teachers should feel free to share any ideas they have.

Persisting means . . .

    . . . to keep going.

    . . . not giving up.

    . . . sticking with it.

    . . . staying on task.

    . . . repeating.

    . . . practicing.

    . . . trying again.

    . . . trying a different way.

Name _____ Class _____ Date _____

Y-Chart for Persisting

> The following is an example of what you are asking teachers to record on the appropriate posters at each station. These answers are simplified. Teachers should feel free to share any ideas they have.

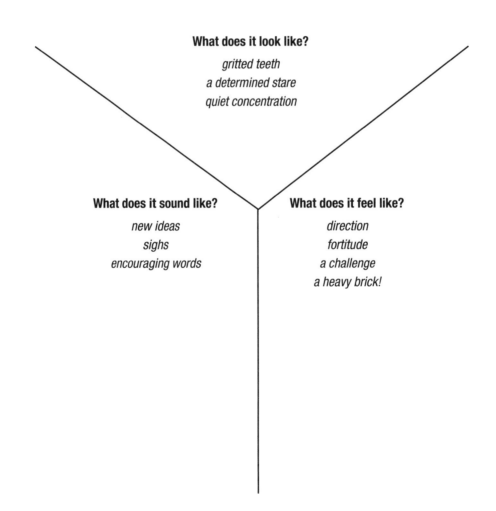

What does it look like?

gritted teeth
a determined stare
quiet concentration

What does it sound like?

new ideas
sighs
encouraging words

What does it feel like?

direction
fortitude
a challenge
a heavy brick!

Classroom Integration for Persisting

> The following is an example of what you are asking teachers to record on the appropriate posters at each station. These answers are simplified. Teachers should feel free to share any ideas they have.

1. It is important to use this Habit of Mind when …

   … students are struggling with new information.

   … students are nervous about something.

   … I'm pushing students to try something new.

2. This Habit of Mind is not useful when …

   … students need to brainstorm.

   … I want students to relax and let things happen.

   … persisting could cause mental, emotional, or physical harm.

3. I could introduce this Habit of Mind by …

   … giving students a task that takes several weeks to complete.

   … giving students a tough group assignment they could figure out together.

   … sharing a personal experience about persistence.

Exploring Meanings

We shall not cease from exploration, and the end of all our exploring will be to arrive where we started and know the place for the first time.

—T. S. Eliot

Understanding the terminology, labels, and definitions of Habits of Mind is an important first step in exploring them and seeing the value they offer. Students report that simply being made aware of the Habits of Mind helps improve their thinking. The language alone seems to act as a cognitive anchor or trigger, allowing students to monitor and describe their own thinking. Once learners know the Habits of Mind, they begin to connect them to their own experiences and recognize them in others. They become able to reflect on times when they have (or should have) used a particular habit.

With the tools in this section, you will be encouraging a solid foundation by helping students gather a range of examples and analogies that relate to the model. Soon they will be able to expand their simple definitions to more complex and complete ones.

CONTENTS

TITLE OF TOOL

Persisting

PURPOSE OF THIS TOOL

Persisting is a Habit of Mind that relates to sticking to a task until it is completed. People who use this habit don't give up easily. They devise methods for analyzing the situation and create a plan for solving problems and accomplishing goals. With this tool, students will have several opportunities to become familiar with persisting as an important habit to develop.

The resources in this tool will enable students to

- Compare characters in literature who do and who do not use persistence.
- Define *persistence* in several ways.
- Identify examples of persistence in everyday life.

HOW TO USE THIS TOOL

The following list of resources includes the suggested sequence for using this tool:

- Condensed version of Aesop's fable "The Tortoise and the Hare" (Motivating Activity)
- Mapping the Characters worksheets (Core Activity)
- Persisting Word Splash worksheet (Reflection Activity)
- Persistence in Everyday Life (Extension Activity)

The activities and tasks included in this tool should take about 45 minutes to complete.

TIPS AND VARIATIONS

1. Motivating Activity

- Read the condensed version of Aesop's fable "The Tortoise and the Hare," provided in this tool, to students. You might wish to give students a copy so they can read along.
- Explain to students that the story's moral that "plodding wins the race" is also sometimes stated as, "Slow and steady wins the race." Ask: What does this moral, or message, mean?

2. Core Activity

- Discuss the characteristics of the tortoise and the hare.
- Have students use one of the two Mapping the Characters diagrams provided in this tool to compare the two characters. If students have trouble comparing the characters, you may wish to provide sample answers on the board.

3. Reflection Activity

- To give students a better sense of the term *persisting*, give them multiple opportunities to define it for themselves. Use the Persisting Word Splash worksheet to further this goal.
- Encourage volunteers to show their word splashes to the class. You may wish to post some of the students' splashes on a bulletin board. You may also wish to allow students to tell or write a story with a character or characters who demonstrate persistence.

4. Extension Activity

- Encourage students to look for examples of persisting in stories, on the news, or among family and friends.
- Invite students to report examples back to the class.

The Tortoise and the Hare
condensed from *Aesop's Fables*

The Hare was once boasting of his speed before the other animals.

"I have never yet been beaten," said he, "when I put forth my full speed. I challenge anyone here to race with me."

The Tortoise said quietly, "I accept your challenge."

"That is a good joke," said the Hare. "I could dance around you all the way."

"Save your boasting till you've won," answered the Tortoise. "Shall we race?"

So a course was fixed and a start was made. The Hare darted almost out of sight at once but soon stopped and, to show his contempt for the Tortoise, lay down to have a nap. The Tortoise plodded on and plodded on, and when the Hare awoke from his nap, he saw the Tortoise just near the winning-post and could not run up in time to save the race.

Then said the Tortoise: "Plodding wins the race."

Name _____ Class _____ Date _____

Mapping the Characters

In the bubbles on the left, list words and phrases that describe the tortoise. Using the bubbles on the right, describe the hare. In the bubbles that connect to both the hare and the tortoise, use terms that apply to both characters.

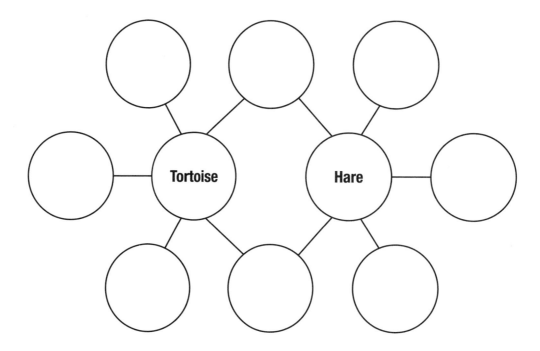

Exploring Meanings

Name _____ Class _____ Date _____

Mapping the Characters

In the bubbles on the left, list words and phrases that describe the tortoise. Using the bubbles on the right, describe the hare. In the bubbles that connect to both the hare and the tortoise, use terms that apply to both characters.

> The following is a sample map. If students have trouble with this exercise, draw the map on the board as an example. Or you could conduct the activity as a group exercise, adding one word at a time and having students contribute their thoughts as you go.

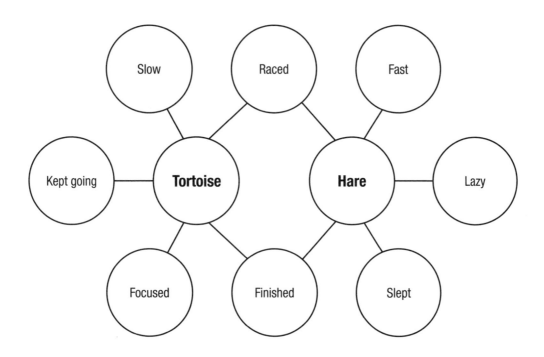

Name _____ Class _____ Date _____

Mapping the Characters

In the circle on the left, list words and phrases to describe the tortoise. Describe the hare in the circle on the right. List characteristics of both in the overlapping portion in the middle of the two circles.

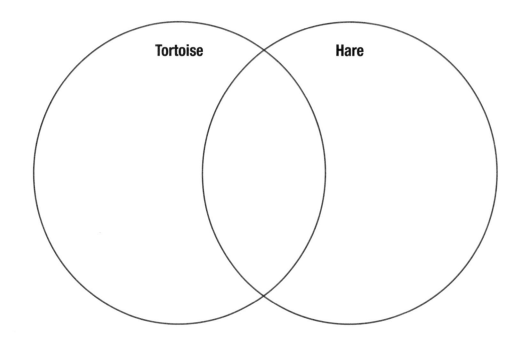

Exploring Meanings

Name _____ Class _____ Date _____

Mapping the Characters

In the circle on the left, list words and phrases to describe the tortoise. Describe the hare in the circle on the right. List characteristics of both in the overlapping portion in the middle of the two circles.

> The following is a sample map. If students have trouble with this exercise, draw the map on the board as an example. Or you could conduct the activity as a group exercise, adding one word at a time and having students contribute their thoughts as you go.

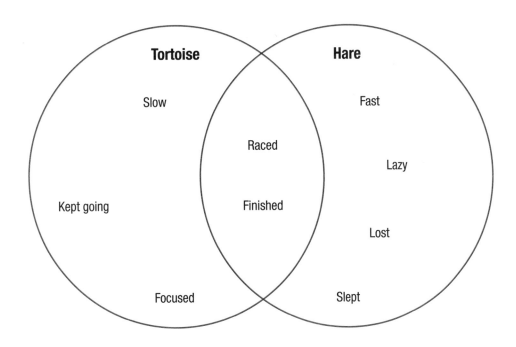

Name _____ Class _____ Date _____

Persisting Word Splash

A word splash starts with one phrase. To complete it, create several different endings for the phrase to fully describe the meaning of the term. Use the space below to create a word splash for the term *persisting*.

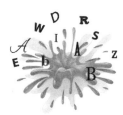

Persisting means . . .

Name _____ Class _____ Date _____

Persisting Word Splash

A word splash starts with one phrase. To complete it, create several different endings for the phrase to fully describe the meaning of the term. Use the space below to create a word splash for the term *persisting*.

> The following is a sample answer. If students have trouble with this exercise, put the following answer on the board as an example. Or you could conduct this activity as a group exercise. List the following answers line-by-line and allow students to contribute their thoughts as you go.

Persisting means . . .

　　 . . . to keep going.

　　 . . . not giving up.

　　 . . . sticking with it.

　　 . . . staying on task.

　　 . . . repeating.

　　 . . . practicing.

　　 . . . trying again.

　　 . . . trying a different way.

Managing Impulsivity

PURPOSE OF THIS TOOL

This tool focuses on the Habit of Mind called Managing Impulsivity. When students learn to manage their desires instead of acting on them immediately, they are better able to prevent problems both in school and in life. They can cooperate with others to achieve goals and develop vision to achieve personal progress. This Habit of Mind teaches students to clarify and understand directions, consider consequences of actions, and develop strategies for solving problems. They are encouraged to make sure they understand a problem or situation before reacting to it and to withhold value judgments until they have a good understanding of the facts and consequences of the situation.

The resources in this action tool will enable students to

- Practice managing an impulse.
- Define the term *impulsive*.
- Identify impulsive behavior and suggest alternatives.

HOW TO USE THIS TOOL

The following list of resources includes the suggested sequence for using this tool:

- Sweets to Eat? (Motivating Activity)
- Candy Color Tally Chart worksheet (Motivating Activity)
- Candy Color Graph worksheet (Motivating Activity)
- Who's Impulsive? worksheet (Vocabulary Activity)
- "The Boy Who Cried Wolf" story (Core Activity)
- Managing Impulsivity Word Splash worksheet or Managing Impulsivity poster (Reflection Activity)

The activities and tasks included in this tool should take about 60 minutes to complete. You will need the following materials:

- Multicolored candies (e.g., M&Ms), about 25 per student or per student work area
- Candy dishes (small paper or plastic bowls or plates will work)
- Pens, pencils, and crayons that are the same colors as the candies (one set per group of 3–4 students)
- Poster board (optional)

TIPS AND VARIATIONS

1. Advance Preparation

- Prepare candy dishes for student work tables. Each dish should contain the same number of candies. Use a candy that comes in many colors, such as M&Ms.

2. Motivating Activity

- Begin a regular lesson for about 10–15 minutes without mentioning the candies. Ignore comments or requests to eat the sweets. If you see a student eat a candy, look the other way.
- Near the end of the lesson, tell students that now you would like them to use the candies in a graphing exercise. Without sounding angry, ask if anyone has eaten any of the candies. Explain that you know how many candies were in each dish, so there is no use lying.
- Ask students who confess to eating the candies why they made that decision. Say: "You were not instructed to do so. What if the candies were unsafe to eat for some reason?"
- Ask students who have not eaten the candies to explain their decision. Ask: Was it difficult not to eat the candies? If students say, "It was OK because those aren't my favorite candies," tell them to imagine that their favorite candies had been in the bowl instead, and repeat the question.
- Use the students' comments to begin discussing the concept of managing impulsivity.
- Divide students into groups of three or four. Give each group a bowl of 20 candies. Ask each group to tally the colors in each packet using the Candy Color Tally Chart.
- Have students use the Candy Color Graph to represent their findings in graph form.

3. Vocabulary Activity

- Ask: What does it mean to be impulsive? What are some characteristics of impulsive behavior?
- Continue the discussion by asking how a person might manage his or her impulsive tendencies.
- Hand out the Who's Impulsive? worksheet. Have students complete the worksheet in small groups, or complete the worksheet as a whole-class activity.

4. Core Activity

- Read aloud the condensed version of Aesop's fable "The Boy Who Cried Wolf," provided in this tool. If you wish, give a copy to students so they can follow along.
- Lead a class discussion by asking the questions provided at the end of the story.

Note: As an alternative, you could read something from Lynley Dodd's *Slinky Malinki* or his *Hairy Maclary* series. These stories also provide examples for discussing the Managing Impulsivity Habit of Mind.

4. Reflection Activity

- Lead students to synthesize what they've learned by having students complete the Managing Impulsivity Word Splash worksheet. You may wish to do this as a whole-class activity, or you may prefer to have students work individually or in small groups.
- Encourage students to share their word splashes with classmates. You may also wish to display the word splashes in the classroom.

Note: As an alternative, you could have students design posters that represent this Habit of Mind with words and pictures.

Name _____ Class _____ Date _____

Candy Color Tally Chart

Tally the number of each color of candy in your dish by making a mark in the "Tally" column beside the appropriate color for each candy you pull from the dish. If you don't see the correct color listed, add it on one of the blank lines. When you are finished tallying all of the candies in your dish, count the total number of each color. Write the number for each color in the "Total" column.

Candy Color Tally Chart

Colors	Tally	Total
Red		
Blue		
Yellow		
Orange		
Brown		
Green		
Total Number of Candies		

Name _____ Class _____ Date _____

Candy Color Tally Chart

Tally the number of each color of candy in your dish by making a mark in the "Tally" column beside the appropriate color for each candy you pull from the dish. If you don't see the correct color listed, add it on one of the blank lines. When you are finished tally-ing all of the candies in your dish, count the total number of each color. Write the total number for each color in the final column.

> The following is a sample answer. You may wish to record at least one row on the board to show students how to complete the chart.

Candy Color Tally Chart

Colors	Tally	Total
Red	///	3
Blue	////	4
Yellow	///	3
Orange	///	3
Brown	/////	5
Green	//	2
Total Number of Candies	20	20

Name _____ Class _____ Date _____

Candy Color Graph

Take the information in your Candy Color Tally Chart and graph it. Look at the number shown in the "Total" column of your chart for the first color. Fill in that number of squares for that color in the graph below. Then repeat for each of the remaining colors. For example, if you counted three red candies, you would color three red squares in the first column below, and so on.

Candy Color Graph

Red	Blue	Yellow	Orange	Brown	Green

Name _____ Class _____ Date _____

Candy Color Graph

Take the information in your Candy Color Tally Chart and graph it. Look at the number shown in the "Total" column of your chart for the first color. Fill in that number of squares for that color in the graph below. Then repeat for each of the remaining colors. For example, if you counted three red candies, you would color three red squares in the first column below, and so on.

> The following is a sample answer. You may wish to use colored chalk to recreate the chart on the board so that students will know how to complete it.

Candy Color Graph

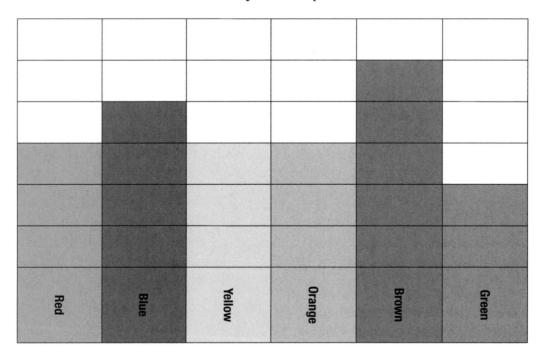

Name _____ Class _____ Date _____

Who's Impulsive?

In the chart below, list four animals that show characteristics of being impulsive. Then list four animals that seem to manage their impulsivity.

Is Impulsive	Manages Impulsivity

Now pick one animal from each column. List characteristics of each animal.

Impulsive Animal:

_____

Animal That Manages Impulsivity:

_____

Name _____ Class _____ Date _____

Who's Impulsive?

In the chart below, list four animals that show characteristics of being impulsive. Then list four animals that seem to manage their impulsivity.

Share the following sample answers with students to help them get started.

Is Impulsive	Manages Impulsivity
chicken	owl
frog	eagle
monkey	turtle
fish	lion

Now pick one animal from each column. List characteristics of each animal.

Impulsive Animal:	**Animal That Manages Impulsivity:**
Frog	*Owl*
Jumps	Searches
Hops	Quiet
Impatient	Careful
Busy	Plans
Silly	Waits
Doesn't pay attention	Wise
Doesn't care	

Exploring Meanings

The Boy Who Cried Wolf
Adapted from *Aesop's Fables*

There was once a young shepherd boy who tended his sheep at the foot of a mountain near a dark forest. It was rather lonely for him all day, so he thought up a plan by which he could get a little company and some excitement.

He rushed down toward the village calling out, "Wolf! Wolf!" The villagers came out to meet him, and some of them stopped with him for a considerable time. This pleased the boy so much that a few days later he tried the same trick, and again the villagers came to his help.

But shortly after this, a wolf actually did come out from the forest, and it began to worry the sheep. The boy, of course, cried out, "Wolf! Wolf!" louder than before. But this time the villagers, who had been fooled twice before, thought the boy was again deceiving them, so nobody stirred to come to his help. The wolf made a good meal off the boy's flock, and when the boy complained, the wise man of the village said: "A liar will not be believed, even when he speaks the truth."

Discussion Questions for "The Boy Who Cried Wolf"

Use these questions to discuss impulses such as the boy's impulse to get the attention of the villagers. Explain that thinking in advance and refraining from doing things that might cause harm or trouble is what it means to manage impulses.

1. Did the boy mean to upset the villagers?

   No.

2. Why did he lie?

   He was bored and having fun.

3. What were the consequences of his lie?

   He lost the respect of his community and lost some of his sheep to the wolf.

4. How might the story have turned out if the boy had thought about the effect of lying before he did it?

   The boy would have realized that he had more to lose than gain.

Name _____ Class _____ Date _____

Managing Impulsivity Word Splash

A word splash starts with one phrase. To complete it, create several different endings for the phrase to fully describe the meaning of the term. Use the space below to create a word splash for the term *managing impulsivity*.

Managing impulsivity means …

Name _____ Class _____ Date _____

Managing Impulsivity Word Splash

A word splash starts with one phrase. To complete it, create several different endings for the phrase to fully describe the meaning of the term. Use the space below to create a word splash for the term *managing impulsivity*.

> The following is a sample answer. If students have trouble with this exercise, put the following answer on the board as an example. Or you could conduct this activity as a group exercise. List the following answers line by line and allow students to contribute their thoughts as you go.

Managing impulsivity means …

    … thinking before acting.

    … getting information.

    … waiting.

    … understanding.

    … considering what might happen.

    … not acting too soon.

Listening with Understanding and Empathy

PURPOSE OF THIS TOOL

This lesson focuses on the Habit of Mind called Listening with Understanding and Empathy. Effective, intelligent people spend time listening to other people and can cue in to oral and body language to understand their feelings. Listening helps people understand diverse perspectives. Listening with understanding and empathy means paying close attention to words and the meaning and feelings beneath the words.

This tool teaches students how to paraphrase another person's ideas, detect cues of their feelings (empathy), and accurately express what the person is trying to say. Students need to practice withholding their own values and opinions in order to really hear and understand another person's thoughts. This complex skill is rarely taught in the classroom, yet it plays a vital role in a healthy life.

The resources in this tool will enable students to

- Listen to sounds and identify feelings about those sounds.
- Identify and portray emotion behind words and phrases.
- Explain the relationship between listening and emotion.
- Explore the concept of empathy by simulating blindness.
- Use empathy to understand others.

HOW TO USE THIS TOOL

The following list of resources and activities includes the suggested sequence for using this tool:

- A Sound Feeling worksheet (Motivating Activity)
- Read It and Weep worksheet (Core Activity 1)
- Blindfolded Walking Tour (Core Activity 2)
- Understanding Empathy discussion (Reflection Activity)

The activities and tasks included in this tool should take about 60 minutes to complete. You will need the following materials:

- A recording of 10 different sounds from around the school or home (you might wish to ask students to create the soundtrack, or you might consider purchasing a commercially available recording).
- A map detailing a short walk around your school or classroom that includes obstacles and different turfs (e.g., students may need to go around corners, up steps, over

Exploring Meanings

grass, through a doorway, or between desks; they might even need to crawl through a tight space or over a chair).

• Blindfolds.

TIPS AND VARIATIONS

1. Motivating Activity

• Play a recording of sounds from around the school or home.
• Have students record their responses to the sounds they hear using the worksheet A Sound Feeling.

2. Core Activity 1

• Divide the class into groups of three or four.
• Give each group a copy of the worksheet Read It and Weep.
• Ask students to silently read the first statement. Give them a few moments to think about the meaning behind the statement. Then ask them to record a word or two to describe the meaning in the final column of the chart.
• Within the small groups, have each member read the statement aloud with the appropriate feeling or emotion. Group members should then briefly discuss the statement.
• Repeat these steps for each statement on the worksheet.
• If time permits, have students add additional statements in the bottom section of the worksheet and repeat the activity.
• Lead a class discussion in which students talk about the types of feelings and emotions they experienced when reading the statements. Ask students whether they experienced similar or different feelings when they listened to the recording of environmental sounds. Discuss with students how listening carefully can enhance the emotional side of an experience.

3. Core Activity 2

• Have a class discussion about what it might be like to be blind. Ask students to describe how blindness would affect their daily lives.
• Divide the class into pairs. Designate one person in each pair to put the blindfold over his eyes. Explain that the other person will serve as the blindfolded person's guide and that the guide's mission is to safely guide his partner student through the walking tour and back to the class.

• Conduct this activity one pair of students at a time. Every three minutes or so, hand another pair of students a map and blindfold, and instruct them begin the course. Prevent students from seeing the map in advance or watching other students complete the course.

• When all pairs have completed the course, ask students how this activity changed their perspective about the challenges of living with blindness.

4. Reflection Activity

• Ask questions such as the following: What does it mean to have empathy for someone? Did the blindfolding activity increase your empathy for people who are blind?

• Continue the discussion by telling students that everyone has problems and difficulties in their lives. Ask if they know someone whose behavior is difficult to understand. Tell students to imagine living a day as that person. For example, they might consider imagining what it would be like to be the teacher all day.

Name _____ Class _____ Date _____

A Sound Feeling

When you hear the sound recording, describe the sound in the first column on the chart below. Then indicate whether hearing the sound made you feel good or not. In the final column, describe in more detail what the sound made you think about or feel.

Sound Chart

Sound	Pleasurable?	Your Feelings or Emotions

Name _____ Class _____ Date _____

A Sound Feeling

When you hear the sound recording, describe the sound in the first column on the chart below. Then indicate whether hearing the sound made you feel good or not. In the final column, describe in more detail what the sound made you think about or feel.

> The following is a sample only. You may wish to begin by listing two or more examples on the board so students will see how to complete the chart.

Sound Chart

Sound	Pleasurable?	Your Feelings or Emotions
Bell ringing	no	It's time to get to class.
Sneezing	yes	My head feels funny.
Chalk on the blackboard	no	I've got shivers up my back!
Water running from a tap	yes	I'm thirsty.

Name _____ Class _____ Date _____

Read It and Weep

Silently read each statement below. Think about what the statement really means. Write a word or two describing how you feel when you read the statement. Then read each statement aloud with the feeling or emotion that matches the statement.

Statement	Feeling or Emotion
I won first prize!	
I left my lunch at home!	
My cat died!	
My homework is too hard!	
I made the highest grade in my class!	
I lost my shoes!	
We won the competition!	
We lost the competition!	

You can record more statements and feelings here if you like:

Statement	Feeling or Emotion

Thinking Flexibly

PURPOSE OF THIS TOOL

This tool focuses on the Habit of Mind called Thinking Flexibly. Effective, intelligent people have control. They are able to change their mind as they receive additional data. They look for unique ways to solve problems, and they have a well-developed sense of humor. They are good at seeing consequences of different options. Thinking flexibly means approaching a problem from a new angle using a novel approach.

Also called lateral thinking, this skill requires thinkers to have confidence in their intuition. They are able to tolerate confusion and ambiguity to a point. They can also let go of a problem, trusting that their subconscious can continue to apply creative strategies for solving it. As students explore this Habit of Mind, they learn to consider alternative points of view and different ways of solving problems. They learn that their initial ideas and strategies are not the only way, and that it is useful to be open-minded and creative.

The resources in this tool will enable students to

- Use flexible thinking to solve riddles.
- Consider alternatives to classic fairy tales.
- Use creativity to rewrite a classic fairy tale.
- Define the term *thinking flexibly*.

HOW TO USE THIS TOOL

The following list of resources and activities includes the suggested sequence for using this tool:

- Riddles worksheet (Motivating Activity)
- Twisted Fairy Tales worksheet (Core Activity)
- Thinking Flexibly Word Splash worksheet (Reflection Activity)

The activities and tasks included in this tool should take about 45 minutes to complete. You will need a clock or watch.

TIPS AND VARIATIONS

1. Motivating Activity

- Give students the Riddles worksheet, and tell them to work through each riddle to find the answer.

- After about three minutes, ask students if they have finished. (They will not likely be done.) Ask if they have solved any of the riddles. (Most will still be struggling to find just one or two answers.)
- Tell students that when solving riddles it is helpful to think flexibly. Ask whether anyone knows what you mean by "thinking flexibly." (Thinking flexibly is thinking about a problem in a new or different way.)
- Allow students to revisit the riddles, this time trying not to approach them in the usual way. Tell them to be open-minded. Suggest that each answer is probably not what they would expect and that they may be making it harder than it is by thinking too much.

2. Core Activity

- Give students the Twisted Fairy Tales worksheet. Explain that on this worksheet they will find summaries of several common fairy tales. Tell them to skim through the stories and pick the one they like best.
- Explain that their mission is to rewrite the story with a twist; that is, they should rewrite the story so that something completely different happens. Emphasize that the story's ending, or outcome, should be completely different from the original story's ending.
- Point out the options listed at the end of the worksheet. Tell students they may use one of these options or create their own alternative ending.
- When students are finished rewriting their stories, discuss this exercise. Pick a story and identify the traditional story line. Then call on a student who chose this story to describe her alternative version of it.
- After several students have shared their story revisions, describe how flexible thinking is needed to produce alternatives to popular stories. Point out that, in the same way, flexible thinking is needed to think about alternative points of view. Tell students that flexible thinking can come in very handy during an argument. Ask why that might be.

3. Reflection Activity

- Have students use the Thinking Flexibly Word Splash worksheet to describe what they believe the term *thinking flexibly* means.
- Allow the students to share their word splashes with classmates. Display the students' word splashes in the classroom, if you wish.

Name _____ Class _____ Date _____

Riddles

Think flexibly to solve each of the following riddles.

1. Karen has $101 made up of two bills. One is not a $1 bill. What are her two bills?

2. All of Jenny's pets are dogs except one. All of her pets are cats except one. How many cats and dogs does Jenny have?

3. Two students are sitting on opposite sides of the same desk. There is nothing between them except the desk. Why can't they see each other?

4. Shaun, who is learning to drive, went down a one-way street in the wrong direction. He did not break the law. How is that possible?

Name _____ Class _____ Date _____

Riddles

Think flexibly to solve each of the following riddles.

1. Karen has $101 made up of two bills. One is not a $1 bill. What are her two bills?

One of the bills is not a $1 bill, but the other is! Karen has one $100 bill and one $1 bill.

2. All of Jenny's pets are dogs except one. All of her pets are cats except one. How many cats and dogs does Jenny have?

She has one dog and one cat.

3. Two students are sitting on opposite sides of the same desk. There is nothing between them except the desk. Why can't they see each other?

They have their backs to the desks.

4. Shaun, who is learning to drive, went down a one-way street in the wrong direction. He did not break the law. How is that possible?

Shaun was walking.

Name _____ Class _____ Date _____

Twisted Fairy Tales

Below you will find a short version of several fairy tales. You will also see several options for rewriting each story with a different twist. Pick one option or come up with your own, and then rewrite the story.

Little Red Riding Hood

Little Red Riding Hood goes through the forest to bring her sick grandmother freshly made cakes. Along the way she runs into a wolf. She's frightened and doesn't know what to do. The wolf wants to eat her but doesn't because a woodcutter is nearby. When the wolf asks her where she is going, Little Red Riding Hood tells him she is taking cakes to her grandmother. She even tells him where her grandmother lives. The wolf then runs ahead and gobbles up the grandmother. When Little Red Riding Hood arrives, the wolf is in the grandmother's bed disguised as the girl's grandmother. Little Red Riding Hood thinks her grandmother looks very different. The disguised wolf plays his part well, however, and encourages the girl to get closer and closer until finally he gobbles her up, too.

Three Little Pigs

Three little pigs each decide to build a home. The first little pig makes a house of straw. A wolf comes along and blows his house down. The second little pig makes a house of sticks. The wolf blows that house down, too. The third little pig builds a house of bricks, and his two brothers come to his house to stay. The wolf tries to blow the house down but is not successful. He tries to trick the pig into coming out but doesn't succeed. Finally, he climbs onto the roof and attempts to slide down the chimney to surprise the pig. The pig is waiting, though. He has boiled water in a pot in the fireplace. So when the wolf slides down the chimney, he lands in the boiling water. Then the pigs have the wolf for dinner!

Jack and the Beanstalk

Jack's mother asks him to sell their only cow so they will have money for food. Jack sells the cow to a stranger for "magical" beans. His mother is mad. Jack sadly takes the beans and plants them outside the house. The next morning he awakes to see that the beans have grown into huge beanstalks that grow up to the clouds. They twist together like a ladder, so Jack decides to climb. At the top, he reaches a new land. A fairy greets him and tells him that he once lived in the beautiful castle on the hill. When the boy was just a baby, a giant came to the village, killed everyone in his family except him and his mother, and took over the castle. The giant still terrorizes the village. The fairy tells Jack to kill the giant and reclaim the village. Jack sneaks into the castle several times and takes items his mother can sell for food. One time the giant hears Jack and chases him. Fortunately, the giant trips and Jack is able to get down the beanstalk first. He chops the stalk down, so the giant falls and dies. Then Jack and his mother are able to move back to the castle and make the village a happy place again.

Hansel and Gretel

Hansel and his sister, Gretel, live with their father and stepmother. Times are tough, and there is barely enough for the family to eat. The stepmother doesn't like the children, so she convinces her husband to take them deep into the forest and leave them. The father doesn't want to but eventually gives in because he has no way to care for them. The lost children eventually happen upon a beautiful house made of chocolate and candies. The owner welcomes them and feeds them well. Soon they discover that she is really a wicked witch who plans to eat them. Gretel gets an opportunity to push the wicked witch into an oven, and they escape. They take treasures they found in the house back to their father. The stepmother has died. The father, who has been deeply grief-stricken about the loss of his children, is overjoyed to see them. They all live happily together.

Options

Little Red Riding Hood: What if Little Red Riding Hood had met a tiger or an anteater and not a wolf?

Jack and the Beanstalk: What if Jack had sold the cow for three wishes?

Three Little Pigs: What if the wolf didn't like eating pigs?

Hansel and Gretel: What if Hansel and Gretel found a kind person in the candy house?

What if . . . ? [Use your own idea!]

Your Fairy Tale Retold (use the back of this sheet or a separate sheet of paper):

Name _____ Class _____ Date _____

Thinking Flexibly Word Splash

A word splash starts with one phrase. To complete it, create several different endings for the phrase to fully describe the meaning of the term. Use the space below to create a word splash for the term *thinking flexibly*.

Thinking flexibly means . . .

Name _____ Class _____ Date _____

Thinking Flexibly Word Splash

A word splash starts with one phrase. To complete it, create several different endings for the phrase to fully describe the meaning of the term. Use the space below to create a word splash for the term *thinking flexibly*.

> The following is a sample only. If students have trouble with this exercise, put this answer on the board as an example. If you wish to conduct this activity as a group exercise, list the following answers line-by-line and allow students to contribute their thoughts as you go.

Thinking flexibly means …

  … thinking outside the box.

  … giving and taking.

  … being bendable.

  … changing your mind.

  … thinking in new ways.

  … using other options.

  … looking beyond what is there.

  … being creative.

  … having an open mind.

Thinking About Thinking (Metacognition)

PURPOSE OF THIS TOOL

This lesson focuses on the Habit of Mind called Thinking About Thinking (Metacognition). This habit focuses on our ability to know what we know and what we don't know. The major components of metacognition are developing a plan of action, maintaining that plan over a period of time, and then evaluating the plan upon its completion.

As students develop their metacognition, they become increasingly aware of their actions and the effects of those actions on others and the environment. They become better able to form internal questions as they search for meaning and information. They develop mental maps and plans for actions, mentally rehearse their plans, and reshape plans as needed during implementation. Finally, students become more skilled at self-evaluation and improving personal performance.

The resources in this tool will enable students to

- Define the term *thinking*.
- Describe thoughts with words and pictures.
- Learn how to brainstorm.
- Use a thinking buddy to assist in the thinking process.
- Learn two additional strategies to think through issues.
- Develop a strategy to solve a brain teaser.

HOW TO USE THIS TOOL

The following list of resources and activities includes the suggested sequence for using this tool:

- Give Me a Minute to Think worksheet (Motivating Activity)
- Thinking Buddy resource sheet (Core Activity 1)
- Think-Aloud Problem Solving worksheet (Extension Activity)
- Two Strategies role-playing activity (Core Activity 2)
- Barrels of Rainwater worksheet (Reflection Activity)

The activities and tasks included in this tool should take about 60 minutes to complete. You will need the following materials:

- Stopwatch or clock with a second hand
- Stuffed animal
- Materials to create a classroom poster

TIPS AND VARIATIONS

1. Motivating Activity

- Lead a group discussion using the following questions: What is thinking? What do you think about?

- Give students the Give Me a Minute to Think worksheet. Time them while they write or draw all the ideas and items they can think of in one minute. If students struggle with this activity, suggest they look around and list or draw what they see in the classroom and out the window. Also encourage them to close their eyes and list the first things that come to mind.

- Afterward, ask students this question: What happened inside your mind during this activity? (They will likely respond with statements such as, "This idea made me think of …, "I pictured it in my mind …," and "I thought of this when I was …."

- Introduce the concept of thinking aloud. Explain to students that thinking aloud is also sometimes called brainstorming. It involves saying the first thing that comes to your mind without really thinking (or planning) what you will say.

2. Core Activity 1

- Tell students that you have brought a thinking buddy to the classroom. Show students a stuffed animal. Give it a name if you wish.

- Explain that together you are going to do a think-aloud, or brainstorming, activity and that you will take the results and make a poster to display in the class. Ask students to finish this sentence: [Animal's name] is a successful problem solver because he ….

- Record student ideas on the board (see the resource page in this tool for samples). Later, create a colorful poster to use as a backdrop for the place in the classroom where you plan to keep the thinking buddy.

Note: Once students have this thinking buddy device in mind, you can use the stuffed animal whenever you pose a challenging question by say, for example, "What would our thinking buddy think?"

3. Extension Activity

- Encourage students to get their own thinking buddy and give it a name if they wish.

- Give students the Think-Aloud Problem Solving worksheet to take home. Encourage them to apply what they've learned about using a thinking strategy.

4. Core Activity 2

• Tell students that there are several ways to carefully think through challenging situations. Write the following on the board:

Strategy A

Before: Describe a plan and strategies for solving the problem or making a decision.
During: Share your thoughts with a trusted friend or adult.
After: Think about your strategies. How effective were they?

• Now list Strategy B on the board, discussing each component of the strategy as you list it.

Strategy B

Check for accuracy.
Clarify details.
Provide data, not answers.
Resist making judgments.
Stay focused on thinking.
Be persistent.

• Call on a couple of students to come to the front of the class and role-play a situation in which they use Strategy A or Strategy B to solve a problem. Suggested scenarios:

You don't think you were graded fairly on an exam.
You don't have much money in your piggy bank, but you'd like to get your
    mother a nice Mother's Day gift.
You aim to surprise your dad by making him breakfast on Father's Day.
You want to start a lawn mowing business in your neighborhood.

5. Reflection Activity

• Give students the Barrels of Rainwater worksheet. Tell them it is a brain teaser, so they will need to develop a strategy to solve it.
• After five minutes, have students pair up to discuss the challenge. If students have solved the problem, suggest they review with each other the strategy they used. If one or both have not yet solved the problem, suggest they work out a strategy together.
• Encourage students to consider the thinking processes they are using. What tools can they use? Diagrams? Lists? Remind students that the focus of this activity is to come up with a good strategy to solve the problem.

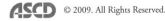

Name _____ Class _____ Date _____

Give Me a Minute to Think

When your teacher says "Go!" write down or draw all of the ideas and objects that come to your mind.

Exploring Meanings

Thinking Buddy: Qualities of a Successful Problem Solver

Our thinking buddy is a successful problem solver because he

- Thinks about thinking and knows what his brain is doing to solve the problem.
- Uses different approaches to the problem.
- Asks for help when he needs it.
- Tries to be neat and accurate.
- Makes plans.
- Thinks flexibly.
- Learns from his mistakes.
- Takes time to understand the problem.
- Makes weak parts stronger.
- Thinks before speaking and tries to be clear.
- Never gives up, even when the problem is really hard.
- Can have a good laugh.
- Remembers things he already knows.
- Uses original ideas and neat thoughts to solve the problem.
- Celebrates cool things.
- Isn't afraid to make mistakes.
- Uses strategies he's learned before.
- Asks himself questions about the problem.
- Listens well to others.
- Gets information from all his senses.

Name _____ Class _____ Date _____

TAPS: Think-Aloud Problem Solving

Get yourself a stuffed animal of some sort. If you don't already have one, make one! Be creative. This stuffed animal is now your thinking buddy. Give it a name if you wish. Whenever you have a problem or need to make a tough decision, your thinking buddy can help.

Here's what to do:

1. Talk aloud to your buddy. Imagine it talks back to you.

2. Once you've gotten the hang of talking to your buddy, *think* to your buddy. Again, imagine that it thinks back to you.

3. Soon you will be able to easily think back and forth with your buddy. At this point, you no longer need to rely on your buddy; you can do your own thinking!

Name _____ Class _____ Date _____

Barrels of Rainwater

Mindy is a wonderful gardener. One of the many ways she protects the environment while gardening is to collect rainwater in big barrels and then use it to water her garden. But now Mindy is moving to an apartment in another city. She no longer has any use for the rain barrels. Jana, Danny, and Sally are Mindy's friends. They all love to garden and have asked if she would donate the barrels to them. Mindy will give away the barrels to her friends only if she can divide them equally three ways. Help Mindy solve this problem using the following details:

- Neither Mindy nor her friends have a measuring tool of any sort.
- There are 7 full barrels of rainwater.
- There are 7 half-full barrels of rainwater.
- There are 7 empty barrels.

Use this space to figure out your answer.

Name _____ Class _____ Date _____

Barrels of Rainwater

Mindy is a wonderful gardener. One of the many ways she protects the environment while gardening is to collect rainwater in big barrels and then use it to water her garden. But now Mindy is moving to an apartment in another city. She no longer has any use for the rain barrels. Jana, Danny, and Sally are Mindy's friends. They all love to garden and have asked if she would donate the barrels to them. Mindy will give away the barrels to her friends only if she can divide them equally three ways. Help Mindy solve this problem using the following details:

- Neither Mindy nor her friends have a measuring tool of any sort.
- There are 7 full barrels of rainwater.
- There are 7 half-full barrels of rainwater.
- There are 7 empty barrels.

Use this space to figure out your answer.

Share the following hints with students one by one as needed:
1. Draw 21 circles to represent the barrels.
2. Use symbols to show the empty, full, and half-full barrels.
3. How might you combine the containers to split them evenly?
4. Sketch different options.
5. Make sure that each person gets exactly the same number of containers. Also make sure you use every container.
Solution: Each person will get three full, one half-full, and three empty barrels. Take two of the half-filled barrels and pour them into other half-filled barrels so that there are nine full barrels, nine empty barrels, and three half-full barrels. These can be split evenly among Jana, Danny, and Sally

Striving for Accuracy

Note: For the elementary grades, we have abbreviated this Habit of Mind from Striving for Accuracy and Precision to Striving for Accuracy.

Exploring Meanings

PURPOSE OF THIS TOOL

This tool focuses on the Habit of Mind called Striving for Accuracy. The habit highlights the accuracy and craftsmanship needed to produce exceptional results. Striving for accuracy means reviewing the rules, criteria, and models relevant to a task and confirming that the work completed matches the specifications given. Exploring this Habit of Mind will motivate students to take pride in their work and ensure that it is complete, correct, and faithful to the requirements of the assignment.

The resources in this tool will enable students to

- Define the term *success*.
- Identify successful people and explain characteristics that led to their success.
- Identify personal characteristics that lead to success.
- Define the term *striving for accuracy*.
- Apply this Habit of Mind to everyday life.

HOW TO USE THIS TOOL

The following list of resources and activities includes the suggested sequence for using this tool:

- Successful People worksheet (Motivating Activity)
- I'm Successful When ... worksheet (Core Activity)
- Striving for Accuracy Word Splash worksheet (Reflection Activity)
- Striving for Accuracy in Daily Lessons (Extension Activity)

The activities and tasks included in this tool should take 30–45 minutes to complete.

TIPS AND VARIATIONS

1. Motivating Activity

- Discuss with students what it means to be successful.
- Give students the Successful People worksheet and ask them to list successful people they know or have heard about. You may wish to help students get started by offering a few examples, such as a current or past president, a favorite movie star or author, an

athlete, an artist, a parent, a teacher, or a medical professional. After about five minutes, encourage volunteers to share one or two examples from their list. Ask: How do you know that person is successful?

• Ask students if thinking about specific successful people has helped them expand their definition of what it means to be successful.

2. Core Activity

• Give students the worksheet I'm Successful When .... Ask them to use this worksheet to describe how they know when they are being successful. Allow students five minutes to individually brainstorm qualities of personal success. Help students get started by personally completing the sentence yourself; for example, say, "I know that I'm successful when I get to work on time, have my lessons properly prepared, spend extra time listening to students with questions, and plan for tomorrow's lessons."

• Ask: What does it mean to "do your best" or "give it your all"? How do you know when you have done your best?

• Ask students if thinking about their own successes has helped them expand their definition of what it means to be successful.

• Introduce Striving for Accuracy as a Habit of Mind. Ask students how this term relates to success. Help students define *striving for accuracy*.

3. Reflection Activity

• Give students the Striving for Accuracy Word Splash worksheet so that they can summarize a definition of this Habit of Mind in several ways.

• Have students create a poster to illustrate what it means to strive for accuracy.

4. Extension Activity

• During regular lessons, reinforce the idea of striving for accuracy. For example, have students review their handwriting and circle their best *s*; then discuss how paying attention to details is part of the Habit of Mind of Striving for Accuracy. Similarly, when leading a math lesson, discuss the importance of accuracy in completing calculations. Talk about how one equation may be dependent upon another, so if the first equation is done correctly, the second has a much better chance of being done correctly, too.

• Explain how many activities in school and in life are dependent upon other activities in this same way.

Name _____ Class _____ Date _____

Successful People

Brainstorm a list of all the successful people you know or have heard about. Write their names below.

Name _____ Class _____ Date _____

I'm Successful When . . .

Finish the sentence stem above by describing some ways that you are successful.

1. _____

2. _____

3. _____

4. _____

5. _____

6. _____

7. _____

8. _____

9. _____

10. _____

Name _____ Class _____ Date _____

Striving for Accuracy Word Splash

A word splash starts with one phrase. To complete it, create several different endings for the phrase to fully describe the meaning of the term. Use the space below to create a word splash for the term *striving for accuracy*.

Striving for accuracy means …

Name _____ Class _____ Date _____

Striving for Accuracy Word Splash

A word splash starts with one phrase. To complete it, create several different endings for the phrase to fully describe the meaning of the term. Use the space below to create a word splash for the term *striving for accuracy*.

> The following is a sample only. If students have trouble with this exercise, put the following answer on the board as an example. If you choose to conduct this activity as a group exercise, list the following answers line by line and allow students to contribute their thoughts as you go.

Striving for accuracy means . . .

    . . . paying attention to details.

    . . . figuring out what is required.

    . . . double-checking work.

    . . . using high standards.

    . . . being correct.

    . . . constantly improving.

    . . . trying to be exact.

    . . . avoiding sloppy work.

    . . . making sure work is complete.

    . . . aiming for excellence.

Questioning and Posing Problems

PURPOSE OF THIS TOOL

This tool, focusing on the Habit of Mind called Questioning and Posing Problems, teaches students the importance of inquiring about the world around them. They learn how to pose questions about alternative points of view, ask questions to help them make causal connections and see relationships, and devise hypothetical (if/then) questions. This Habit of Mind helps students realize that questions vary in complexity, structure, and purpose. It also reinforces the value of asking good questions in order to find solutions and expand understanding.

The resources in this tool will enable students to

- Ask questions to solve a problem.
- Learn how to ask high-quality questions.
- Explore the difference between thin and thick questions.
- Apply what they have learned.

HOW TO USE THIS TOOL

The following list of resources and activities includes the suggested sequence for using this tool:

- 20 Questions (Motivating Activity)
- T-Chart worksheet (Core Activity)
- 20 Questions with Animals (Reinforcement Activity)

The activities and tasks included in this tool should take 30–45 minutes to complete.

TIPS AND VARIATIONS

1. Motivating Activity

- Play the game 20 Questions. Tell the class that you are thinking of a number between 1 and 100 and that they should figure out what it is by asking only questions that require a yes or a no answer. (Examples: Is the number above 50? Is it even? Is it a prime number?) When a student thinks he knows the number, he should stand up. Once several students are standing, call on one of them at a time to provide the answer until someone gets it right.
- Next, tell students to choose a partner. One partner should pick a number between 1 and 100, and the other should ask yes/no questions until she can guess the number.

Have students tally the number of questions asked. When all students have determined their partner's mystery number, have them total the number of questions they asked before guessing the number.

• Have the student who asked the fewest questions describe some of the questions he used. Likewise, ask one or two of the groups that required the most questions to share a few examples of questions they asked.

• Conduct a class discussion about the differences between the types of questions asked. Lead students to reflect on the quality of the questions asked.

2. Core Activity

• Introduce the idea of two types of questions: thin (or factual) and thick (or inferential). Describe thin questions as questions whose answers can be found in the text and can be completed with a few words or short sentences. Describe thick questions as questions that readers have to think about more fully because the answers require some thought, not simply recall from the text.

• Give students the T-Chart worksheet to allow them to practice asking thin and thick questions. Have students ask questions about a topic you have recently studied in class. Get them started by offering a few examples.

Note: As an alternative, have a group discussion, creating the T-chart on the board. Let students provide questions and discuss why each question is thick or thin.

• Point out that some thin questions have only one answer. Example: Which legs do frogs use to jump? (Answer: The rear legs.) Other thin questions may have multiple answers. Example: What color are frogs? (Answer: Green, yellow, red, spotted, etc.)

• If students have trouble coming up with thick questions, demonstrate how to change a thin question into a thick one. For example, change the thin question "Who is Captain Underpants?" (Answer: The principal) into the thick question "Why is the principal in *Captain Underpants* so funny?" (Answer: Principals don't usually come to school in their underwear; it is funny to see a character who is normally an authority figure become ridiculous.)

• Ask: How can you tell if a question is truly a thick question? (The answer cannot be found directly in the book; a person must form an opinion to answer it.) Make sure students understand that when they ask thick questions they are using their own creative thought and not just recalling facts (as with thin questions).

3. Reinforcement Activity

• Have students work in pairs again to play the 20 Questions game using an animal or object. This time encourage them to use as many high-quality (thick) questions as possible.

• Have students again keep a tally of the number of questions asked and compare the total with the total number of questions asked in their previous game of 20 Questions. Then ask what conclusion they can draw. (They should note that high-quality questions are more effective and efficient at getting needed answers.)

• Ask students whether they can think of an example in real life when thick questions proved (or would have proved) to be more effective than thin questions.

Name _____ Class _____ Date _____

T-Chart

List at least four **thin** questions and at least four **thick** questions in the following chart.

Thin	Thick

Name _____ Class _____ Date _____

T-Chart

List at least four **thin** questions and at least four **thick** questions in the following chart.

> The following are sample questions. You may wish to guide students by having them ask questions about something you have recently completed in class. For example, the following questions relate to Roald Dahl's *Charlie and the Chocolate Factory*.

Thin	Thick
Who is Charlie?	*What kind of person is Charlie?*
Who lives in the house with Charlie?	*Why does Charlie want to win the golden ticket?*
Who is Willy Wonka?	*Why is Willy Wonka so strange?*
What does Willy Wonka do?	*Why does Willy Wonka like Charlie so much?*

> Answers to thin questions are fact-based; they can be found in the text.

> Answers to thick questions are open to argument. However, they should be supported by the text and by good reasoning.

Applying Past Knowledge to New Situations

PURPOSE OF THIS TOOL

This lesson focuses on the Habit of Mind called Applying Past Knowledge to New Situations. With this tool, students learn the importance of drawing forth experience from the past when dealing with new situations. They begin to use their past experiences as sources of data to support, theories to explain, and processes to solve new challenges. With this Habit of Mind, students learn to abstract meaning from one experience and apply it in a new situation.

The resources in this tool will enable students to

- Define the term *past knowledge*.
- Use metaphors to explore the concept of using past knowledge.
- Explore thoughts and feelings about an old experience.
- Apply the knowledge of a past experience to help others.

HOW TO USE THIS TOOL

The following list of resources and activities includes the suggested sequence for using this tool:

- Use What You've Learned (Introductory Discussion)
- Past-Knowledge Metaphors worksheet (Motivating Activity)
- First Day at School worksheet (Core Activity)
- What to Expect brochure (Core Activity)

The activities and tasks included in this tool should take two 60-minute class periods to complete. You will need materials for creating brochures, either with construction paper and markers or by using a computer.

TIPS AND VARIATIONS

1. Introductory Discussion

- Tell students that this Habit of Mind means accessing prior knowledge and transferring that knowledge beyond the situation in which it was learned. Put simply, it means: Use what you have learned.
- Generate class discussion with questions such as the following: What is past knowledge? How do you use knowledge from the past? How do you use knowledge that you have learned?

2. Motivating Activity

• Give students the Past-Knowledge Metaphors worksheet. Encourage them to think about how they feel in each situation and then find an animal, object, or experience that reminds them of that feeling.

• Encourage volunteers to share their responses aloud.

3. Core Activity

• Give students the First Day at School worksheet. To get them thinking, recall for them what that first day of school was like for you.

• When students have finished their worksheets, discuss their responses as a class.

• Explain that being nervous on the first day of school is very normal. Ask if anyone has ever had an older sibling or friend who offered reassurance with specific examples about the school or class. Tell students that you would like them to create brochures to offer reassurance to students who will be in this class next year.

• Have students work in teams of two or three to plan and create "What to Expect" brochures for your grade level, so that next year's students will have some clues about what the class will be like. Remind students that their goal is to help younger students, so the brochures should be fun and encouraging.

• Conclude the activity with a class discussion about this question: How did your past experience help you create the "What to Expect" booklet for new students?

Name _____ Class _____ Date _____

Past-Knowledge Metaphors

Complete the sentences below to create metaphors about past knowledge.

1. Forgetting what I've done before is like _____

_____

because _____

_____

_____ .

2. Sort of remembering something I've done before is like _____

_____

because _____

_____

_____ .

3. Drawing on past knowledge is like _____

_____

because _____

_____

_____ .

Exploring Meanings

Name _____ Class _____ Date _____

Past-Knowledge Metaphors

Complete the sentences below to create metaphors about past knowledge.

> The following are sample answers only. Students' answers will vary.

1. Forgetting what I've done before is like _an empty box of Valentine's Day candies_ because _it's no good when it's empty_.

2. Sort of remembering something I've done before is like _plants I keep watering but they won't grow_ because _they don't have what they need_.

3. Drawing on past knowledge is like _celebrating my birthday_ because _everyone and everything I need is there_.

Name _____ Class _____ Date _____

First Day at School

Think back to your first day and first week of school. Remember what it was like ending your vacation and getting ready to start back to class. How did you feel? Think about it, and then answer the questions below.

1. How did you feel on the first day of school?

2. What were you afraid of or worried about?

3. What would you have liked to know about school?

4. What kind of help did you want?

Name _____ Class _____ Date _____

First Day at School

Think back to your first day and first week of school. Remember what it was like ending your vacation and getting ready to start back to class. How did you feel? Think about it, and then answer the questions below.

> The following are sample answers. You may want to encourage students to close their eyes and think quietly for a few moments before beginning this activity.

1. How did you feel on the first day of school?

   I was really nervous.

2. What were you afraid of or worried about?

   I didn't think I would have any friends. I was worried that school would be hard. I thought I would be bored.

3. What would you have liked to know about school?

   That it was really pretty and fun, and my teacher is super nice.

4. What kind of help did you want?

   I'm not sure. Maybe a short day at first just to see what everything was like. Maybe if I could have just gone for one hour the first day, that would have been good.

Thinking and Communicating with Clarity and Precision

PURPOSE OF THIS TOOL

This Habit of Mind describes effective thinking as the process of simultaneously enriching the complexity and specificity of language. The habit stresses the importance of using precise language, clearly defined terms, correct names, and universal labels and analogies to communicate accurately in both written and oral forms. In this lesson, students learn to avoid vague and imprecise language and start supporting their statements with explanations, comparisons, quantification, and evidence.

The resources in this tool will enable students to

- Determine how listening is related to thinking and communicating.
- Rely on language alone to accomplish a task.
- Discuss the value of using precise language.
- Describe what it means to think and communicate with clarity and precision.

HOW TO USE THIS TOOL

The following list of resources and activities includes the suggested sequence for using this tool:

- Chain Whispers (Motivating Activity)
- Making Patterns worksheet (Core Activity)
- Thinking and Communicating with Clarity and Precision Word Splash worksheet (Reflection Activity)

The activities and tasks included in this tool should take 60 minutes to complete. You will need the following materials:

- Scissors
- Books or screens to prevent students from seeing each other across a desk
- Plastic sandwich bags

Note: See Tips and Variations for details about and alternatives to the materials needed for the Core Activity.

Exploring Meanings

TIPS AND VARIATIONS

1. Motivating Activity

- Have students stand in a straight line.
- Whisper a message into the first student's ear. Ask that student to pass the message along by whispering it into the next person's ear. That person should then whisper the message into the next person's ear, and so on. The last person to hear the message should say it aloud. (The message will likely be much different from the original one.)
- Tell students that someone once said, "Nature gave us one tongue and two ears so that we could listen twice as much as we could speak." Ask: How does this statement apply to the activity we just completed?
- Tell students that in this lesson they will be learning about the Habit of Mind called Thinking and Communicating with Clarity and Precision.

2. Core Activity

- Give each student a copy of the Making Patterns worksheet and a pair of scissors. You could precut the shapes and give each student a baggie containing the 10 shapes, if you prefer.
- Direct students to arrange themselves in pairs; each pair should share one desk, with each partner on one side. Place a book or screen in the center of the desk to prevent each student from seeing the other's work. If you prefer, you could have students sit at separate desks with their backs to each other. The partners will need to be close enough to be able to hear each other clearly when they talk.
- Tell Student A to make a pattern with the shapes. Then ask Student A to explain to Student B what the pattern looks like. Direct Student B to use his set of shapes to try to make the same pattern. When Student B thinks he has the pattern right, let the students view each other's work.
- Repeat the activity but direct the partners to switch roles.
- Discuss the results with the class by asking questions such as these: What made this activity difficult? How successful were you? Did the second person who directed the activity have a better sense of what words to use to guide the other person? Explain. How does the language we use help with the effectiveness of our communication?

3. Reflection Activity

- Have students complete the Thinking and Communicating with Clarity and Precision Word Splash worksheet to consolidate their understanding of this Habit of Mind.
- Lead a discussion about how this Habit of Mind applies to students' schoolwork or to situations in life outside the classroom.

Name _____ Class _____ Date _____

Making Patterns

Cut out the following shapes. Then arrange the shapes into a pattern. Your partner will use clues from you to arrange his or her own shapes into the same pattern.

Name _____ Class _____ Date _____

Thinking and Communicating with Clarity and Precision Word Splash

A word splash starts with one phrase. To complete it, create several different endings for the phrase to fully describe the meaning of the term. Use the space below to create a word splash for the term *thinking and communicating with clarity and precision*.

Thinking and communicating with clarity and precision means ...

Name _____ Class _____ Date _____

Thinking and Communicating with Clarity and Precision Word Splash

A word splash starts with one phrase. To complete it, create several different endings for the phrase to fully describe the meaning of the term. Use the space below to create a word splash for the term *thinking and communicating with clarity and precision*.

> The following is a sample answer. If students have trouble with this exercise, put the following answer on the board as an example. If you prefer, you could conduct this activity as a group exercise by listing the following answers line by line and allowing students to contribute their thoughts as you go.

Thinking and communicating with clarity and precision means . . .

   . . . using precise language.

   . . . defining words.

   . . . using correct names.

   . . . using explanations.

   . . . being specific.

   . . . not using slang.

   . . . not using vague words.

   . . . avoiding fuzzy language.

Gathering Data Through All Senses

PURPOSE OF THIS TOOL

The Habit of Mind called Gathering Data Through All Senses relates to getting information into the brain through sensory pathways: gustatory, olfactory, tactile, kinesthetic, auditory, and visual. Those whose sensory pathways are open and alert absorb more information from the environment than those who are oblivious to sensory stimuli. With this tool, students learn to explore the textures, rhythms, patterns, sounds, and colors around them.

The resources in this tool will enable students to

- Remember details about a holiday.
- Categorize memories.
- Observe how we remember sensory details of events.
- Define and describe the five senses.
- Classify statements according to the senses.
- Discuss the importance of using all the senses to gather data.

HOW TO USE THIS TOOL

The following list of resources and activities includes the suggested sequence for using this tool:

- Noting Memories (Motivating Activity)
- The Five Amazing Senses worksheet (Core Activity)
- Dorria Said . . . worksheet (Core Activity)
- "The Blind Men and the Elephant" story (Read-Aloud Activity)
- Story discussion (Think-Pair-Share Activity)

The activities and tasks included in this tool should take 75 minutes to complete. You will need two or three pads of self-adhesive notes.

TIPS AND VARIATIONS

1. Motivating Activity

- Group the class into teams of three students.
- Give each student 4–6 self-adhesive notes. Ask them to write their memories of their last Halloween. Students should write each recollection on a separate self-adhesive note and place their notes randomly all over their table. Explain that there will be no

discussion, but each time a student places a note on the table, she should read the note aloud to her group members.

• Have student groups order the notes according to any categories they choose.

• When all groups are finished, lead a class discussion about how the various groups categorized their memories. Steer the conversation toward the senses. Explain that we often remember with our senses—we remember the way things sounded, tasted, felt, looked, and smelled.

2. Core Activity

• Give students the worksheet The Five Amazing Senses. Tell them to follow the directions on the worksheet to describe each sense using words or pictures. Encourage them to be creative—brainstorming ideas for each sense and then representing those ideas with powerful words or fun images.

• After students have defined the senses on their own, discuss the senses as a class. Make sure everyone has a correct understanding of the five senses.

• Give students the worksheet Dorria Said .... Ask them to classify each object by listing the correct sense described in each statement. If you wish, write additional statements on the board and have students provide the answers.

3. Read-Aloud Activity

• Tell students that you are going to read them a very old parable, which is a story with a lesson. The story is called "The Blind Men and the Elephant." Many countries have an old version of this story, but it probably originated in China sometime during the Han dynasty (202 BC–220 AD). The story can be found on page 99. Give students the story to follow along, if you wish.

4. Think-Pair-Share Activity

• Conduct a Think-Pair-Share activity as follows:

Think: Ask students to think about why each man in the story reached his conclusion.
Pair: Have students pair up and sit knee-to-knee with their partner.
Share: Ask students to discuss why each blind man reached the conclusion he reached. Students should discuss various possibilities with their partners.

• Lead a class discussion with questions such as the following: Why didn't the blind men investigate further to discover the whole truth? Why is it important to use all of our senses?

The Five Amazing Senses

Name _____ Class _____ Date _____

The Five Amazing Senses

List words or draw pictures to describe each of the five amazing senses.

Sight	Hearing	Touch
Taste	**Smell**	

Exploring Meanings

Exploring Meanings

Name _____ Class _____ Date _____

Dorria Said . . .

As part of a school exercise on the senses, Drake made a list of all the things his sister Dorria said after she got home from school yesterday. Help him finish his assignment by classifying each statement. To do so, choose the best sense for each statement. Write that sense in the blank next to the statement.

> The Five Senses:
>
> Sight
>
> Hearing
>
> Touch
>
> Taste
>
> Smell

Yesterday, Dorria said . . .

1. "I love the sound of the school bell at the end of the day!" _____

2. "Spaghetti is my favorite. This is yummy!" _____

3. "Drake, I can always tell when you forgot to take out the trash. Pee-eu!" _____

4. "Ewwww! I can't stand it when that crazy lizard licks me!" _____

5. "What are you writing there? It looks like it is about me! Why, you little . . . ."

_____

The Blind Men and the Elephant

Once upon a time, there lived six blind men in a village. One day the villagers said to them, "Hey, there is an elephant in the village today!"

The blind men had no idea what an elephant was. They decided that even though they would not be able to see it, they would go and feel it anyway. All of them went to find the elephant and learn what it was. Each touched the elephant in turn.

"Hey, the elephant is firm like a tree," said the first blind man after touching the elephant's round, strong leg.

"No, the elephant is like a rope," said the second man, who touched the thin, long tail.

"Oh, no! It is like a snake," said the third man as he touched the long, squirming trunk of the elephant.

"It is like a big hand fan," said the fourth bind man, who touched the elephant's gentle flapping ear.

"It is like a huge wall," said the fifth man, who touched the strong, wide side of the elephant.

"It is like a sharp spear," said the sixth man upon touching the elephant's smooth ivory tusk.

The blind men began to argue about the elephant, each insisting that he was right. They were getting louder and louder as they squabbled back and forth. A wise man was passing by, and he saw the argument taking place. He stopped and asked, "What is the matter?" The blind men replied, "We cannot agree about what the elephant is like." Each man then described what he thought the elephant was like. The wise man then calmly explained to them, "You are all right! Each one of you is talking about the elephant differently because each one of you touched a different part of the elephant. The elephant has all those features that you have described."

"Oh!" said all the blind men, and suddenly there was no more fighting. They felt happy that they were all right.

Note: The moral of the story is that there may be some truth to what someone says. Sometimes we can see that truth but sometimes we cannot, because the person may have a different perspective than we do. So, rather than arguing like the blind men, we should say, "Maybe you have your reasons." This way we don't get into arguments.

Creating, Imagining, and Innovating

PURPOSE OF THIS TOOL

The Habit of Mind called Creating, Imagining, and Innovating speaks to the inherent ability of all human beings to generate new, original, and clever ideas, solutions, and techniques. When this habit is well developed, a person is adept at solving problems because he or she can view a situation from many angles and offer numerous alternative possibilities. Such a person can also jump into new roles, using analogies, vision, and perspective to take charge of each new role.

People who are good at creating, imagining, and innovating are not afraid to take risks. They can push the boundaries of what is considered the norm. With this tool, students are encouraged to eliminate "can't" from their vocabulary and believe in their own creative potential.

The resources in this action tool will enable students to

- Review several popular board games to study creative elements of the games.
- Work with a team to design a board game to meet specific criteria.
- Plan, sketch, and finalize a design for a unique piece of furniture.
- Self-evaluate the furniture design.
- Discuss the creative process.
- Find opportunities for creative expression.

HOW TO USE THIS TOOL

The following list of resources and activities includes the suggested sequence for using this tool:

- Comparing Games worksheet (Motivating Activity)
- Planning Our Game worksheet (Motivating Activity)
- It's All That worksheet (Core Activity)
- Furniture Sketches worksheet (Core Activity)
- Check It Out worksheet (Core Activity)
- How It Feels to Be Creative (Reflection Activity)

The activities and tasks included in this tool should take three or four 60-minute class periods to complete. You will need the following materials:

- Sketch paper, color pencils, erasers, and rulers
- Furniture magazines or magazines with photos of different types of furniture and décor (modern, classic, eco-friendly, etc.)

TIPS AND VARIATIONS

1. Motivating Activity

- Ask: What is your favorite board game? Call on students to answer; record their ideas on the board as you go.
- Give students the Comparing Games worksheet. Have them work in small groups to complete the worksheet.
- Hold a class discussion about what students like in board games.
- Have students work in their groups to create a simple board game. Give each team the Planning Our Game worksheet to help guide their ideas. Students may wish to center their game on a topic recently covered in class. Encourage creativity and let students follow ideas that occur to them. Remind them to include the positive attributes of a great board game.

2. Core Activity

- Give students the It's All That worksheet. Allow them to work independently to plan a piece of furniture that can be used as a bed, table, and storage space. Have magazines available that students can review for ideas. Also have sketch paper, colored pencils, erasers, and rulers available for students to use.
- Hand out the Furniture Sketches worksheet to allow students to begin sketching some initial furniture ideas. Encourage them to sketch out several ideas and to label the various parts of their design and even add a caption if an explanation is needed. If students are concerned that they can't draw, tell them not to worry—it doesn't have to be perfect. Let students take this worksheet and the It's All That worksheet home to further think about and sketch their plan.
- The next day, have students use the Check It Out worksheet to self-evaluate their furniture designs. Help students see this as a positive tool for improving their designs. Encourage them not to be hard on themselves but to simply evaluate their designs objectively.
- Have a class discussion about this project so far. Without asking anyone to share their actual design, encourage students to talk about what they learned from the self-evaluation. This exercise may help students expand their own evaluations.
- Once again, allow students to take the assignment home and rethink their idea. Give each student two or more pieces of sketch paper so they can create a final sketch of their improved idea.
- When students arrive in class the next day, paste their designs on the walls. Encourage students to take a look at everyone's imaginative ideas.

Exploring Meanings

3. Reflection Activity

• Have a class discussion about the process of coming up with an original idea, sketching out some ideas, thinking about those plans, and revising as necessary. Ask questions such as the following: Did you enjoy this process? Was it difficult? What helped you? What hindered you? Did you find that being in a certain environment was useful? Did you create better when you were alone, or when you had the music on, or in some other circumstances?

Name _____ Class _____ Date _____

Comparing Games

Make a table to compare several board games that you play or know about. Begin by filling in the column headings of columns 2, 3, and 4 with features that you like about board games in general. Then, in the first column, list the names of several games, with your favorite first. Fill in the rest of the table by briefly writing what you think about each feature of each game on your list.

Name of Board Game	Feature 1:	Feature 2:	Feature 3:

Name _____ Class _____ Date _____

Comparing Games

Make a table to compare several board games that you play or know about. Begin by filling in the column headings of columns 2, 3, and 4 with features that you like about board games in general. Then, in the first column, list the names of several games, with your favorite first. Fill in the rest of the table by briefly writing what you think about each feature of each game on your list.

> The following are sample answers. You may wish to give students several examples of features and list one or more game comparisons on the board to help them get started.

Name of Board Game:	Feature 1: Good characters	Feature 2: Funny	Feature 3: Challenging
Monopoly®	Yes. I like the top hat.	Not really.	Yes, depending on whom you play with.
Operation®	Yes. I love the guy on the operating table.	I laugh a lot when I play this game.	Yes
Risk®	I guess different countries make good characters!	No	Yes
Scrabble®	No	Sometimes	Yes
Pictionary®	?	Yes!	Yes!

All of the foregoing registered trademarks are the property of their respective owners.

Name _____ Class _____ Date _____

Planning Our Game

Use this worksheet to help you plan a terrific board game!

Our game is designed for the following type of person:

The basic idea of this game is:

It's going to look like:

We need to keep in mind:

Additional thoughts:

Name _____ Class _____ Date _____

Planning Our Game

Use this worksheet to help you plan a terrific board game!

The following are sample ideas. Encourage creativity! Make sure pencils and erasers are on hand so that students can revise their plans as necessary. You may also wish to have extra worksheets and sketching paper available.

Our game is designed for the following type of person:

Boys and girls, ages 6–12

The basic idea of this game is:

It will be a taco stand. Everyone starts out with a certain amount of money. They can use the money to buy supplies for their stand. The game will be timed with a large hourglass. They will roll a die. If they roll a two, four, or six, they get a "Bad Luck" card. If they role a one, three, or five, they get an "Opportunity" card. Bad luck usually means they lose money or spaces. Opportunity cards give them stuff to make tacos, improve their taco stand, or earn money. Whoever has the most tacos by the end of the game wins.

It's going to look like:

It will have a cartoony look. The game will have little pieces that resemble the parts of the taco or taco stand they can use.

We need to keep in mind:

How big do we want the hourglass to be? (How much time is needed?) How many cards will we have time to write?

Additional thoughts:

Whenever we can, we should make the game funny. We aren't sure of a name, but may call it Taco Stand.

Name _____ Class _____ Date _____

It's All That!

Your challenge is to design a piece of furniture that is a bed, a table, and a storage space. You won't need to actually build the furniture, just create a detailed drawing that shows what it will look like and explains how it will work. Use this worksheet to help you plan your design. Then sketch your design using sketch paper.

What style will my furniture be?

What are some ways I could have it be a bed, a table, and a storage space all at once? (Brainstorm your ideas here.)

What do I need to keep in mind? (Brainstorm a list of factors to consider here.)

Name _____ Class _____ Date _____

It's All That!

Your challenge is to design a piece of furniture that is a bed, a table, and a storage space. You won't need to actually build the furniture, just create a detailed drawing that shows what it will look like and explains how it will work. Use this worksheet to help you plan your design. Then sketch your design using sketch paper.

What style will my furniture be?

> Help students decide whether they want their furniture to be fancy, colorful, modern, antique-looking, natural-looking, environmentally friendly, or some other style. Provide furniture magazines for them to look through for ideas. Tell students that this part of the process is called "looking for inspiration."

What are some ways I could have it be a bed, a table, and a storage space all at once? (Brainstorm your ideas here.)

> Encourage students to write down each and every idea that occurs to them. They may be tempted to run with one idea, but suggest that the brainstorming process is a very important way to come up with the coolest, niftiest ideas.

What do I need to keep in mind? (Brainstorm a list of factors to consider here.)

> Again, encourage students to jot down every question they may have about the process. Examples:
> How big can this piece of furniture be?
> Can I use any material I want?
> Could the table and storage space be together?
> How can I make my furniture different from everyone else's?

Name _____ Class _____ Date _____

Furniture Sketches

Use this space to draw some sketches of your furniture. Leave room to sketch several different designs. Then you can choose the best design later. Also, be sure to use pencil and have an eraser handy so you can revise your designs as you think about them!

Name _____ Class _____ Date _____

Exploring Meanings

Check It Out

Use the following questions to evaluate your furniture idea so far.

1. Is my idea practical?

2. Can my piece of furniture be easily made?

3. Is my idea as simple as possible?

4. Is it safe?

5. Is my idea original?

6. Will my furniture piece be easy to use, or will it break easily?

7. Will people want to have this type of furniture?

8. Can I do anything to make my design better?

Responding with Wonderment and Awe

PURPOSE OF THIS TOOL

The Habit of Mind known as Responding with Wonderment and Awe recognizes the "I can" and "I enjoy" attitude of intelligent people. It relates to the creative and passionate force that drives individuals to enjoy solving challenges and problems. As students develop this Habit of Mind, they learn to cultivate and appreciate their curious nature. They learn to enjoy communing with the world around them, feel charmed by natural forces, and appreciate the logical simplicity of mathematics.

This tool gets students started on the path of being passionate lifelong inquirers. Art Costa says that this Habit of Mind is "caught, not taught." With this tool, you can help inspire kids and teach them how to be open to inspiration.

The resources in this tool will enable students to

- Experience wonderment.
- Show the meaning of the terms *wonderment* and *awe* with words and pictures.
- Plan and execute a magic show.
- Observe others as they express wonderment and awe.
- Synthesize meaning from activities to create a new definition for the terms *wonderment* and *awe*.
- Work independently to learn another magic trick.

HOW TO USE THIS TOOL

The following list of resources and activities includes the suggested sequence for using this tool:

- Magic Trick (Motivating Activity)
- Wonderful Definitions worksheet (Vocabulary Activity)
- Magic Show (Core Activity)
- Wonderment and Awe Word Splash worksheet (Reflection Activity)
- Tablecloth Trick (Extension Activity)

The activities and tasks included in this tool should take three to four 60-minute class periods to complete. You will need the following materials:

- A dictionary and a thesaurus per student group
- Books with magic tricks (optional)
- Materials for creating a magic show environment (optional)

You may want to plan a trip to the school library for students to get ideas for magic tricks. If so, meet with the librarian in advance to ensure that such books are available.

TIPS AND VARIATIONS

1. Motivating Activity

- Perform a simple magic trick for the class. Use the Internet to locate and select one that you like and that would be appropriate for your students—for example, a coin or card trick.
- Perform a few other magic tricks for students if you wish. Then ask: How did you feel watching me do those tricks? (Students will likely say it was exciting to watch and exclaim that they were very surprised you could do the tricks. They may also express a desire to figure out how you did the tricks.)
- At this point, tell students they are describing the Habit of Mind called Responding with Wonderment and Awe. Say that this habit is all about being surprised, excited, and astonished to see or learn something new.

2. Vocabulary Activity

- Divide the class into groups of three or four. Give each group a dictionary and a thesaurus.
- Give each student the Wonderful Definitions worksheet. Tell students to share the dictionary and thesaurus but work independently to complete the worksheet. Encourage creativity. Some students may want to be abstract in their expression of the term.
- If the meaning of a student's image is not immediately clear, encourage the student to explain.
- When all groups are finished, discuss student answers as a class.

3. Core Activity

- Tell students you would like them to prepare a magic show for a group of younger students. Have each group of three or four plan a magic act. Explain that to create their act, students will need to research and learn several magic tricks. Have students do this research on the Internet or at the library, or have several magic books available for students to use in the classroom.
- Give students time to practice their tricks. Students may also want to decorate the classroom and create costumes for the show. When the show is ready, invite a younger class to come see it.

• After the younger students have left, ask students to discuss any wonderment and awe they noticed in audience reactions. Then ask: Did you feel any wonderment and awe personally as you watched your classmates perform? How about when you discovered new tricks?

4. Reflection Activity

• Help students synthesize what they have learned by having them complete the Wonderment and Awe Word Splash worksheet.
• Allow students to share and discuss their definitions of the terms.
Give students time to add to their word splash after hearing some other students' ideas.

5. Extension Activity

• Ask if anyone has ever seen a magician pull a tablecloth out from under a fully set table, leaving the cups and saucers safe and sound on the table. Tell students that they could try a version of this trick on their own. Explain that this is not a good trick to try on the family dinner table, as many dishes would likely get broken. However, students could ask an adult to help them try the activity at home, outside, using a plastic cup filled with water. They should place the cup on a sturdy sheet of paper close to the edge of the table. At least one-third of the paper should be over the edge of the table. Then students should practice until they are able to remove the paper without spilling the water.
• Allow students to report back to the class on what they tried, how their trick turned out, what they learned, and whether they saw wonderment in their siblings' or friends' faces when they performed the trick.

Name _____ Class _____ Date _____

Wonderful Definitions

Use a dictionary or thesaurus to look up the following words. Think about the definitions you find; then use four or five words to describe the term. Next, draw a picture to show what the word means.

My definition of *wonderment* is:

Wonderment looks like this:

My definition of *awe* is:

Awe looks like this:

Exploring Meanings

Name _____ Class _____ Date _____

Wonderment and Awe Word Splash

A word splash starts with one phrase. To complete it, create several different endings for the phrase to fully describe the meaning of the term. Use the space below to create a word splash for the terms *wonderment* and *awe*.

Wonderment and *awe* mean ...

Name _____ Class _____ Date _____

Wonderment and Awe Word Splash

A word splash starts with one phrase. To complete it, create several different endings for the phrase to fully describe the meaning of the term. Use the space below to create a word splash for the terms *wonderment* and *awe*.

> The following is a sample answer. If students have trouble with this exercise, put the following answer on the board as an example. Or you could conduct this activity as a group exercise. List the following answers line-by-line and allow students to contribute their thoughts as you go.

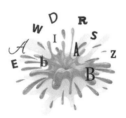

Wonderment and *awe* mean . . .

> . . . *astonishment and surprise.*

> . . . *intense curiosity.*

> . . . *excitement.*

> . . . *wanting to know the answer.*

> . . . *wanting to figure something out.*

> . . . *being very impressed.*

> . . . *enjoying something you can't figure out right away.*

Taking Responsible Risks

Exploring Meanings

PURPOSE OF THIS TOOL

As students study the Habit of Mind called Taking Responsible Risks, they learn that flexible people frequently go beyond established limits and put themselves in situations where the outcome is not known. They accept confusion, uncertainty, and the risk of failure as necessary, challenging, and rewarding. But when flexible people take risks, their risks are educated.

In this tool, students learn that there is a responsible way to take risks. Through repeated experiences, they gain knowledge that allows them to make educated decisions about when and how to risk.

The resources in this tool will enable students to

- Try a new and difficult experience.
- Analyze how the concepts of learning and failing are related.
- Define the term *risk* and distinguish between responsible and irresponsible risks.
- Brainstorm and evaluate personal risks.

HOW TO USE THIS TOOL

The following list of resources and activities includes the suggested sequence for using this tool:

- The Maze Game (Motivating Activity)
- Three Topics discussion (Core Activity)
- What's a Risk? worksheet (Core Activity)
- I'd Love to Try This! worksheet (Reflection Activity)

The activities and tasks included in this tool should take two 60-minute class periods to complete. You will need the following materials:

- A watch or clock
- Sturdy tape (such as duct tape or painter's tape)

See the Tips and Variations section for advance preparation details.

TIPS AND VARIATIONS

1. Advance Preparation

- Use tape to create a maze grid on the floor of your classroom. If you prefer, make a portable maze by using paint or colored tape on a large sheet of plastic.
- Follow this pattern or create your own:

2. Motivating Activity

- Organize students to play the Maze Game by dividing the class into groups of 10–15 and having all gather around the grid. Explain that the object of the game is to find the path through the maze. Tell them that you will say "beep" if a student stands in an incorrect space; a student who is beeped must retrace her steps off the maze using only the correct path, and yield her turn to another student. Team members should support one another's efforts as they travel through the maze. If you wish to add an extra challenge, enforce a "no talking" requirement so that students will have to support each other visually only.
- Some students may be very afraid to make a mistake. They may be tentative and eager to get help from others. Explain that the only way to get through the maze is to make mistakes and that the faster they make the mistakes, the faster they can learn.
- Point out to students how this game can apply to many real-life situations. For example, when people are asked to try something new and out of their comfort zone, they often get fearful and afraid of failing in front of others. Ask students: How did you feel when I first told you the rules of the game? How did you feel the second time you went through the maze? The third? Explain how your behavior changed over time, and why. How might what you learned relate to your daily life?

3. Core Activity

- Lead a class discussion about some of your students' favorite TV programs or movies. As volunteers suggest names of programs or movies, write them on the board. Then ask: How long do you suppose each scene takes to film (or, in an animated movie, how long does each scene take to get animated)? Tell students that, believe it or not, filmmakers and animators usually rework scenes many times. In fact, they will keep shooting or drawing until they get the scene right! The director shouts "Cut!" if a film scene is not correct, usually provides feedback and details about things that need to be corrected, and then asks the actors and crew to do the scene again. The director may even demonstrate what needs to be done.

- Lead a class discussion about the process of learning to walk. Ask: How did you learn to walk? (Typical student answer: I fell down, then got up again. Then I fell down and got up again.) Affirm that such a response is exactly right: people learn to walk by simply getting up again after they fall. Ask whether anyone in class fell so much they decided, "That's it, I'm just going to crawl for the rest of my life!"

- Lead a class discussion about taking risks and making mistakes. Sample questions: What does it mean to take a risk? What happened when you were learning to ride a bike? What about learning to read? Learning to write? Learning to tie your shoelaces? Point out that in every situation students probably failed a few times before they got it right, because humans are designed to learn by making mistakes. Conclude the discussion by soliciting responses to the following question: How do you feel about making mistakes?

- Shift the discussion to encompass the concept of responsible risk taking. Ask students to suggest examples of responsible and irresponsible risks. Record their ideas in a T-chart as each is introduced and described.

- Give students the What's a Risk? worksheet and ask them to complete it.

4. Reflection Activity

- Give students the I'd Love to Try This! worksheet. Give them five minutes to brainstorm a list of risks. Then have students categorize the risks they listed into responsible and irresponsible risks.

- Allow volunteers the opportunity to share their responses aloud.

Name _____ Class _____ Date _____

What's a Risk?

Take a moment to think about and answer the following questions.

What is a risk?

What is a responsible risk?

What is a nonresponsible, or irresponsible, risk?

Name _____ Class _____ Date _____

What's a Risk?

Take a moment to think about and answer the following questions.

> The following are sample answers. You may wish to discuss these questions as a class, or have students work in small groups to complete the worksheet.

What is a risk?

Taking a chance, trying something new.

What is a responsible risk?

Being smart about taking a chance. You should prepare first or make sure you have some experience to draw from. You should make sure the risk is not unsafe.

What is a nonresponsible, or irresponsible, risk?

Not preparing—being impulsive when taking a chance and doing something unsafe.

Name _____ Class _____ Date _____

I'd Love to Try This!

When your teacher gives you the word, list as many risky actions as you can think of that you might like to take. If you run out of room, use the back of this worksheet. When your teacher says to stop, go through your list and write "R" next to risks that are responsible and "I" next to risks that are irresponsible.

Risks I Would Like to Take	Responsible (R) or Irresponsible (I)?

Exploring Meanings

Name _____ Class _____ Date _____

I'd Love to Try This!

When your teacher gives you the word, list as many risky actions you can think of that you might like to take. If you run out of room, use the back of this worksheet. When your teacher says to stop, go through your list and write "R" next to risks that are responsible and "I" next to risks that are irresponsible.

> The following are sample answers. Allow students to work independently to complete this activity and stress that no one will see these worksheets.

Risks I Would Like to Take	Responsible (R) or Irresponsible (I)?
I would like to go skydiving.	*I*
I would like to write a comic book but I'm scared I can't draw.	*R*
I would like to ride my mountain bike to my friend's house several blocks away.	*I*
I want to learn how to build a rocket and shoot it up miles into the air.	*I*
I want to ask Misha to be my girlfriend.	*R*

Finding Humor

PURPOSE OF THIS TOOL

The Habit of Mind called Finding Humor is an essential characteristic of intelligent people. The ability to find humor in a situation has many positive physiological benefits, such as stress release and decreased blood pressure. In addition, this Habit of Mind can provoke creative and higher-order thinking, allowing a person to see powerful visual imagery and make analogies.

People who find ways to infuse humor into situations have the ability to perceive situations from an original and often interesting vantage point. Some people, however, find humor in all the wrong places, such as human differences, ineptitude, injurious behavior, vulgarity, violence, and profanity. With this tool, students can begin to distinguish between situations that require compassion and those that are truly funny.

The resources in this tool will enable students to

- Share jokes with the class.
- Explore the concept of finding humor with a Y-chart.
- Analyze a cartoon.
- Describe why finding humor is important.
- Practice finding humor by creating a funny logo.

HOW TO USE THIS TOOL

The following list of resources and activities includes the suggested sequence for using this tool:

- Sharing Jokes (Motivating Activity)
- Finding Humor Y-Chart worksheet (Core Activity)
- Watching a Cartoon (Core Activity)
- Finding Humor Word Splash worksheet (Reflection Activity)
- Creating a Finding Humor Logo (Extension Activity)

The activities and tasks included in this tool should take 75–90 minutes to complete. You will need a short, animated cartoon to complete this activity.

TIPS AND VARIATIONS

1. Motivating Activity

- Ask students if they know any good, clean jokes. (For example, a six-year-old came up with the following: "Where do bees wait? At the buzz stop!") If a student shares an inappropriate joke, have a discussion about finding humor in the wrong places. To avoid this problem, you could come to class with several jokes to share.
- Tell students that one very important characteristic of intelligent people is their ability to find humor in ordinary and even difficult situations. Ask students why finding humor is an important Habit of Mind. (It can help us relax. If we are more relaxed, we can think better. Humor can also inspire creative thinking.)

2. Core Activity 1

- Divide the class into groups of three or four. Give each group one copy of the Finding Humor Y-Chart worksheet.
- Ask students to work together, using the chart, to define the importance of the Finding Humor Habit of Mind. For example, students could ask themselves questions such as the following:

What does it look like when someone in my class finds humor? What facial expressions might I see? What body language? What does Finding Humor look like outside my classroom? On the baseball field? In a chess tournament? At the airport? At the beach?

What does it feel like when I find humor? Is there just one feeling or emotion, or several? Do my feelings change as I find humor? Does everyone experience the same feelings when they find humor?

What does it sound like when someone finds humor? What speech might I hear? What other noises? How might I talk to myself? What advice might I offer a friend who needs to find humor? How might the sounds change—for example, from the classroom to the football field?

- When students have finished, have each group discuss their Y-chart with the class. Ask: Is the Habit of Mind called Finding Humor just about being funny?

3. Core Activity 2

• Bring in a short, funny cartoon to show the class. You can record any number of funny animated shorts from TV, rent them in a video store, or even find many available for download on the Internet. You might enjoy showing the class a very old, classic cartoon.

• Ask students why the video is a good example of the Finding Humor Habit of Mind. Encourage them to discuss why the cartoon was funny. Then ask: Why do so many people enjoy cartoons?

4. Reflection Activity

• Give students the Finding Humor Word Splash worksheet to synthesize learning about this Habit of Mind.

• Allow volunteers to share their word splashes with the class. Use various students' ideas as springboards to a discussion of how this Habit of Mind applies to everyday life situations that students have had or seen.

5. Extension Activity

• Have students design and draw a logo for the Finding Humor Habit of Mind. Encourage students to be silly or wacky, if they wish, to express humor in their artwork.

• Display students' logos in the classroom or as part of a schoolwide display. You could also assemble students' logos into a booklet to share with another class or to place in the school library.

Name _____ Class _____ Date _____

Finding Humor Y-Chart

Use this chart to explore your thoughts about the Habit of Mind called Finding Humor.

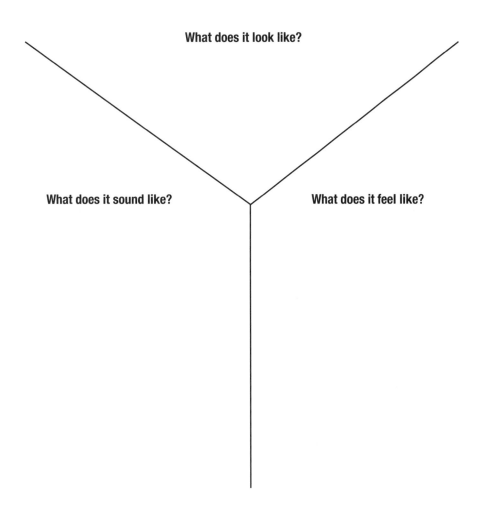

What does it look like?

What does it sound like?

What does it feel like?

Name _____ Class _____ Date _____

Finding Humor Word Splash

A word splash starts with one phrase. To complete it, create several different endings for the phrase to fully describe the meaning of the term. Use the space below to create a word splash for the phrase *finding humor*.

Finding humor is a useful skill because it . . .

Name _____ Class _____ Date _____

Finding Humor Word Splash

A word splash starts with one phrase. To complete it, create several different endings for the phrase to fully describe the meaning of the term. Use the space below to create a word splash for the phrase *finding humor*.

> If students have trouble with this exercise, put the following answer on the board as an example. If you prefer, you could conduct this activity as a group exercise by listing the following answers line by line and allowing students to contribute their thoughts as you go.

Finding humor is a useful skill because it . . .

 . . . *makes people smile.*

 . . . *makes people feel good.*

 . . . *explains things without being too harsh.*

 . . . *brings people closer together.*

 . . . *makes boring things more interesting.*

 . . . *helps people connect ideas.*

 . . . *helps people be creative.*

 . . . *helps people relax.*

 . . . *reminds people not to be so serious.*

Thinking Interdependently

PURPOSE OF THIS TOOL

The Habit of Mind called Thinking Interdependently relates to the fact that human beings are by nature social beings. Individuals who have developed this Habit of Mind understand that people can often accomplish a lot more intellectually, physically, or both by working together than they can by working alone. With complex problems, many people bring many sources of experience and data. They also bring alternative points of view and ideas.

As students develop this Habit of Mind, they learn to try out and justify ideas on others. They also develop a willingness to be open to feedback, and they become motivated to help others via constructive critiques. With this tool, students learn that listening, consensus seeking, giving up one idea to work on someone else's idea, developing empathy and compassion, leading, and supporting are all behaviors of cooperative human beings.

The resources in this tool will enable students to

- Work with classmates to create a classroom mural.
- Discuss the principles of thinking interdependently.
- Brainstorm times when more was accomplished with a group than could have been accomplished alone.
- Evaluate the performance of peers in the group activity.

HOW TO USE THIS TOOL

The following list of resources and activities includes the suggested sequence for using this tool:

- Classroom Mural (Motivating Activity)
- Working Together (Core Activity)
- We Did It! worksheet (Reflection Activity)
- Peer Evaluation (Extension Activity)

The activities and tasks included in this tool should take 60–75 minutes to complete. You will need the following materials:

- Color pencils or markers
- Copies of a colorful image
- Transparent tape

Advance preparation guidelines are included in the Tips and Variations section.

Exploring Meanings

Exploring Meanings

TIPS AND VARIATIONS

1. Advance Preparation

• Make a black and white copy of a colorful card or picture. Cut it into equal-size pieces such that every student will have a piece.

• Enlarge each piece to 8 ½" x 11" so that you will have one colorful original and 20–30 enlarged copies of various sections of the image. *Do not reveal the original image to the students!*

2. Core Activity

• Tell students they will create a classroom mural. Give each student an 8 ½" x 11" copy of the image. Ask them to use their best judgment to color their piece using colors appropriate to what they are viewing. Assure them that the classroom mural they make together will be really neat.

• When everyone has finished coloring, join the pieces together into one large image. Then reveal the original image and have students compare their work to it.

• Discuss the importance of each person's contribution to the creation of the mural.

• Discuss the activity with the class. Ask questions such as the following: What was it like not knowing how the mural would look when it was finished? Did you like the final outcome? If you had completed the activity by yourself, how do you think the end result might have been different? What benefits do you see to working cooperatively? Is the mural perfect? Does it look really neat anyway? Is there something about that mural that wouldn't be as neat if it were done perfectly by one person?

3. Reflection Activity

• Give students the We Did It! worksheet. Ask them to brainstorm a list of times when they were able to accomplish more by working with others as a group than they would have been able to accomplish alone. Students can consider classroom activities completed this year and in years past, as well as activities with family and in extracurricular venues.

• Allow volunteers to share some of the ideas as a springboard to a summarizing class discussion. You might ask how many students wrote similar things on the worksheet. You could ask students which of the accomplishments they listed were their biggest and best, or which one they were most proud of. You could ask for students' thoughts about the importance of this Habit of Mind in today's global society.

4. Extension Activity

- Discuss how important it is for group members to be able to talk to each other about their individual performances. Give a few examples of positive feedback and constructive criticism. An example of positive feedback might be, "You are really good at coloring" or "You choose colors very well." An example of constructive criticism might be, "You are a good leader, but if you aren't the chosen leader it's better for you to ask for direction rather than give it."

- Have volunteers offer compliments to class members on things they did well during the creation of the class mural and helpful ideas for improving their general ability to work well in a group to effectively complete a task.

Name _____ Class _____ Date _____

We Did It!

Brainstorm a list of times when you were able to accomplish more by working with others as a group than you would have been able to accomplish alone. Think about activities you completed in the classroom this year. You can also consider activities you completed in school in years past. Think, too, about goals you've accomplished with your family or other groups.

When I was working with a group I was able to . . .

Exploring Meanings

Name _____ Class _____ Date _____

We Did It!

Brainstorm a list of times when you were able to accomplish more by working with others as a group than you would have been able to accomplish alone. Think about activities you completed in the classroom this year. You can also consider activities you completed in school in years past. Think, too, about goals you've accomplished with your family or other groups.

> Share the following sample answers with students to help them get started.

When I was working with a group I was able to ...

... *plant a tree.*

... *plant a vegetable garden.*

... *build a playhouse.*

... *put on a magic show.*

... *go through a walking course blindfolded.*

... *make neat posters.*

... *make a board game.*

Learning Continuously

Exploring Meanings

PURPOSE OF THIS TOOL

The Habit of Mind called Learning Continuously relates to the importance of staying in a continuous learning mode. People with this Habit of Mind regularly look for ways to improve, grow, learn, and otherwise modify and improve themselves. They look upon problems and complicated circumstances as opportunities to grow and learn. Many people confront learning opportunities with fear. With this tool, students can begin to look upon challenges with wonder and intrigue.

The resources in this tool will enable students to

- List skills learned in the last year.
- Self-evaluate their willingness to learn.
- Reflect on quotations about learning.
- Provide personal examples of learning experiences.
- Help decorate a bulletin board that will make remembering the Habits of Mind easier.

HOW TO USE THIS TOOL

The following list of resources and activities includes the suggested sequence for using this tool:

- My New Skills worksheet (Motivating Activity)
- Do I Like to Learn? worksheet (Core Activity)
- It's So True! worksheet (Reflection Activity)
- Using the Habits of Mind (Extension Activity)

The activities and tasks included in this tool should take 60–90 minutes to complete. You will need the following materials:

- Color pencils and markers
- Paper
- Other art materials students could use to create a bulletin board

TIPS AND VARIATIONS

1. Motivating Activity

- Give students a copy of the My New Skills worksheet. Have them list at least three examples of new skills they have learned in the past year or so.
- Call on students to identify some of the skills they've learned. Explain that we are all continuously learning new skills.

2. Core Activity

- Give students the Do I Like to Learn? worksheet. Encourage them to think carefully about each statement and to be honest.
- If you prefer, have a one-on-one conversation with each student about his or her answers to these questions. Together, you can discuss the importance of remaining open to continuous learning and explore obstacles to doing so. Alternatively, you can have a whole-class discussion about the importance of remaining open to continuous learning.

3. Reflection Activity

- Tell the class you'd like them to work in pairs for this next activity. When they've paired off, give them each a copy of the It's So True! worksheet.
- Tell the pairs of students to discuss the quotes on the worksheet with their partner until they feel that they really understand each one.
- Then direct students to work on their own. Tell them to first pick the quote they like best and then, beneath the quote, write an example of how the quote is true for them. If time permits, ask students to provide a sample for each quote.

4. Extension Activity

- Have students help you decorate a bulletin board to describe the 16 Habits of Mind. They could incorporate logos for each icon and use symbols, quotes, and examples of activities they did while studying the habits. You may wish to provide the basic structure for the bulletin board and let students enhance it with images that will help them remember to apply the habits continuously.
- Call on volunteers to explain what they have drawn to symbolize various Habits of Mind and why. Another option is to restate or summarize what each Habit of Mind means as the students post their work on the bulletin board.

Name _____ Class _____ Date _____

My New Skills

Brainstorm a list of new skills you have learned in the past year or so. Think about things you've learned at school, at home, with friends, and with other groups.

New Skill	How did you feel about learning this skill?

Exploring Meanings

Name _____ Class _____ Date _____

My New Skills

Brainstorm a list of new skills you have learned in the past year or so. Think about things you've learned at school, at home, with friends, and with other groups.

> Share the following sample answers with students to help them get started.

New Skill	How did you feel about learning this skill?
I learned to ride my new mountain bike over the hills behind my house.	*I was scared at first, but it was really exciting— even when I fell a couple of times.*
I learned how to play the violin.	*I feel like I was born to play the violin! It's a very natural and easy thing for me to do.*
I learned why my mother wants me to take my shoes off before coming into the house if it's been raining.	*Ugggh. I got in a lot of trouble when I tracked mud through the living room. It was not fun cleaning it up!*

Name _____ Class _____ Date _____

Do I Like to Learn?

Check the statements below that are true about you.

_____ I like learning new skills.

_____ I like learning new skills only if they are related to something I'm interested in, like sports or music.

_____ I like learning new skills only if I can immediately see how they will help me.

_____ I like learning new skills if I can use them to help other people.

_____ I like learning about new technologies, like the latest video games and cell phones.

_____ I like learning new skills if the person showing me demonstrates them first.

_____ I like learning new skills only if I get a chance to practice before I have to use them.

_____ I like learning new skills only if I absolutely need to have those skills.

Name _____ Class _____ Date _____

It's So True!

Below are some quotes about the Habit of Mind called Continuous Learning. Discuss the quotes with a partner. Pick the quote you like best. Beneath that quote, write an example of how it is true for you.

"To learn is to change."
  —George B. Leonard, Author, Editor, Educator

"I think success has no rules, but you can learn a lot from failure."
  —Jean Kerr, Author

"Every person you meet—and everything you do in life—is an opportunity to learn something."
  —Tom Clancy, Author

Name _____ Class _____ Date _____

It's So True!

Below are some quotes about Continuous Learning. Discuss the quotes with a partner. Pick the quote you like best. Beneath that quote, write an example of how it is true for you.

> The following are sample answers. If time permits, have students provide personal examples for each quote.

"To learn is to change."
   —George B. Leonard, Author, Editor, Educator

Every time I come back from summer break I feel different somehow. I feel like I know a lot more than the kids in the grade below me. It may not be true, but it's a good feeling—like I'm making progress.

"I think success has no rules, but you can learn a lot from failure."
   —Jean Kerr, Author

I made up a joke and shared it with a few people. Nobody really laughed. My brother suggested a little change, and now people really laugh when I tell it!

"Every person you meet—and everything you do in life—is an opportunity to learn something."
   —Tom Clancy, Author

It seems like you never know when you're going to learn something. My Aunt Maggie, whom I didn't think I really liked that much, taught me how to play chess. I was amazed because it was so much fun and she was so much fun. I didn't think I was smart enough to learn chess, but she taught me I could. Now I really like Aunt Maggie and see her differently than I did before.

Expanding Capacities

We don't learn from our experiences; we learn from our capacity for experience.

—Buddha

This section builds upon the foundation established in the Exploring Meanings section. Teachers and students should now be familiar with all 16 Habits of Mind and have an understanding of what each one means. At this stage, however, students aren't expected to be able to recall all of the habits by memory. In addition, they haven't really assessed themselves in relation to the habits.

Expanding capacities with the Habits of Mind occurs when learners realize that they need to call upon a particular habit and consider the different ways they can use it. With the tools in this section, students will become able to select and deploy habits as appropriate, use different strategies to employ the habits, and see changes in their own lives and learning experiences because of an application of the habits. Costa and Kallick put it this way:

As students learn and practice the Habits of Mind, they become more skillful. They develop a large repertoire of strategies that they can call upon.... Learners begin to develop internal, metacognitive strategies and "self-talk" about using the Habits of Mind when confronted with problems, decisions, and ambiguous situations.... Persistence, for example, is not just a word. Rather, it is found to be a composite of numerous skills and strategies. Learners employ techniques that help them stay with a task in the face of uncertainty. When it is difficult to complete a task, learners develop new ways of encouraging themselves to stick with it. (Costa & Kallick, 2008, p. 61)

PORTFOLIO OPPORTUNITY

This section is a good place for students to begin building a portfolio to document their Habits of Mind learning experiences. They can later look back upon their initial exploration of the habits and appreciate how they have deepened their understanding.

CONTENTS

TITLE OF TOOL

Expanding Capacities

Persisting

PURPOSE OF THIS TOOL

This tool gives students opportunities to find examples of persisting in the world around them. They draw analogies and create visual portraits, and then connect their understanding to literature. As students further apply the concept of persisting, they form a deeper understanding and begin to make it a true Habit of Mind.

The resources in this tool will enable students to

- Relate an animal or object to persisting in some way.
- Visually portray how the animal relates to persisting.
- Identify examples of persistence in literature.

HOW TO USE THIS TOOL

The following list of resources includes the suggested sequence for using this tool:

- Persisting Metaphors (Introductory Discussion)
- Persisting posters (Core Activity)
- Connections to Persistence (Reflection Activity)

The activities and tasks included in this tool should take about 45 minutes to complete. You will need the following materials:

- Poster board
- Markers

TIPS AND VARIATIONS

1. Introductory Discussion

- Write the following sentences on the board:

  A cat is like the Habit of Mind called Persisting because it waits patiently for its prey. An army of ants is like the Habit of Mind called Persisting because they keep going and going to create an anthill.

- Tell students to look at these comparisons of animals to the Habit of Mind of Persisting. Ask: Do these comparisons make sense to you? Can you imagine the cat quietly waiting for the bird to land in the yard? Can you see a long row of ants slowly carrying bits of soil up a hill to create a mound?

Expanding Capacities

• If students have trouble visualizing the second scenario, ask for a volunteer to come to the board and draw what the ants and anthill might look like.

2. Core Activity

• Refresh students' minds about the meaning of the term *persisting*. Suggest that they refer to the word splash they created when they were first introduced to this Habit of Mind. If you prefer, have students create a new word splash together as a class. (For a sample answer, see page 37.)

• Give students a few minutes to think about these meanings and, individually, choose an animal or object that relates to one meaning in some way.

• Tell students to create a poster to show how their chosen animal or object relates to the Habit of Mind of Persisting.

3. Reflection Activity

• To help students make further connections with this Habit of Mind, ask them to name characters from fiction or people they know or have heard of that show characteristics of being persistent. Examples:

Horton, from *Horton Hatches the Egg*, by Dr. Seuss

The chicken, in *Are You My Mother?* by P. D. Eastman

George, in *Curious George*, by H. A. Rey

The engine, in *The Little Engine That Could*, by W. Piper

The hen, in *The Little Red Hen*, by P. Galdon

Sir Edmund Hillary, a New Zealand mountain climber, who was the first
person to reach the summit of Mount Everest

Lance Armstrong, cancer survivor and seven-time winner of the Tour de
France cycling competition

• Give students a minute or two to think about occasions in their own lives when they have shown persistence. Ask them to also think of upcoming events or situations that they know will require them to be persistent. Allow volunteers to share their thoughts with the class.

Managing Impulsivity

PURPOSE OF THIS TOOL

This lesson gives students opportunities to find examples in the world around them of the Habit of Mind called Managing Impulsivity. They learn the Stop, Think, Go model for managing impulsivity. They also learn that following directions and plans are methods for managing impulsivity. As they further apply the concept of managing impulsivity, they form a deeper understanding and begin to make it a true Habit of Mind.

The resources in this tool will enable students to

- Discuss how a character in a story could have managed his impulsivity.
- Learn the Stop, Think, Go model for managing impulsivity.
- Learn the value of following directions.
- Interview an adult to determine how they follow a plan.

HOW TO USE THIS TOOL

The following list of resources includes the suggested sequence for using this tool:

- "The Boy Who Cried Wolf" story (Motivating Activity)
- Traffic Light worksheet (Motivating Activity and Core Activity 1)
- A Simple Test worksheet (Core Activity 2)
- Following a Plan discussion (Reflection Activity)
- Planning on the Job worksheet (Extension Activity)

The activities and tasks included in this tool should take about 30 minutes to complete.

TIPS AND VARIATIONS

1. Motivating Activity

- Reread "The Boy Who Cried Wolf" to students. You can find the story in the Exploring Meanings section on page 47.
- Ask: Did the boy manage his impulsivity? Why or why not? (No. He wanted attention, so he called out to the people in town without thinking about the harm it might cause.)
- Give students a copy of the Traffic Light worksheet. Ask: What does the red light mean to a driver? (Stop.) Have students write the word *Stop* on the line at the left of the top light on their worksheet. Next ask: What does the yellow light mean? (Wait. The light is about to turn red.) Have students write the word *Wait* on the line to the

left of the middle light. Finally, ask: What does the green light mean? (Go.) Have students write the word *Go* on the line next to the bottom light.

2. Core Activity 1

- Say to students: We're going to use this traffic light to help us create a model for managing impulsivity. Ask: How could the story have turned out better for the boy? (If he had waited and thought about what was going to happen, he might not have lost the support of the villagers.)
- Tell students that to use the traffic light model for managing impulses, they need to change one word. Instruct them to write *Think* on the line to the right of the middle light, then *Stop* on the line to the right of the top light and *Go* on the line to the right of the bottom light. Explain that the new model they have just created—Stop, Think, Go—will help them manage impulsivity.
- Ask: How might the boy in the story have used the Stop, Think, Go model to manage his impulsivity? (He could have stopped his impulse to call to the villagers, thought about what might happen when they realized there wasn't really a wolf, and then gone on with his responsibilities of tending the sheep.)

3. Core Activity 2

- Give students the worksheet A Simple Test and tell them to complete the test. Remind them they must carefully follow the directions and stay quiet until everyone is finished. Say that you will be watching them carefully to make sure they are following directions. (All students need to do to pass this test is read through all the questions, put their name at the top of the page, and stay quiet. It will quickly become clear who has not followed directions.)
- Walk around the room, pretending to be taking notes on the students' performance. Observe who reads the test first and who does the activities. When it is clear who has followed directions and who has not, tell students time is up.
- Lead a discussion by asking questions such as the following: What happened? (Some people followed the directions and others did not.) How does following directions help us in the classroom? (We are better able to complete our tasks and maintain order so we can learn.) How will following directions help us in our lives? (Order is maintained and people can work better together to get things done.) When is it important to follow instructions? (In the classroom, at home, at work.) When is it OK not to follow directions? (When someone's safety is in danger or when something inappropriate or harmful is happening.)

4. Reflection Activity

• Tell students that successful people show a certain amount of deliberateness. This means that they have a plan and they stick to the plan. Explain that as a teacher you follow a plan—you start class with announcements, then call roll, then launch into the lesson you have created for the day.

• Ask students to think about other professions: What other professionals might follow a plan at work? What about an air traffic controller? A hairdresser? A pilot? A lawn mowing professional? A house cleaner? A doctor? A lawyer? A police officer? Discuss the types of plans these professionals might follow.

5. Extension Activity

• Tell students you would like them to interview a parent, guardian, or other adult about the job he or she does.

• Give students the Planning on the Job worksheet to direct their questions and help them keep track of answers.

• When they have completed their interviews, ask students to tell the class what they learned and how it relates to the Managing Impulsivity Habit of Mind.

Name _____ Class _____ Date _____

Traffic Light

What do the various lights mean in a traffic light?

Name _____ Class _____ Date _____

A Simple Test

1. Put your name at the top of the page.

2. Before answering any other questions, read to the bottom of the page.

3. Draw a circle.

4. Put an x in the circle.

5. What does 2+2 equal? _____

6. Find a yellow crayon, pencil, or felt pen.

7. Color in the circle.

8. Tap your pencil on the desk three times.

9. Stand up and turn around three times.

10. Once you have read this test, do nothing except answer question 1.

Name _____ Class _____ Date _____

Planning on the Job

Interview your parent, guardian, or another adult about the type of planning he or she does on the job or in handling responsibilities.

I interviewed _____

Questions	Answers
1. What kind of planning goes into your job?	
2. Do you follow any systems or directions?	
3. Is there a deliberateness to what you do?	
4. In what ways do you manage impulsivity on the job?	

Name _____ Class _____ Date _____

Planning on the Job

Interview your parent, guardian, or another adult about the type of planning he or she does on the job or in handling responsibilities.

Share the following sample answers with students to help them get started.

I interviewed _____ *Mom* _____

Questions	Answers
1. What kind of planning goes into your job?	*I begin my day by thinking about what needs to be done. What will we have for breakfast? Lunch? Dinner? What household repairs need to be done? Do I need to run errands? Pay bills? Water plants? Shop for groceries? Once I've answered these questions, I map out a plan for my day so that I can get everything done.*
2. Do you follow any systems or directions?	*Yes. There are certain ways to do things so that everything turns out right. For example, I follow recipes when I cook and I use certain methods to wash, fold, iron, and hang clothes. If I overwater or underwater the plants, they die. If I don't repair things properly, they get worse.*
3. Is there a deliberateness to what you do?	*Yes. I try very hard to get as much done during the day as I can so that our family can stay healthy, happy, and motivated.*
4. In what ways do you manage impulsivity on the job?	*I try to stick to my daily schedule so I get everything accomplished that I need to do. Sometimes I write a list to help me stay focused.*

Listening with Understanding and Empathy

PURPOSE OF THIS TOOL

This lesson allows students to identify examples of empathetic behavior. In addition, students receive several opportunities to practice effective listening skills. They are introduced to the Pause, Paraphrase, and Probe strategy to help them learn specific listening behaviors. As students further apply the concept of listening with understanding and empathy, they form a deeper understanding and begin to make it a true Habit of Mind.

The resources in this tool will enable students to

- Identify characters that show empathy.
- Use the Pause, Paraphrase, and Probe listening strategy to improve listening skills.
- Evaluate their listening skills in the classroom.
- Evaluate their ability to use listening skills outside the classroom.

HOW TO USE THIS TOOL

The following list of resources includes the suggested sequence for using this tool:

- *Rainbow Fish and the Big Blue Whale* (Motivating Activity)
- P-P-P Listening worksheet (Core Activity)
- Listening Checklist worksheet (Reflection Activity)
- Listening Self-Evaluation worksheet (Extension Activity)

The activities and tasks included in this tool should take about 45 minutes to complete. You will need a clock or a watch with a second hand.

TIPS AND VARIATIONS

1. Motivating Activity

- Read students the book *Rainbow Fish and the Big Blue Whale*, by Marcus Pfister. If you don't have this book readily available, you could select another short book that would demonstrate the concept of empathy.
- Define and explain for students what *empathy* means.
- Ask: Who shows empathy in this story? (Rainbow fish.) Who doesn't show empathy? (His friends.)
- Ask volunteers to share an example of a time when they felt misunderstood. Ask: How does it feel to be misunderstood? Can you think of a time that you may have

Expanding Capacities

misunderstood someone else? How might listening with understanding and empathy help you prevent misunderstandings? In class, what can we do to ensure that we do not misunderstand each other?

2. Core Activity

- Give students the P-P-P Listening worksheet. Explain that P-P-P stands for "Pause, Paraphrase, and Probe" and is a good strategy for remembering how to be a good listener. Review the worksheet with students to help them understand the strategy.
- Ask students to sit in pairs and choose which person will be the speaker and which the listener. Then explain that they will have a chance to practice the P-P-P listening strategy. Tell the speaker in each pair of students to begin talking to the listener about the school year so far. You may wish to put a conversation-starting sentence on the board such as, "This year I am most excited about . . ." or "This year, I am most proud of . . ."
- Let the speaker talk for 1–2 minutes while the listener uses the P-P-P listening strategy. You may need to remind students that this activity is a dialogue between the partners, not a monologue.
- When time is up, ask students: What are some of the strategies you used to make sure you listened well? Have the students record their answers in the "Examples" column of the P-P-P Listening worksheet.

3. Reflection Activity

- Ask students: How do you know when you have been listening well?
- Explain that a checklist is a good tool for thinking about whether they are using strategies for listening. Give students the Listening Checklist worksheet and have them use it to evaluate how well they listened to their partner. (With older students, you may wish to use the Listening Self-Evaluation worksheet form instead of the Listening Checklist.)
- Have students sit with their partners again and talk for another minute or two. Tell students this is another opportunity for them to practice their listening skills.
- Have students rate their performances in the worksheet column marked "2nd Time."
- Have students use this checklist any time you would like them to reflect on their listening skills. Give them several opportunities to practice listening so they can get the hang of the P-P-P method.

4. Extension Activity

- Encourage students to practice applying their new listening skills the rest of the day at school and that evening at home.
- The next day, give students the Listening Self-Evaluation worksheet and have them review their application of the P-P-P strategy so far.

Name _____ Class _____ Date _____

P-P-P Listening

Use these strategies to help you develop good listening skills.

Strategy	Explanation	Examples
Pause	Stop and listen to the person who is speaking without interrupting him or her.	
Paraphrase	Reword what the person said to show that you are trying to understand him or her.	
Probe	Ask questions if you are not sure about what the person has said.	

Expanding Capacities

Name _____ Class _____ Date _____

P-P-P Listening

Use these strategies to help you develop good listening skills.

Strategy	Explanation	Examples
Pause	Stop and listen to the person who is speaking without interrupting him or her.	*Use eye contact.* *Nod my head.* *Block out other noise.* *Make a list inside my head about what my partner is saying.*
Paraphrase	Reword what the person said to show that you are trying to understand him or her.	Students should list an example or two from their conversation here.
Probe	Ask questions if you are not sure about what the person has said.	Students should list an example of a question or two they asked during the conversation.

Name _____ Class _____ Date _____

Listening Checklist

Place a check in the appropriate column if you have used one of the listed listening strategies. You can add additional strategies in the blank spaces.

Checklist for Good Listening Skills

Did you . . .	1st Time	2nd Time	3rd Time
Turn your head toward the speaker?			
Nod?			
Take turns speaking?			
Use eye contact?			
Question (probe) for clarity?			
Paraphrase what the person said?			
Use facial expressions similar to the speaker's expressions?			

Expanding Capacities

Name _____ Class _____ Date _____

Listening Self-Evaluation

Use the following chart to evaluate your listening skills.

Behavior	Often	Sometimes	Not Yet
Verbal			
I restate or rephrase a person's idea before offering my opinion.			
I ask questions to make sure I understand the speaker's concepts or ideas.			
I express empathy for the speaker's feelings or emotions.			
I express a personal interest in what the speaker is saying.			
I do not interrupt the speaker.			
Nonverbal			
I face the person who is speaking.			
I establish eye contact with the speaker (if appropriate).			
I nod my head to show understanding.			
I show facial expressions similar to the speaker's.			

Thinking Flexibly

PURPOSE OF THIS TOOL

At the beginning of this tool, students realize that things are not always what they seem. Using a model, they explore an idea from many angles to make sure they really understand it before forming an opinion about the idea. Students also have an opportunity to describe real-life situations in which they have used flexible thinking.

As they further apply the concept of thinking flexibly, students form a deeper understanding and begin to make it a true Habit of Mind. They learn that their initial ideas and strategies are not the only way and that being open-minded and creative is a useful skill.

The resources in this tool will enable students to

- Realize things are not always what they seem.
- Explore an idea from many angles.
- Describe a time when they used flexible thinking in real life.

HOW TO USE THIS TOOL

The following list of resources includes the suggested sequence for using this tool:

- Rat Tails and Snail Guts discussion (Motivating Activity)
- Thumbs Up, Thumbs Down, What If worksheet (Core Activity)
- Wait a Minute worksheet (Reflection Activity)
- Background Information for Teachers (resource page)

The activities and tasks included in this tool should take about 45 minutes to complete. You will need a clock or watch with a second hand. To prepare for using this tool, you may wish to read the Background Information for Teachers resource page (see page 165).

TIPS AND VARIATIONS

1. Motivating Activity

- Ask students: What does the "thumbs up" sign mean? (Demonstrate for the class.) What about the "thumbs down" sign? (Again, demonstrate.)
- Say to students: "I've got a brilliant idea! I'm going to call the lunchroom and ask them to serve rat tails and snail guts for lunch! What do you think about that idea—thumbs up or thumbs down?" (Most students will show thumbs down.) Then say: "OK, what if the rat tails and snail guts were really spaghetti and meatballs disguised for Halloween?" (Most students will show thumbs up.)

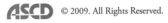

Expanding Capacities

Expanding Capacities

• Explain that things are not always what they seem. Say: "When I first mentioned rat tails and snail guts, you might have thought I was suggesting you eat nasty, contaminated food. But when I explained a little further, you could see that I was just having a little fun. It's always a good idea to think about things from several angles before you form an opinion."

2. Core Activity

• Divide the class into small groups. Give them the Thumbs Up, Thumbs Down, What If worksheet.

• Explain that the worksheet is a model students can use to think flexibly about an idea or an issue. Point out the thumbs-up image and explain that they will write good things about the idea in that area. Then tell them they will use the thumbs-down section to write things that might not be so great about the idea. Finally, tell them they will brainstorm new ideas related to the initial idea and record their thoughts in the What If section.

• For one minute, have the groups discuss the question listed at the top of the page from a thumbs-up perspective and record their thoughts in the thumbs-up section.

• Then give the groups one minute to discuss and record their thoughts from a thumbs-down perspective.

• Finally, give the groups one minute to think about the idea in a totally different way. Ask: What new ideas occur to you when thinking about this one? Can you think of any ideas that are similar to this one but perhaps solve some of the thumbs-down issues? Have students record new ideas they brainstorm in the What If section of the worksheet.

3. Reflection Activity

• Lead a discussion about what students have learned. Ask: Did you like the Thumbs Up, Thumbs Down, What If model? How is this model a good tool for thinking flexibly? Can you think of some examples of when the model could be useful? What was the hardest part of this exercise?

• Then give students the Wait a Minute worksheet and have them complete it to demonstrate a time when they were flexible in their thinking. Share the scenario on page 170 to help students get started. If they still can't think of any examples, encourage them to make up a scenario that demonstrates flexible thinking and is something they might actually do in the future.

Background Information for Teachers

One of the world's leading experts in lateral thinking is Edward de Bono. He has written numerous books about lateral thinking, creative thinking, and other thinking skills. One of the most famous of de Bono's thinking tools is called Six Thinking Hats. Check out the book that goes by the same name, *Six Thinking Hats*, for more information and ideas on flexible thinking.

Many of the major shifts in our society have come from lateral thinking. For example, in the early 19th century many people believed the only way humans would ever be able to travel long distances quickly and efficiently was by breeding faster horses. However, nothing really made long-distance travel faster until the steam train was invented.

In 1930, Michael Cullin revolutionized shopping by putting goods on accessible shelves and allowing customers to help themselves. Instantly, he created the idea of the supermarket!

For more information on lateral thinking strategies, look for books by Edward de Bono or Paul Sloane.

Expanding Capacities

Name _____ Class _____ Date _____

Thumbs Up, Thumbs Down, What If

Consider the idea below. Record your thoughts from a thumbs-up, or positive, perspective on the issue. Then record your thoughts from a thumbs-down, or negative, perspective. Finally, consider the idea as a starting point for a brainstorming session. Come up with new ideas that stem from the original.

Idea:

I could have an alligator as a pet!

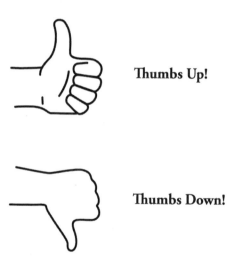 **Thumbs Up!**

Thumbs Down!

 **What If . . .**

Name _____ Class _____ Date _____

Thumbs Up, Thumbs Down, What If

Consider the idea below. Record your thoughts from a thumbs-up, or positive, perspective on the issue. Then record your thoughts from a thumbs-down, or negative, perspective. Finally, consider the idea as a starting point for a brainstorming session. Come up with new ideas that stem from the original.

Idea:
I could have an alligator as a pet!

 Thumbs Up!

Share the following sample answers with students to help them get started.

It would be a unique pet.

All my friends would be impressed.

It would be fun.

Maybe I could ride it to school!

Expanding Capacities

Thumbs Down!

I'd probably have to clean up its messes.

I'd also have to feed it.

Where would it sleep?

Would it eat the cat?

It might not be as cuddly as a dog would be.

What If . . .

. . . all my friends got alligators and they could hang out and play.

. . . I visited the zoo a lot to see the alligators—I could really get to know them.

. . . I volunteered at the zoo to help with the alligators.

. . . I offered to stop asking for an alligator if I could have two dogs instead.

Name _____ Class _____ Date _____

Wait a Minute

Think of a time when you used flexible thinking. Perhaps you changed your mind about something or changed strategies to get a different result. Use words to describe what happened. Then draw illustrations or create a comic strip to show what happened.

Description

Illustration

Expanding Capacities

Name _____ Class _____ Date _____

Wait a Minute

Think of a time when you used flexible thinking. Perhaps you changed your mind about something or changed strategies to get a different result. Use words to describe what happened. Then draw illustrations or create a comic strip to show what happened.

> Share the following sample answers with students to help them get started.

Description

I really wanted to rent a video game. I planned to ask my mom to take me to the video rental place as soon as I got up. But then I thought about it for a minute. She hates it when I want to start playing video games right after I wake up—especially if it involves her first taking me to rent or buy one! So I decided to have breakfast with her. I was sweet the whole time. I even offered to help clean the kitchen! She was in a good mood. Then I asked her to take me to the video game rental place, and she didn't mind at all! It just cost me a few minutes and was much better than her getting mad at me!

Illustration

Thinking About Thinking (Metacognition)

Expanding Capacities

PURPOSE OF THIS TOOL

Students jump into this tool with a significant and enticing challenge: to design the ultimate classroom. They are asked to create a purpose and design for their room and give it a definite style. They get an $11,000 budget and a comprehensive shopping list to manage. Later in the lesson, students are asked to create a new line of currency, incorporating symbols that reflect five important Habits of Mind for the nation.

Throughout this tool, students think through problems and form rationales for their decisions. As a result, they exercise the major components of metacognition: developing a plan of action, maintaining that plan over a period of time, and then evaluating the plan upon its completion. As students flex their metacognitive muscles, they form a deeper understanding of the concept of thinking about thinking and begin to make it a solid Habit of Mind.

The resources in this tool will enable students to

- Think about, plan, and design the ultimate classroom.
- Think about, plan, and design money notes using the Habits of Mind as a theme.
- Explain their design goals and objectives.
- Observe how people use thinking strategies in literature.

HOW TO USE THIS TOOL

The following list of resources includes the suggested sequence for using this tool:

- Ultimate Shopping, Ultimate Classroom Design, and Ultimate Goals and Plans worksheets (Core Activity)
- Money Metacognition and Money Design worksheets (Reflection Activity)
- Summary of 16 Habits of Mind worksheet (Reflection Activity)—found in Appendix B
- Thoughtful Characters (Extension Activity)

The activities and tasks included in this tool should take about 90 minutes to complete. You will need the following materials:

- Several calculators
- Pencils and erasers
- Scratch paper

TIPS AND VARIATIONS

1. Core Activity

- Invite students to pretend that they are a teacher who is competing on a TV reality show about designing rooms. Tell them they have the opportunity to design the ultimate classroom and that they have a budget of $11,000 to spend on the project.
- Give students the following worksheets for this project: Ultimate Shopping, Ultimate Classroom Design, and Ultimate Goals and Plans. Have them take a look at the purpose of each worksheet, and then get started.
- Explain to students that they need to think about what the whole room is going to look like. Caution them that rather than just picking items they like, they should have a goal in mind and design around that goal.
- Remind students that they will need to buy several of some items, such as student desks. Tell them they will need two gallons of paint to cover the entire room (more than that if they want to use several different colors). Tell them that if they want an item in their room but don't see it, they can add it at the end of the shopping list. They should then ask you or do research to find a reasonable cost estimate for that item.
- Either have students bring their shopping lists to you to calculate their totals or loan calculators to students so they can compute their own totals.
- While students are creating their designs, walk around and peer over their shoulders. Help them with proportion and make sure they are accounting for everything on their shopping lists.
- When students have finished the worksheets, post all of the designs on the walls and let students look at them. You may wish to number each design, have students pick a favorite design as if they were the director of the TV show, and then place the number of that design in a box. After everyone has voted, you can announce the name of the person the "directors" chose as the winner.
- Discuss how students thought through this activity with questions such as the following: What were you trying to achieve with your plan? What went well, and why? What would you do differently next time? Did you feel like you needed help?

2. Reflection Activity

- Tell students to imagine that they have been asked to create a new set of money for their country. Alert them to incorporate the Habits of Mind into their designs.
- Give students the Summary of 16 Habits of Mind (Appendix B), and the Money Metacognition worksheet.

- Ask them to choose five Habits of Mind that they believe would be useful for everyone in the country to be aware of and adopt. They should then think about symbols they can use to depict each. Have them summarize their ideas using the Money Metacognition worksheet.
- Give students the Money Design worksheet and have them translate their ideas onto the money design templates.
- Post students' final designs on the walls and have students evaluate them by pointing out specific strengths.

3. Extension Activity

- Ask students to consider books they've read recently. Ask questions such as the following about the main characters: How did they think about problems? How did they solve problems? Were they concerned with facts? Did they get help from friends? Encourage students to pay attention to different strategies people use to solve problems and make decisions.

Expanding Capacities

Name _____ Class _____ Date _____

Ultimate Shopping

Pretend you are a teacher who is competing on a TV reality show about designing rooms. You have the opportunity to design your ultimate classroom for your grade level. The following is a shopping list for items available to you. Circle the items you want, specify how many of each you will order, and compute the total cost of each item. Then add your totals to arrive at one grand total. Remember, you can't spend more than $11,000.

Shopping List

Item	Cost	How many?	Total Item Cost	Item	Cost	How many?	Total Item Cost
desk	$20			telescope	$250		
chair	$10			toy box	$220		
carpet mat	$50			whiteboard	$150		
desk computer	$2000			board games	$150		
laptop computer	$1500			portable stereos	$100		
TV	$600			drum kit	$250		
DVD player	$100			costumes	$50		
swimming pool	$3000			kitchen	$90		
microwave	$100			guitar	$100		
telephone	$20			couch	$150		
stereo	$200			basketball hoop	$40		
video game equipment	$150			science station	$250		
popcorn maker	$20			teacher chair	$50		

Expanding Capacities

Ultimate Shopping

Shopping List, *continued*

Item	Cost	How many?	Total Item Cost	Item	Cost	How many?	Total Item Cost
water cooler	$30			electric pencil sharpener	$50		
data projector	$2000			piano	$700		
art equipment	$200			slide	$75		
PE equipment	$300			swing	$75		
math games	$150			wooden blocks	$60		
book shelves	$80			trampoline	$300		
disco ball	$25			potted plant	$15		
table	$65			pet mouse and cage	$40		
wall paint, 1 gallon	$25			aquarium and fish	$60		
juice bar	$100			large video screen	$2000		
fountain	$100			playhouse	$150		
COLUMN TOTALS:							
GRAND TOTAL:	$			*Remember, your total can't be greater than $11,000.*			

Expanding Capacities

Name _____ Class _____ Date _____

Ultimate Classroom Design

The following is the shape of your classroom. Sketch a design, showing where you want everything to go. Label the items and wall colors.

windows along this entire wall

storage closet	bathroom	
		d o o r

Name _____ Class _____ Date _____

Ultimate Goals and Plans

Answer the questions to describe your ultimate classroom goals and plans.

1. Describe your goal for the ultimate classroom. What do you want to achieve? Remember, you are a teacher!

2. What design challenges do you face?

3. What style will you use for layout and colors?

4. Is there anything you want to do but can't? Explain.

5. What is your best design feature going to be?

Expanding Capacities

Name _____ Class _____ Date _____

Ultimate Goals and Plans

Answer the questions to describe your ultimate classroom goals and plans.

> Share the following sample answers with students to help them get started.

1. Describe your goal for the ultimate classroom. What do you want to achieve? Remember, you are a teacher!

   I want a fun classroom that is technology oriented.

2. What design challenges do you face?

   I have to fit a lot of ugly desks in the room!

3. What style will you use for layout and colors?

   I want a very modern room, so I'll use grays and reds and modern furniture.

4. Is there anything you want to do but can't? Explain.

   I'd love to have a swimming pool, but there isn't enough room and it doesn't fit with my technology theme.

5. What is your best design feature going to be?

   The big-screen TV/projector screen.

Name _____ Class _____ Date _____

Money Metacognition

In the space below, list the five Habits of Mind you want to show on the money you design. Provide a reason for each decision. Then sketch or explain the symbol you will use.

Habit of Mind	This Habit of Mind is important for this cause because ...	The symbol I will use to show this Habit of Mind is ...

ASCD © 2009. All Rights Reserved.

Expanding Capacities

Name _____ Class _____ Date _____

Money Metacognition

In the space below, list the five Habits of Mind you want to show on the money you design. Provide a reason for each decision. Then sketch or explain the symbol you will use.

> Share the following sample answers with students to help them get started.

Habit of Mind	This Habit of Mind is important for this cause because ...	The symbol I will use to show this Habit of Mind is ...
Thinking Interdependently	*Many different kinds of people live in this world. We need to learn how to get along and work together.*	*a globe*
Responding with Wonderment and Awe	*We should show respect and appreciation for our environment and for the tremendous potential of humans and other animals.*	*a tree*
Creating, Imagining, and Innovating	*We are a nation that is known for innovation. We should continue to be world leaders in inventions and in creative solutions to problems.*	*a light bulb*
Applying Past Knowledge to New Situations	*Nations that don't learn from their mistakes will repeat them. We can also learn from the mistakes other nations make.*	*a pyramid*
Listening with Understanding and Empathy	*We need to value and respect each other so we can live in peace.*	*peace symbol*

Expanding Capacities

Name _____ Class _____ Date _____

Money Design

Use these templates to design your bills.

5

10

20

50

100

Striving for Accuracy

Note: For the elementary grades, we have abbreviated this Habit of Mind from Striving for Accuracy and Precision to Striving for Accuracy.

PURPOSE OF THIS TOOL

In this lesson, students learn that some good can come from making mistakes. They discuss how much of what we learn comes from trial-and-error experiences. In addition, they discuss how they have personally learned from their mistakes. They also focus on personal accuracy by adopting and becoming a checking buddy.

As they further apply the concept of striving for accuracy, they form a deeper understanding and begin to make it a true Habit of Mind. As students continue to study this habit, they will be further motivated to take pride in their work and learning experiences.

The resources in this tool will enable students to

- Discuss the value of making mistakes.
- Create a poster to show a mistake from which they learned something.
- Discuss how a buddy can help them check their work.
- Describe how several animals demonstrate accuracy.
- Join with buddies to check one another's work.

HOW TO USE THIS TOOL

The following resource can be used with this tool:

- Animal Accuracy worksheet (Reinforcement Activity)

The activities and tasks included in this tool should take 30–45 minutes to complete. You will need poster board and markers.

TIPS AND VARIATIONS

1. Introductory Discussion

- Tell students that today you would like to talk about making mistakes. Ask: No one likes to make mistakes, right? (Students will agree.) Then ask: There is absolutely no value in making mistakes, right? (Students will likely agree again.)
- Explain that there is a lot of value in making mistakes. In fact, a significant way people learn is through a process called trial and error, which is essentially making mistakes and then correcting them.

- Share the following example with students: Imagine a child learning to walk. What does she do? She falls down, gets up, falls down, and gets up. Ask: Did anyone here ever fall down so many times that you decided to crawl from then on? (No, of course not! We all learned from our mistakes.)

- Ask students to apply the same logic to riding a bicycle: When the training wheels come off, what happens? (You wobble a lot and may fall.) Discuss with students how the wobbly feeling is natural, but eventually most people learn to balance and ride on their own without much trouble.

2. Core Activity 1

- Share a true personal experience of a time when you made a mistake, learned from it, and corrected it. Explain that trusted friends and family can often help a person work through mistakes.

- Invite students to make a poster of a time when they made a mistake and learned from it. Encourage them to label their poster with a caption or captions that explain in words what their mistake was and what they learned from it.

- When students are finished, display their posters. You may need to make space by taking down some of the class's previous Habits of Mind products and having students put them in their portfolios.

3. Core Activity 2

- Reinforce the idea of striving for accuracy by telling students they should always check their work before handing it in. Ask: What would happen if the people who wrote textbooks didn't recheck their work, and the books you learn from in school were filled with mistakes? (No one would learn correctly, or at least they wouldn't trust their textbooks.) Then have students think about and discuss this question: Is it easier to find your own mistakes or the mistakes of someone else? (It is often easier to spot other people's mistakes than to see our own.)

- Write the following letters on the board: C3B4ME. Ask students to guess what these letters might mean.

- Tell them textbook writers always get other writers and people called editors to check their work, and that they are now going to do the same thing.

- Group students together in fours, such that every student has three buddies. Say: The people around you right now are your checking buddies. Before you hand in any work to me, I want you to have your checking buddies look at it first. They need

Expanding Capacities

to sign off by putting their initials in the bottom corner. This process makes you all accountable for helping each other learn from mistakes.

• If students have not unraveled the message on the board yet, redirect their attention to the letters. Explain that from now on they should "see three (C3) buddies before (B4) me." That's C3B4ME.

4. Reinforcement Activity

• To give students an opportunity to practice the C3B4ME technique right away, give them a copy of the Animal Accuracy worksheet.

• Ask students to pick four animals from the list that they think do a good job striving for accuracy. They should list the four animals in the chart and explain why they chose each one.

• After students have completed the worksheet individually, have them meet with their buddies to exchange worksheets and check one another's work.

Name _____ Class _____ Date _____

Animal Accuracy

Take a look at the list of animals below. Circle the animals you think probably do the best job of striving for accuracy.

Owl	Dolphin	Cheetah	Bee	Butterfly	Horse
Monkey	Dog	Eagle	Elephant	Bear	Snail	Swan
Tortoise	Pig	Dragon	Octopus	Fish	Ant	Beaver
Ox	Chicken	Tiger	Crab	Cat	Donkey	Fox

Now choose four of the animals you circled and explain why you think those animals are good examples of the Habit of Mind called Striving for Accuracy.

Expanding Capacities

Animal	Explanation

Remember: Before you hand this work in, C3B4ME and have them put their initials here:

Name _____ Class _____ Date _____

Animal Accuracy

Take a look at the list of animals below. Circle the animals you think probably do the best job of striving for accuracy.

Owl	Dolphin	Cheetah	Bee	Butterfly	Horse
Monkey	Dog	Eagle	Elephant	Bear	Snail	Swan
Tortoise	Pig	Dragon	Octopus	Fish	Ant	Beaver
Ox	Chicken	Tiger	Crab	Cat	Donkey	Fox

Now choose four of the animals you circled and explain why you think those animals are good examples of the Habit of Mind called Striving for Accuracy.

> Share the following sample answers with students to help them get started.

Animal	Explanation
Cheetah	I think cheetahs strive for accuracy by being among the fastest creatures on Earth. They work really hard to run fast—they must've practiced a lot and perfected a good technique.
Fox	It seems like foxes are in a lot of stories. Sometimes they outsmart humans or other animals, so I think they must be really smart. I imagine them working very hard to hunt and capture their prey.
Owl	Owls are known for their good vision. I think they must do a lot of striving for accuracy, because they hunt at night when it is the most difficult to see!
Dolphin	I have always heard that dolphins are very intelligent. I've seen them at the water park—they can make perfect leaps out of the water. I think their dives are very accurate too, especially when they are diving for fish!

Remember: Before you hand this work in, C3B4ME and have them put their initials here:

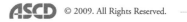

Expanding Capacities

Questioning and Posing Problems

PURPOSE OF THIS TOOL

With this tool, students continue to learn the value of asking good questions in order to find solutions and expand understanding. They apply the thick/thin questioning technique they learned in the Exploring Meanings section by asking questions about a story of an absentminded family. Then they explore reasons why the family may be absentminded, and they learn a new technique for avoiding absentmindedness themselves. As students further apply the concept of questioning and posing problems, they form a deeper understanding and begin to make it a true Habit of Mind.

The resources in this tool will enable students to

- Explore a story by asking thin and thick questions about it.
- Use questions to consider all of the factors in a situation.
- Apply the C-A-F (Consider All Factors) model at home.

HOW TO USE THIS TOOL

The following list of resources includes the suggested sequence for using this tool:

- "The Absentminded Borgs" story (Motivating Activity)
- The C-A-F Model worksheet (Core Activity)
- The C-A-F Model template (Extension Activity)

The activities and tasks included in this tool should take about 30 minutes to complete. You will need two packages of self-adhesive notes to complete this activity.

TIPS AND VARIATIONS

1. Motivating Activity

- Tell students that you are going to read a short story. Explain that while you are reading, they should write questions about the story on self-adhesive notes. Tell them to use a separate note for each question.
- On the board, create a T-chart to use later for posting thin and thick questions. Next to the chart, write the words *Who? What? When? Where? Why? How?* Explain that these words are called "the 5Ws and 1H" and that they are great words to use when asking questions.
- Tell students to carefully listen as you read and to silently write their questions.

• Read the story, which is provided on page 190. When you've finished reading, have students review their self-adhesive notes. Remind them of the differences between thin and thick questions, which they learned earlier. (If necessary, review the concept of thick and thin questions by referring to the Questioning and Posing Problems tool in the Exploring Meanings section, page 80.) Then ask students to classify their notes by writing either *thin* or *thick* on each one.

• Suggest that students convert some of their thin questions into thick questions if necessary to create a balance of both types. Then have them post their notes in the appropriate columns of the T-chart on the board.

• Have students review where their classmates have placed their questions. (Suggest students point thumbs up or thumbs down to gently express their opinions.) Decide as a class where controversial questions should be placed.

• Group similar questions together for convenience in answering them later.

Note: The primary purpose of this activity is to give students practice in forming questions, hearing others' questions, and giving and receiving feedback. It is not necessary to answer all of the questions at this time.

2. Core Activity

• Ask: What does it mean to be absentminded? Explain the importance of thinking before acting. Tell students the C-A-F model is a great tool for helping to prevent absentmindedness.

• Explain that C-A-F stands for "Consider All Factors." The model encourages students to ask good questions before making an important decision. It is also a good metacognition tool, as it helps students think about the thinking process.

• Give students the C-A-F Model worksheet with scenarios. Work through one of the scenarios as a class to help students get the hang of the tool. Then have students work in pairs to complete the other scenarios. One student can write questions as they brainstorm. When they have finished brainstorming, they should answer their questions and come up with a solution to the dilemma. Allow students 5–10 minutes per scenario to generate questions.

• Stimulate metacognitive discussion by encouraging students to talk about how the C-A-F model can help them.

3. Extension Activity

- Give students the C-A-F Model template to take with them. Suggest that students use it whenever they need to solve a problem or make an important decision.
- Keep extra copies of the template handy in the classroom as a reference for students to use as necessary.

The Absentminded Borgs

Mr. and Mrs. Tim and Nancy Borg and their kids—Susie, Arlo, and Kit—make up the Borg family. For some reason, the Borgs never quite seem to have it together. They are never on time, and they never have what they need when they get someplace!

Mr. Borg works very hard. He doesn't have as much time to spend with his kids as he would like. One day, Mr. Borg promises Susie, Arlo, and Kit that soon they will go to the mountains for a hike and a picnic. Unfortunately, he has to cancel the date a couple of times because of pressing business. Finally, the day is right and the trip to the mountains is really going to happen! The Borgs are determined to do everything right. They make a list of everything they need for the trip. Then they work together to get ready, crossing items off the list as they go. They prepare food and drinks, and they get a picnic blanket, hiking shoes, hats, insect repellent, and everything else they can possibly think of for the trip. They carefully place all the items in the car, pile in, and fasten their seat belts. It's going to be a great trip!

But when Mr. Borg puts the key in the ignition and tries to start the car, nothing happens! He sighs a heavy sigh, and says, "It looks like I'm the absentminded person in this family!"

> The following are sample questions for the T-chart:

Thin	Thick
Who are the Borgs?	Why can't Mr. Borg start the car?
Where are the Borgs going?	Why is Mr. Borg so absentminded?
What did the Borgs pack for their trip?	Do you think the Borgs will have what they need when they finally get to the mountains?
How did the family organize for the trip?	How could the family better prepare for their trip?

Name _____ Class _____ Date _____

The C-A-F Model: Consider All Factors

To consider all the factors in a situation, it's important to ask yourself good questions. Choose one or more of the scenarios below. Then brainstorm a list of questions and answer them to solve the dilemma.

Scenario 1: You are going to the grocery story to get something for an adult. On the way, you meet a friend who is going to play with some other kids you know. He asks you to come along. You would like to play but aren't sure if it's the right thing to do.

Scenario 2: You want to get a new pet but don't think your parents will be crazy about the idea.

Scenario 3: You want to get a birthday present for a friend. You have no idea what to get her.

Expanding Capacities

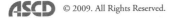

Name _____ Class _____ Date _____

The C-A-F Model: Consider All Factors

To consider all the factors in a situation, it's important to ask yourself good questions. Choose one or more of the scenarios below. Then brainstorm a list of questions and answer them to solve the dilemma.

Scenario 1: You are going to the grocery story to get something for an adult. On the way, you meet a friend who is going to play with some other kids you know. He asks you to come along. You would like to play but aren't sure if it's the right thing to do.

Scenario 2: You want to get a new pet but don't think your parents will be crazy about the idea.

Scenario 3: You want to get a birthday present for a friend. You have no idea what to get her.

Sample Answers for Scenario 1

Key Questions:

What factors are involved?
Time, adult expecting me to return, safety, fun with friends.

Who is affected by my decision?
Me, my friends, and the adult I'm helping.

Have I thought of everything?
How long will my friends play? How far away is the playground? Should I go back and let the adult know? Am I allowed to do this? If I play now, will I still have time to run my errand?

Do I have everything I need?
Permission?

Name _____ Class _____ Date _____

The C-A-F Model: Consider All Factors (Template)

Use the C-A-F model when you need to make a decision. To consider all the relevant factors, brainstorm a list of questions to ask yourself. The following are a few questions to get you started. You can add more questions. When you are finished brainstorming, answer the questions to help you make a decision.

Key Questions:

What factors are involved?

Who is affected by my decision?

Have I thought of everything?

Do I have everything I need?

Expanding Capacities

Applying Past Knowledge to New Situations

PURPOSE OF THIS TOOL

This tool offers students a fun challenge: to rewrite a classic fictional tale with a new plot. The characters are to demonstrate in some way that they can apply their past knowledge to a new situation.

With this dynamic activity, students abstract meaning from one experience and apply it in a new situation. Next, they get an opportunity to be creative, as they find images in magazines and draw pictures to express feelings they have about this Habit of Mind. Finally, students reflect on a famous quotation from Thomas Edison. As students further apply the concept of applying past knowledge to new situations, they form a deeper understanding of it and begin to make it a true Habit of Mind.

The resources in this tool will enable students to

- Write a story in which the characters apply things they've learned before in a new way.
- Use images and creativity to express an understanding of this Habit of Mind.
- Reflect on what Thomas Edison meant when he said he learned from experience.

HOW TO USE THIS TOOL

The following list of resources includes the suggested sequence for using this tool:

- Old Story, New Take (Motivating Activity)
- Design a Poster (Core Activity)
- Who Me? Make a Mistake? discussion (Reflection Activity)

The activities and tasks included in this tool should take two 60-minute class periods to complete. You will need the following materials:

- Collection of classic stories (optional)
- Magazines
- Poster-making supplies (tape or glue, markers, poster board, and scissors)

TIPS AND VARIATIONS

1. Motivating Activity

- Have students choose a classic story such as "The Three Little Pigs," "Little Red Riding Hood," "Cinderella," "Sleeping Beauty," "Rumpelstiltskin," or a classic story of their own choosing. Students probably already know these stories, but you may wish to have a collection of the classics available for reference.

- Ask students to rewrite their chosen story, using the same characters but a completely different plot. The characters should benefit in some way from the experience they had in the original story. Tell students they may present their new spin on the classic tale in a written, pictorial, or comic strip format.

- After the student presentations, discuss students' ideas as a class. Ask: How did your characters apply past knowledge in the new situation you created for them? Did they learn from their mistakes? Did they use what they learned?

2. Core Activity

- Have students design a poster to illustrate this Habit of Mind. Provide magazines, tape or glue, markers, and poster board. Encourage creativity.

- Suggest that students look for images that express what they feel when they think about applying past knowledge to new situations. Allow them the option to portray a realistic situation, if they wish, in which someone is applying past knowledge to a new situation.

Note: If students prefer and the resources are available, you could allow students to create an electronic presentation to represent this Habit of Mind instead of the poster.

3. Reflection Activity

- Write the following quotation from Thomas A. Edison on the board: "I've never made a mistake. I've only learned from experience."

- Lead students in a discussion about what this quotation means to them. Ask: How do Edison's words relate to the Habit of Mind called Applying Past Knowledge to New Situations? (We can learn from our mistakes and apply that knowledge in new situations. If the result is good, it's almost as if the mistake never occurred.)

Thinking and Communicating with Clarity and Precision

PURPOSE OF THIS TOOL

This tool helps students continue to understand that effective thinking is the process of simultaneously enriching the complexity and specificity of language. They learn why thinking and communicating with clarity and precision is so important by first observing and discussing an example of poor communication. Then they have an opportunity to communicate clearly to teach a fellow student. As students further apply the concept of thinking and communicating with clarity and precision, they form a deeper understanding of it and begin to make it a true Habit of Mind.

The resources in this tool will enable students to

- Decipher a newspaper headline.
- Discuss the importance of clear, accurate language.
- Use precise language to guide a partner.
- Describe why it is important to think and communicate with clarity and precision.

HOW TO USE THIS TOOL

The following list of resources includes the suggested sequence for using this tool:

- Parents for Breakfast worksheet (Motivating Activity)
- Tying Shoelaces (Core Activity)
- Thinking and Communicating Word Splash II worksheet (Reflection Activity)

The activities and tasks included in this tool should take 30–45 minutes to complete. You will need several pairs of shoes with laces.

TIPS AND VARIATIONS

1. Motivating Activity

- To illustrate what happens when we do not use precise language, give students the Parents for Breakfast worksheet.
- Have students work alone or in pairs to answer the questions on the worksheet.
- Lead a class discussion about why using precise language is so important. Ask: Can you think of a time when you were confused because instructions were not clear? In the article, which words have a double meaning, making the headline confusing?

2. Core Activity

- Tell students to find a partner for this activity and to decide which partner will be person A and which will be person B.
- Explain that you would like person A to teach person B how to tie a shoelace, without demonstrating. In other words, person A can use only words to communicate the explanation. Person B must follow the instructions exactly.
- When partners have finished, ask them to discuss with each other what was helpful, what was frustrating, and what worked or didn't work as they proceeded.
- Lead a whole-class discussion in which various teams can share their experiences and what they learned about communicating with clarity and precision.

3. Synthesis Activity

- Have students complete the Thinking and Communicating Word Splash II worksheet to consolidate their understanding of this Habit of Mind.
- Display students' word splashes if you wish.

Name _____ Class _____ Date _____

Parents for Breakfast

Read only the headline of the newspaper clipping shown below and then answer the first question below. After you have completed your answer, read the rest of the article and answer the remaining questions.

Students Cook and Serve Parents

As part of their farewell activities, the graduating class of Brentford Academy hosted the first-ever Gratitude Day on Wednesday, June 11. All sixth grade parents and guardians were invited to be guests of honor at a pancake breakfast in the school cafeteria. Under the guidance of their teachers, student teams worked as greeters, chefs, servers, and clean-up crews for the event. Other students coordinated and provided background music and entertainment in the form of skits and a talent show. Still other teams designed and printed the invitations, and kept track of parents' replies; they also designed and printed place cards, souvenir menus, and name tags.

The celebration served as a culminating activity for a grade-level project that involved all curricular areas and a lot of teamwork. Students and teachers began the project in February and say they all learned from the experience. They hope to make Gratitude Day an annual event as part of graduation week activities.

---

1. By itself, what does the headline appear to be saying?

2. Now read the rest of the article. What is the article really about?

3. Rewrite the headline to better reflect what the article is really about.

Name _____ Class _____ Date _____

Parents for Breakfast

Read only the headline of the newspaper clipping shown below and then answer the first question below. After you have completed your answer, read the rest of the article and answer the remaining questions.

Expanding Capacities

Students Cook and Serve Parents

As part of their farewell activities, the graduating class of Brentford Academy hosted the first-ever Gratitude Day on Wednesday, June 11. All sixth grade parents and guardians were invited to be guests of honor a pancake breakfast in the school cafeteria. Under the guidance of their teachers, student teams worked as greeters, chefs, servers, and clean-up crews for the event. Other students coordinated and provided background music and entertainment in the form of skits and a talent show.

The celebration served as a culminating activity for a grade-level project that involved all curricular areas and a lot of teamwork. Students and teachers began the project in February and say they all learned from the experience. They hope to make Gratitude Day an annual event as part of graduation week activities.

Share the following sample answers with students to help them get started.

1. By itself, what does the headline appear to be saying?

   It would seem that a bunch of kids are going to cook their parents and then serve them to someone to eat!

2. Now read the rest of the article. What is the article really about?

   Graduating students cooked and served breakfast to thank and honor their parents.

3. Rewrite the headline to better reflect what the article is really about.

   Local Graduates Honor Parents, or *Homemade Breakfast for Parents,* or *Graduating 6th Graders Sponsor Gratitude Day Event*

Name _____ Class _____ Date _____

Thinking and Communicating Word Splash II

A word splash starts with one phrase. To complete it, create several different endings for the phrase to fully describe the meaning of the term. Use the space below to create a word splash for the term *thinking and communicating with clarity and precision.*

Thinking and communicating with clarity and precision is really important because …

Expanding Capacities

Name _____ Class _____ Date _____

Thinking and Communicating Word Splash II

A word splash starts with one phrase. To complete it, create several different endings for the phrase to fully describe the meaning of the term. Use the space below to create a word splash for the term *thinking and communicating with clarity and precision*.

> The following is a sample answer. If students have trouble with this exercise, put the sample answer on the board. If you prefer, you could conduct this activity as a group exercise, listing the sample answers line by line and allowing students to contribute their thoughts as you go.

Thinking and communicating with clarity and precision is really important because …

> *… people can get confused.*

> *… someone could get hurt.*

> *… feelings could be hurt.*

> *… people could learn something that is incorrect.*

> *… people don't want to struggle to understand.*

Gathering Data Through All Senses

PURPOSE OF THIS TOOL

This tool helps students determine how they can best use their senses to learn in the classroom. Then they express their understanding of the senses creatively by writing a poem. Finally, students are encouraged to look for uses of the senses in literature. As they further apply the concept of gathering data through all the senses, students form a deeper understanding of it and begin to make it a true Habit of Mind. In the process, they become more open and alert to the environment around them.

The resources in this tool will enable students to

- Brainstorm ways to use the senses in different school subjects.
- Write a poem using the five senses.
- Find examples of the importance of the senses in literature.

HOW TO USE THIS TOOL

The following list of resources includes the suggested sequence for using this tool:

- Using Our Senses worksheet (Motivating Activity)
- A Poem for the Senses worksheet (Core Activity)
- More Stories (Extension Activity)

The activities and tasks included in this tool should take 30–45 minutes to complete. You will need markers and colored pencils.

TIPS AND VARIATIONS

1. Motivating Activity

- Tell students: "It is said that we remember 20 percent of what we read, 30 percent of what we hear, 40 percent of what we see, 50 percent of what we say, and 60 percent of what we do. If you see, hear, say, and do, the brain will remember 90 percent!"
- Give students the Using Our Senses worksheet. Have them work in small groups to complete the worksheet, and then discuss the answers as a class. You may wish to create a master list on a poster in the classroom.

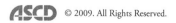

Expanding Capacities

2. Core Activity

• Ask students to choose a theme, or use a theme you are working with in class. For example, students may choose springtime or the seasons.

• Give students the worksheet A Poem for the Senses. Have them write a poem using their chosen theme and addressing one sense in each line of the poem. Tell them they can move the senses from one line to another if they wish, as long as they include all of the senses.

• When students are finished, you may wish to have them copy their poem to a clean piece of paper and decorate it with colorful illustrations. You may also want to take the poems and frame them together in a display called Gathering Data Through All Senses.

3. Extension Activity

• Have students think back to the story about the three blind men and the elephant. (If necessary, retell the story or reread it to the students—see page 99 in the Exploring Meanings section.) Tell them that many books reinforce the concept of using all the senses. Ask students if they can think of any examples.

• Suggest some additional reading students could do on their own to help them think more deeply about this Habit of Mind. Examples:

There's a Nightmare in My Cupboard, by Mercer Mayer
Charlotte's Web, by E. B. White
James and the Giant Peach, by Roald Dahl
The Diary of a Young Girl, by Anne Frank

Name _____ Class _____ Date _____

Using Our Senses

Brainstorm ideas for engaging your senses in each of the following categories. You can add additional categories at the bottom of the chart if you wish.

Subject Area	How We Can Use Our Senses
Spelling	
Reading	
Mathematics	
Science	
All subjects	

Expanding Capacities

Name _____ Class _____ Date _____

Using Our Senses

Brainstorm ideas for engaging your senses in each of the following categories. You can add additional categories at the bottom of the chart if you wish.

Share the following sample answers with students to help them get started.

Subject Area	How We Can Use Our Senses
Spelling	• We can look up the spelling of a word. • We can sound out a word and base our spelling on that. • We can listen while someone explains why a word is spelled a certain way. • We can practice by writing words out.
Reading	• We can practice reading by sight. • We can listen to someone else read to us and follow along. • We can practice by writing words out. • We can read and talk about different reading strategies.
Mathematics	• We can read about how to do a math problem before we do it. • We can talk about a math problem. • We can listen while someone else explains a math problem. • We can practice by doing math. • We can look up answers to practice questions.
Science	• We can read and talk about science. • We can listen while someone explains a science topic. • We can practice by answering questions about science. • We can learn about nature and other things by looking through a microscope or telescope, touching things, tasting things, and doing experiments.
All subjects	• We can listen very carefully. • We can read and make observations about things. • We can practice doing things. • We can brainstorm. • We can listen and share ideas. • We can do experiments and see what happens.
Art	• We can use our sense of sight to distinguish colors. • We can use textures to make things feel neat. • We can listen to unique sounds and add music to our projects.

Name _____ Class _____ Date _____

A Poem for the Senses

Write a poem using the following format, referring to each sense in its designated line.

Title:

Line 1: [Sight] _____

Line 2: [Smell] _____

Line 3: [Hearing] _____

Line 4: [Taste] _____

Line 5: [Touch] _____

Name _____ Class _____ Date _____

A Poem for the Senses

Write a poem using the following format, referring to each sense in its designated line.

> You may wish to share a sample poem such as the following to help students get started.

Title: *Spring*

    Line 1: *I see tiny shoots poking from the rich, brown earth,*

    [Sight]

    Line 2: *The scent of rain mixes with blossoms in the air,*

    [Smell]

    Line 3: *Birds chirp with newfound vibrato in the trees,*

    [Hearing]

    Line 4: *Succulent strawberries ripen in the sun,*

    [Taste]

    Line 5: *All is warm, fresh, and beautiful in the world.*

    [Touch]

Expanding Capacities

Creating, Imagining, and Innovating

PURPOSE OF THIS TOOL

In this tool, students are encouraged to observe nature, noticing oddities and fascinating qualities in plants and animals. Then they brainstorm how those features might be translated into a product for human use. In this way, they gain more experience to suggest that indeed all humans can generate original and clever ideas, solutions, and techniques. In addition, they gain more motivation to eliminate "can't" from their vocabulary and believe in their own creative potential. As students further define the terms and apply the concepts of creating, imagining, and innovating, they form a deeper understanding of this Habit of Mind and begin to make it their own.

The resources in this tool will enable students to

- Explore the meaning of the terms *creating, imagining,* and *innovating.*
- Learn how one man was inspired to create a very useful product after a nature hike.
- Observe unique adaptations found in nature.
- Brainstorm how ideas from nature can inspire new products.
- Find opportunities for creative expression.

HOW TO USE THIS TOOL

The following list of resources includes the suggested sequence for using this tool:

- Defining Terms discussion (Vocabulary Activity)
- A Burr-y Good Idea! worksheet and field trip (Core Activity)
- Looking for Opportunities to Create (Extension Activity)

The activities and tasks included in this tool should take one or two 60-minute class periods to complete. You will need pencils and small sketchpads or notebooks. For the field trip, you could plan a simple walk around the school grounds or organize a field trip to a local botanical garden, nature center, zoo, aquatic center, or other natural area.

TIPS AND VARIATIONS

1. Vocabulary Activity

- Write the words *creating, imagining,* and *innovating* on the board, leaving room to write beside each term.
- Ask students to define the term *creating.* Write their answers next to the term on the board. (Examples: Making something or saying something that wasn't present

before; coming up with new ideas and novel ways of doing things.) Tell students that the word in English and most other European languages comes from the Latin word *creatus*, which translates as "to have grown."

• Next, ask students to define the term *innovating*. (This term takes the concept of creating one step further. It means creating something new that is also useful.)

• Finally, ask students to define the term *imagining*. (Examples: Allowing one's mind to wander to follow and originate creative thoughts; forming new ideas, images, and pictures.) Explain that when imagining, the mind makes subconscious leaps and follows patterns that are unique to the person imagining. Imagining is its own activity. It does not result in an actual product.

• Tell students that the term *creativity* encompasses all three terms. Creativity is an important skill and a valuable habit. Being able to think of original ideas is a skill students can use throughout their lives. Reassure students that everyone can be creative. It just takes an understanding of the thinking involved and practice.

2. Core Activity

• Read the story provided in the worksheet A Burr-y Good Idea! Do not give the worksheet to the students.

• Plan a field trip to a natural area where students can observe various types of trees, plants, and insects that live in the area. You could lead the class on a simple nature walk around the school grounds, or you could conduct this activity at a botanical garden, zoo, or nature center. Encourage students to really observe their surroundings. Suggest they bring along a sketchpad and pencil to take notes and draw pictures of things they want to remember.

• When students have had a chance to look at a number of natural objects up close, give them the worksheet A Burr-y Good Idea! and have them work in pairs to complete it. The point of this activity is not so much for students to come up with a great idea as for them to think about what they've seen and imagine an innovation that might correspond.

3. Extension Activity

• If anyone came up with a solid invention idea during the field trip or as they completed the worksheet, encourage them to pursue the idea by creating sketches and researching whether the idea might work. Encourage students to look for additional opportunities to practice creating, imagining, and innovating, such as by making up their own endings to stories they know or creating a new piece of music.

• Consider offering extra credit points for creative projects turned in within a specific time period.

Name _____ Class _____ Date _____

A Burr-y Good Idea!

Read the following passage about the history of Velcro. Then answer the questions that follow.

> One day in 1948, a Swiss mountaineer and inventor named George de Mestral went for a nature hike with his dog. They both returned home covered with burrs. These seed sacs, which cling to animal fur for transport to fertile new planting grounds, fascinated Mestral. He looked at one of the burrs under the microscope to see what kind of structure would allow the seeds to cling so well to fabric and fur. What he saw surprised him—a bunch of tiny hooks! It also inspired him. He set out to design a two-sided fastener that would be just as good as or better than the zipper. So he created a product that had one side with stiff hooks like burrs and another side with soft loops like fabric. Initially, many people laughed at Mestral's idea. But he persisted, worked with a weaver in France, learned by trial and error, and by 1955 had perfected and patented his design. Today Velcro is a multimillion dollar industry. And it all began with a walk in nature!

1. Brainstorm a list of things in nature that are unique and interesting to you.

2. Now brainstorm how one or more of these natural objects might inspire a new product. If you can't think of anything, brainstorm something you would like to see invented, such as a product that would solve a problem you've noticed.

Name _____ Class _____ Date _____

A Burr-y Good Idea!

Read the following passage about the history of Velcro. Then answer the questions that follow.

One day in 1948, a Swiss mountaineer and inventor named George de Mestral went for a nature hike with his dog. They both returned home covered with burrs. These seed sacs, which cling to animal fur for transport to fertile new planting grounds, fascinated Mestral. He looked at one of the burrs under the microscope to see what kind of structure would allow the seeds to cling so well to fabric and fur. What he saw surprised him—a bunch of tiny hooks! It also inspired him. He set out to design a two-sided fastener that would be just as good as or better than the zipper. So he created a product that had one side with stiff hooks like burrs and another side with soft loops like fabric. Initially, many people laughed at Mestral's idea. But he persisted, worked with a weaver in France, learned by trial and error, and by 1955 had perfected and patented his design. Today Velcro is a multimillion dollar industry. And it all began with a walk in nature!

After students have had a chance to observe nature, have them brainstorm. You may want to share a few sample ideas such as these.

1. Brainstorm a list of things in nature that are unique and interesting to you.

I saw a palm tree that had a bunch of flowers shooting out of it at the top. There was a set of flowers resting on top of the leaf. It's really neat looking.

I saw huge, round, green seedpods that are as hard as a small baseball. I wonder how they break open to release seeds?

Some flowers have long stalks with lots of tiny flowers coming from them. They are in pretty colors—to attract butterflies, I guess.

Expanding Capacities

2. Now brainstorm how one or more of these natural objects might inspire a new product. If you can't think of anything, brainstorm something you would like to see invented, such as a product that would solve a problem you've noticed.

I could design an umbrella or a fan a lady might use that would have flowers lying across it. I even like the colors I saw—a green leaf with yellowish white flowers on top.

I think it would be neat to have a sculpture that had something big at the bottom, then something shooting up out of it with little tiny miniature versions of it on the stalk. Maybe it could have little peace symbols on the stalk and the sculpture could be about world peace. Or better, maybe it could have little flags or symbols for countries coming off the shoot.

Expanding Capacities

Responding with Wonderment and Awe

PURPOSE OF THIS TOOL

In this tool, music and lyrics stimulate students to celebrate wonderful things about the world around them. They express their sense of wonder by creating a poster showing things to see and do in the world around them. Then they are encouraged to regularly post questions about things they wonder about on a classroom bulletin board. As students pay more attention to their experiences of wonderment and awe, they form a deeper understanding of this Habit of Mind and begin to make it their own. As they do, they further cultivate and appreciate their curious nature and enjoyment of the world around them.

The resources in this tool will enable students to

- Listen to an artist express his experience of wonder in the world.
- Brainstorm a list of things they think are wonderful about the world.
- Create a poster to express wonderful things about their world to alien visitors.
- Ask questions about things they've wondered about.
- Continue to ask questions when they wonder about something.
- Share their experiences of wonderment and awe with the class.

HOW TO USE THIS TOOL

The following list of resources includes the suggested sequence for using this tool:

- "What a Wonderful World" or other appropriate song (Motivating Activity)
- Wonderful World poster (Core Activity)
- Wonder Board (Ongoing Activity)
- Share Your Wonderment and Awe (Extension Activity)

The activities and tasks included in this tool should take about 60 minutes to complete. You will need the following materials:

- Travel brochures and magazines
- Materials for making a poster: poster board, markers, scissors, glue
- Materials to create a classroom bulletin board

Note: Please read the Advance Preparation notes for the Core Activity.

TIPS AND VARIATIONS

1. Motivating Activity

- Have students listen carefully to a song with inspirational lyrics, such as "What a Wonderful World," (written by George David Weiss and Bob Thiele, and most famously recorded by Louis Armstrong). If students know the song, have the class sing along, if you wish.
- Ask students to brainstorm a list of amazing qualities the song lyrics made them think about (e. g., amazing qualities about our world). You may wish to have them do this individually, in small groups, or as a whole-class activity.
- Discuss student responses as a class.

2. Advance Preparation for Core Activity

- Many cities have a local board of tourism. Check to see if you can get a few brochures or magazines that students may use to find and cut out images for their posters.
- If you don't have a local board of tourism, call a board of tourism at a larger city nearby, or even your state board of tourism, and request they mail you brochures. These materials are often provided free of charge.

3. Core Activity

- Have students design a Wonderful World poster that advertises our wonderful world to outer space visitors. Ask: What attractions do you think the aliens should visit? What can you imagine might cause the aliens to say "Wow!"?
- Direct students to use pictures from magazines or draw wonderful things for the alien space visitors to see and do.

4. Ongoing Activity

- Ask: What do you wonder about? Have you ever wondered who invented the TV and why? What about how a plane flies? Why fruit spoils?
- Create a Wonder Board for the classroom. Attach a pocket that contains self-adhesive notes or papers students can write on and pin to the board. Tell students they can use this board to post notes about the things they wonder about.
- Each week, choose one topic to discuss and explore as a class.

Expanding Capacities

5. Extension Activity

• Look for unique opportunities to provoke wonderment and awe in your students. For example, one teacher was taking her daily walk along the beach one morning when she stumbled upon a baby shark that had recently died. She bundled the shark up and took it to school. There her class investigated the animal and discovered small fish inside its mouth. Then they wrote stories about the adventures the shark may have had.

Note: If you do an activity such as this, make sure you comply with health regulations. You may need to get special authorization to conduct an activity such as this. Also be sure students wear appropriate safety gear.

• Encourage students to share experiences they have had that provoked wonderment and awe.

Taking Responsible Risks

PURPOSE OF THIS TOOL

This tool helps students learn how to communicate with other people and, along the way, with themselves about value that can come from failure. They reinforce this understanding by reading about a literary character that was willing to take a risk. A class discussion about the many things that never would have been accomplished without risk solidifies student understanding about the value of risk.

As students put more thought into the notion of taking responsible risks, they form a deeper understanding of this Habit of Mind and begin to make it their own. As they do, they gain knowledge that allows them to make educated decisions about when and how to risk.

The resources in this tool will enable students to

- Show how a person's failure could be interpreted as an opportunity to learn and grow.
- Read a book or story and describe how a character took a risk.
- Distinguish between responsible and irresponsible risks.
- Discuss the importance of taking risks.

HOW TO USE THIS TOOL

The following list of resources includes the suggested sequence for using this tool:

- Relabeling Mistakes worksheet (Motivating Activity)
- A Risky Character worksheet (Core Activity)
- What If No One Risked? discussion (Reflection Activity)

The activities and tasks included in this tool should take two or three 60-minute class periods to complete. You may wish to organize a trip to the school library so students can choose an appropriate book. Alert the librarian in advance so she can have some books with risk-taking characters available.

TIPS AND VARIATIONS

1. Motivating Activity

- Give students the Relabeling Mistakes worksheet. Have them take a moment to think about each statement. They should ask themselves: How can what this person has done be seen as a learning opportunity?

 © 2009. All Rights Reserved.

- Have students respond in the second column with a reassuring answer.

2. Core Activity

- Give students an opportunity to read a book or story about a character that took a risk. Each of the following books has a relevant theme. Your librarian may be able to suggest others.

  Crash! The Story of Poddy, by William Taylor

  The Man Whose Mother Was a Pirate, by Margaret Mahy

  Danny, the Champion of the World, by Roald Dahl

  Don't Step on the Crack, by Colin McNaughton

  The *Harry Potter* series, by J. K. Rowling

- Give students the worksheet A Risky Character and have them complete it to describe a scene from their book in which a character took a risk.

3. Reflection Activity

- Have several students talk about their "risky" character. Then ask: What would the world would be like if no one took risks? (The character would not have achieved what he or she achieved. This world would be a different place, too, if no one took risks.) How different would this country be if Christopher Columbus had never risked his life to sail away and find new lands? Could a man have walked across the surface of the moon without taking a risk?

- Encourage students to think about risks in their own lives. Ask: Do you take risks in your life? (We may not be walking on the surface of the moon, but everyone is faced with risks throughout life.) What happens if we avoid risks altogether? (We may miss out on opportunities to grow our experiences and talents.) What happens if we rush into risks without thinking through the consequences for others and ourselves? (Any number of things could go wrong—for example, we could be hurt or could hurt someone else.)

- Stress to students that risks may be significant, and we must calculate what we may gain against what we might lose. Tell students that as they learn about the Habit of Mind called Taking Responsible Risks, they will become more skilled at measuring risks and knowing how to take a responsible risk.

Name _____ Class _____ Date _____

Relabeling Mistakes

Suppose friends or family members shared with you the statements in the chart below. Point out the good that came from each person's willingness to risk.

A friend or family member said:	You point out the good that came from the experience by saying:
"I can't believe I can't get down this ski slope without falling!"	
"I can't believe I thought I would be a good cheer-leader. I finished my routine facing the wrong direction. I must've looked so ridiculous. The squad was nice but said I didn't cut it."	
"I asked Jenna to be my girlfriend and she said no."	
"I thought I would be some great inventor, but look—this thing I designed doesn't do anything it's supposed to do!"	
"I entered a poetry contest and didn't even get honorable mention. I heard that nearly everyone who enters gets honorable mention."	
"I thought I would be a great lifeguard, but I didn't pass the test!"	

Name _____ Class _____ Date _____

Relabeling Mistakes

Suppose friends or family members shared with you the statements in the chart below. Point out the good that came from each person's willingness to risk.

Share the following sample answers with students to help them get started.

A friend or family member said:	You point out the good that came from the experience by saying:
"I can't believe I can't get down this ski slope without falling!"	*My ski instructor said, "If you aren't falling, you aren't trying hard enough!" I'm sure you're learning a lot from those falls and will be a better skier because of them.*
"I can't believe I thought I would be a good cheerleader. I finished my routine facing the wrong direction. I must've looked so ridiculous. The squad was nice but said I didn't cut it."	*Be proud of yourself for trying! Now you know cheerleading is not for you. Or maybe you know you need to concentrate on your routine's ending for next time. Either way, I know you can learn and grow from this!*
"I asked Jenna to be my girlfriend and she said no."	*Don't worry. I know there is a girl out there who will appreciate you. Just think of Jenna as practice, so next time you won't be so nervous.*
"I thought I would be some great inventor, but look—this thing I designed doesn't do anything it's supposed to do!"	*Keep at it. Edison said he never made a mistake—he only learned from his experiences. It took him a long time to invent the lightbulb, right?*
"I entered a poetry contest and didn't even get honorable mention. I heard that nearly everyone who enters gets honorable mention."	*First of all, don't believe everything you hear! Then remind yourself that you took a risk and that's a good thing. You were brave, and I know you can learn from this. Just keep trying.*
"I thought I would be a great lifeguard, but I didn't pass the test!"	*I've heard those tests are really tough. They have to make absolutely sure the lifeguards are capable of saving lives. Let's figure out where you fell short so you can try again.*

Expanding Capacities

Name _____ Class _____ Date _____

A Risky Character

Use this worksheet to help you analyze a book or story.

1. What is the name of the book you are reading?

2. Pick a scene from the book that shows a character taking a risk.

    a. What page number does this scene begin on?

    b. Describe the risk the character took.

    c. Was the risk responsible or irresponsible? Explain.

3. What happened after the character took the risk?

4. What would you like to say to the character about the risk he or she took?

Name _____ Class _____ Date _____

A Risky Character

Use this worksheet to help you analyze a book or story.

> The following are sample answers. You may wish to share these examples with students to help direct their analysis.

1. What is the name of the book you are reading?
Harry Potter and the Sorcerer's Stone

2. Pick a scene from the book that shows a character taking a risk.

  a. What page number does this scene begin on?
  000

  b. Describe the risk the character took.
  When Hagrid, a giant man and complete stranger to Harry, entered the lighthouse, Harry was nervous but willing to go away with him on a flying motorcycle. That was a big risk!

  c. Was the risk responsible or irresponsible? Explain.
  It was responsible, because he had read the letters from Hogwarts and realized that everything in his life was starting to make sense. He learned that his parents were good people and good witches. He learned that he had that gift. And he learned that his aunt and uncle were not being honest with him.

3. What happened after the character took the risk?
Harry went to Hogwarts and spent the rest of his school years there. He had tons of adventures, met really cool people, and got out of a house that was not nourishing to him.

4. What would you like to say to the character about the risk he or she took?
Way to go, Harry! I don't know if I would have been brave enough to get on a flying motorcycle with a giant, hairy stranger who was constantly pulling weird stuff out of his pockets. But you made the right decision. Hagrid turned out to be one of your best friends after all!

Finding Humor

PURPOSE OF THIS TOOL

With this tool, students laugh a lot. They share old jokes and create new ones, and they translate funny information into even funnier comic strips. By creating a Joke Wall to post these and future funny materials, students begin to think of humor as an important part of life. They are challenged to put themselves in others' shoes before sharing jokes; their previous lessons in empathy become relevant.

As students make finding humor a way of life, they form a deeper understanding of this Habit of Mind and begin to make it their own. As they do, they learn to assume the responsibility that comes along with finding humor, and they distinguish between situations that require compassion and those that are truly funny.

The resources in this tool will enable students to

- Translate a joke into a cartoon strip.
- Discuss what makes something funny.
- Explore individual reactions to humor.
- Discuss the responsibility that goes along with sharing humor.
- Create a knock-knock joke.

HOW TO USE THIS TOOL

The following list of resources includes the suggested sequence for using this tool:

- Finding a Good Joke (Advance Activity)
- Jokes-to-Comic Strips (Core Activity)
- Why Are Clowns Funny? discussion (Reflection Activity)
- Knock-Knock Jokes (Extension Activity for Students)
- Finding Humorous Books and Resources (Extension Activity for Teachers)

The activities and tasks included in this tool should take 45–60 minutes to complete. You will need the following materials:

- Self-adhesive notes or white board
- Materials to create a Joke Wall—drawing paper, and markers or colored pencils

TIPS AND VARIATIONS

1. Advance Activity

- Invite students to do some research and bring in a funny, clean joke they can share.

2. Core Activity

- Rather than having students share their jokes out loud, have them create a comic strip of the joke.
- Then create a Joke Wall, where students can post their comic strips. You may want to attach a pad of blank self-adhesive notes or incorporate a white board, so that students can add new jokes and funny sayings to the wall throughout the year.
- Encourage students to read the jokes before or during break time.

3. Reflection Activity

- Ask: Why are clowns funny? (Because they dress up in bright costumes and act silly to make people laugh.) Does everyone think clowns are funny? (No. Some people find clowns scary or think their jokes are too silly.) How do you feel about that?
- Make sure students understand that it is important to respect people's differences. Tell students that it's OK to think something is funny even though someone else does not. Neither person is right or wrong—just different. Discuss how humor can be a very individual experience. It should not be used to put people down or make people feel uncomfortable. Healthy humor is humor that helps people feel good.
- Explain that students can apply what they've learned about empathy to using humor. Caution them that when sharing humor they should be aware of the perspectives of the people who are listening, and that by attempting to feel what the audience might feel they can avoid hurting people's feelings. Tell students to ask themselves: If I were the target of this joke, how would I feel? Say that if the answer is "bad," then they shouldn't share the joke. Remind students to be honest with themselves.

4. Extension Activity for Students

- Have students work in small groups to create knock-knock jokes.
- Add the students' knock-knocks to the Joke Wall.

5. Extension Activity for Teachers

- Do some research to find funny books and Web sites for kids. Recommend these to students.
- Periodically bring in funny puzzle books, joke books, or Internet resources to allow students to have some fun.

Thinking Interdependently

PURPOSE OF THIS TOOL

This tool gives students another opportunity to complete a group activity. Before beginning, they recall what they have learned about thinking interdependently so far. They discuss important behaviors for team members to exhibit. Then they demonstrate those behaviors and reflect on their performance. As students continue to practice thinking interdependently, they form a deeper understanding of this Habit of Mind. They become more open to feedback and more motivated to help others via constructive critiques.

The resources in this tool will enable students to

- Discuss the principles of teamwork.
- Create and solve a puzzle with classmates.
- Evaluate their teamwork capabilities.

HOW TO USE THIS TOOL

The following list of resources includes the suggested sequence for using this tool:

- Teamwork (Motivating Activity)
- 4 x 4 Puzzle (Core Activity)
- Teamwork Self-Evaluation worksheet (Reflection Activity)

The activities and tasks included in this tool should take 45–60 minutes to complete. You will need the following materials:

- 1 copy of puzzle cut into pieces per student group
- Plastic sandwich bags
- 8 felt-tip pens of different colors per student group
- At least 1 pair of scissors per student group

Note: Some advance preparation must be completed prior to conducting the Core Activity.

TIPS AND VARIATIONS

1. Motivating Activity

- Ask: What kinds of teams do you belong to or have you belonged to in the past? (Students may mention groups such as sports teams, academic teams, orchestra, band, Girl Scouts, and Boy Scouts.) Explain that there are many types of teams. Help

Expanding Capacities

students see that even their classroom could be considered a team, as well as their family and even their entire school. Say that any group that works together to achieve a common goal is a team.

• Ask: What are important things to remember when working in a team? (To give positive, encouraging feedback; be respectful of other people's feelings; do your part; participate fully; offer ideas; follow directions.) Then tell students that today they are going to work in a team. Ask: What are some behaviors that will help your team have great teamwork? (Accept all reasonable answers.)

• Give students the Teamwork Self-Evaluation worksheet. Explain that the behaviors listed are some good qualities for team members to have. Encourage students to suggest additional qualities they thought of or learned about during the discussion just completed. Tell them that after the next activity, they will have an opportunity to evaluate their own performance as a team member, so they should keep these good qualities and behaviors in mind.

2. Advance Preparation for Core Activity

• Select a photograph of a scene or landscape or a photographic reproduction of a suitable artwork (or take a photograph yourself)—for example, Van Gogh's *The Olive Trees*. Many are available on the Internet, such as at www.awesome-art.biz, if you wish to purchase high-resolution reproductions. Also, your school's art teacher or librarian may be able to provide a suitable image.

• Determine how many teams will result when your class is divided into teams of four. Make one copy of the photograph or image you have selected to create one 4 x 4 Puzzle worksheet per student group. For each worksheet, cut the image into four strips. Put each puzzle into a baggie, so you will end up with one baggie per student group.

3. Core Activity

• Divide the class into groups of four students. Give one 4 x 4 Puzzle baggie to each group. Tell each group member to take one strip of the puzzle.

• Out of a package of eight different-color felt-tip pens, give each team player two pens. Instruct students to color their strip using only their two colors.

• Tell students to cut their strips into four boxes and to place their boxes on the table.

• Tell students they must work together with their group members to create a picture out of all the boxes, but that each person may touch only his or her own boxes.

4. Reflection Activity

• Discuss this activity with the class. Ask: Was it difficult not being able to touch the other puzzle pieces? How did you work together to solve the puzzle? What did you learn about teamwork during this activity?

• After the discussion, refer students again to the Teamwork Self-Evaluation worksheet. Ask them to complete a self-evaluation of their performance in the group activity. You may wish to keep this checklist handy for students to use regularly after group activities.

• Walk around the room and offer a constructive review of students' self-evaluations when you think it is necessary.

Expanding Capacities

Name _____ Class _____ Date _____

Teamwork Self-Evaluation

For each item in the chart below, show whether you did a good job, average job, or poor job by checking the column with the correct symbol. Feel free to add good teamwork behaviors to the chart.

Good Teamwork Behaviors	☺	😐	☹
Take turns.			
Listen to each other.			
Respect the ideas of team members.			
Be flexible in your thinking.			
Participate.			
Follow directions.			

Expanding Capacities

Learning Continuously

PURPOSE OF THIS TOOL

This tool challenges students to relax and enjoy learning no matter what the situation. First they explore the meaning of the word *continuously*. Then they discuss times they may have learned when they didn't know they were learning and other times they may have chosen not to learn something new when they could have.

As students further apply and develop this Habit of Mind, they begin to integrate it and make it their own. They naturally and unknowingly look for ways to improve, grow, learn, and otherwise modify and improve themselves. They don't fear problems and complicated circumstances as much as they used to; instead, they see them as opportunities to grow and learn.

The resources in this tool will enable students to

- Define the term *continuously*.
- Reflect on when, where, and how open they are to learning.
- Challenge themselves to remain open and have fun during a game.
- Discuss how they feel when challenged.

HOW TO USE THIS TOOL

The following list of resources includes the suggested sequence for using this tool:

- *Continuously* discussion (Motivating Activity)
- Word Frenzy worksheet (Core Activity)
- Just Relax discussion (Reflection Activity)

The activities and tasks included in this tool should take 30–45 minutes to complete. You will need a clock or watch with a second hand.

TIPS AND VARIATIONS

1. Motivating Activity

- Ask: What does the word *continuously* mean? (Constantly, regularly, consistently, all the time.) What do you think it means to be *continuously* open to learning new things? (It means that you are always ready to learn.) Do you expect to learn on the playground? How about in front of the TV? At the grocery store? While driving in a car? While laughing with friends? (Yes!)

Expanding Capacities

• Continue by asking students to think about these questions: Are you always ready and open to learn? Have you ever been in a situation where you were really frustrated and just wanted the problem to go away? Is it possible that you were not exercising patience and persistence to see the problem through or get help? Have you ever thought something looked hard and asked someone to do it for you even though you probably could have figured out how to do it yourself?

• Assure students that being open to learning continuously is not easy at first. It is easy to get frustrated and to rely too heavily on other people. Assure students that the more they can develop this Habit of Mind, the better they will get at it and the more they will benefit from this skill throughout their entire life.

2. Core Activity

• Divide the class into groups of three or four. Tell them they will be playing a game, and the person who wins will get a prize.

• Write the following rules on the board:

Brainstorm as fast as you can.

Don't use proper nouns, such as names of people and places.

Don't use bad words.

Stick to the subject.

Don't write the same word in different forms (e.g., boy, boys).

• Place the Word Frenzy worksheet face down on each student's desk. Tell students not to turn the worksheet over until you give them the OK.

• When everyone has a worksheet, tell students to turn their papers over but to immediately use a second piece of paper to cover everything but the title. Explain that they will have 30 seconds to brainstorm as many examples as they can for each category listed on the worksheet.

• Direct students' attention to the rules on the board. Ask if anyone has any questions. Tell students when you say "Go!" they can slide their cover paper down to reveal only the first category and start brainstorming. Tell them they must stop writing immediately when you say "Stop."

• When everyone is ready, say "Go!" At the end of 30 seconds, say "Stop!" Ask: How are you doing? Is this a little scary? What thoughts and feelings did you have while you were doing Category 1? Students may confess that they feel a little anxious. Even if they don't, give them a few reassuring words. Tell them that if they fear they are not doing well in this game or that they might mess up in front of everyone, those feelings are perfectly normal and OK.

• Then say that it might help to think of this as just another opportunity to test themselves and learn something. Have students repeat these words after you: "It doesn't really matter if I'm perfect at this game. It's just about having fun and being open." Tell students that by being open-minded and relaxed, they are more likely to have fun and may even learn something.

• Repeat this process for the remaining categories on the worksheet.

• When students are finished, collect all papers. Cross out identical words and words that don't follow the rules. Tally the total number of words on the page and list the number at the top. Then determine who had the most correct words and declare a winner. Give the winner a small prize.

3. Reflection Activity

• Discuss this activity with questions such as the following: Did your attitude change any after doing the first category? Why? Did you have fun? Was this activity easy or difficult? Were you nervous when you learned you were going to be competing against other students? What about when you learned you needed to remember words really quickly? Does the idea of having to think quickly scare you a little bit? Did it help to take a moment to relax and be open to the fun of something new?

• Ask students how they might apply what they learned today in future situations.

Expanding Capacities

Name _____ Class _____ Date _____

Word Frenzy

Work by yourself to complete this activity. Cover up all the text below with a second piece of paper. When your teacher says "Go!" reveal only one category and brainstorm to do what it says. Work as fast as you can. Don't worry about being neat or orderly; it's fine to scribble the words out quickly. Stop immediately when your teacher says "Stop." Your teacher will guide you from one category to the next. In the meantime, don't peek!

Category 1: Write words that begin with the letter A:

Category 2: Write words that begin with the letter M:

Category 3: Write examples of contractions:

Category 4: Write words that are fun to say:

Increasing Alertness

Example is not the main thing in influencing others. It is the only thing.

—Albert Schweitzer

This section takes the Expanding Capacities section one step further. By this time, students can identify the habits and their value and use them in specific situations. It is time for them to see the importance of developing the habits in and for themselves. Therefore, this section starts a shift away from teacher-led growth to student-led growth. It serves as a bridge between having an external understanding of the habits and forming a true internal, personal understanding. By the end of this section, the locus of control will begin to move from the teacher to the students. As a result, students will be empowered to use the habits to strengthen their skills as learners at school and in the world beyond.

This transfer of responsibility represents a key step in achieving student buy-in. Recognizing the Habits of Mind is not sufficient to generate personal activation. Students must see significant personal advantage in order to truly adopt and cultivate these habits. This section helps students become more alert to applications of the habits outside the classroom.

With the tools in this section, students will investigate people and situations that matter to them: famous people, world leaders, local people they respect, and significant global and local issues. As students identify applications of the Habits of Mind in the world around them via case studies, interviews, and research projects, they better understand that the habits can truly be beneficial to them in learning and in life.

In integrating the resources of this section into daily classroom practice, it is important to use as many personal, school, and local examples as possible. Continue to look for opportunities to integrate the Habits of Mind into your curriculum. Doing so will further increase the relevance of the habits to students.

CONTENTS

TITLE OF TOOL

Increasing Alertness

Looking Around Us

PURPOSE OF THIS TOOL

This tool focuses on specific examples of people using the Habits of Mind. First, students research a world leader as a group; then they conduct individual research on a famous person they admire. Finally, with a partner, they interview someone in the local area. With each activity, students explore how influential people adopt and apply various Habits of Mind to make contributions to society. As students look closely at people they admire and observe, they discover that these people use Habits of Mind to great benefit; this discovery ignites a greater desire in students to use the habits themselves.

The resources in this tool will enable students to

- Identify Habits of Mind as they are used by various people and in specific situations.
- Do a case study of a world leader to analyze how he or she uses or used Habits of Mind.
- Do a case study of a famous person to analyze how he or she uses or used Habits of Mind.
- Do a case study of a local leader to analyze how he or she uses or used Habits of Mind.
- Compare global, celebrity, and local examples in the application of Habits of Mind.

HOW TO USE THIS TOOL

This tool will support student understanding of how Habits of Mind apply to the world beyond the classroom, especially to their own direct experiences as well as observations of their environment. The following list of resources includes the suggested sequence for using this tool:

- Observing Others (Introductory Discussion)
- Case Study of a World Leader worksheet (Core Activity 1: Group Research)
- Key Research Questions worksheet (Core Activities 1 and 2)
- Habits of Mind Research worksheet (Core Activities 1 and 2)
- Case Study of a Famous Person worksheet (Core Activity 2: Independent Research)
- Case Study of a Local Leader worksheet (Core Activity 3: Partner Interviews)
- Looking for Habits of Mind (Reflection Activity)
- Obstacles on the Path worksheet (Extension Activity)

Increasing Alertness

The activities and tasks included in this tool should take several weeks, including research time, to complete. You will need access to a library or Internet resources. In addition, you will find Key Research Questions and Habits of Mind Research worksheets to aid students in all three research projects.

TIPS AND VARIATIONS

1. Introductory Discussion

- Ask: Can you identify other people's use of Habits of Mind? Can you name a few situations that were positively affected by somebody's use of a Habit of Mind? Have you seen other people benefit when one person used the habits?

2. Core Activity 1: Group Research Project

- Say to students: We can increase our alertness to the Habits of Mind by looking at case studies of people who have clearly used them. Analyzing case studies will help us identify the habits in others and pick up cues about when to use them.
- Introduce the first research project—a case study of a few famous people whose lives illustrate the potential of the habits. Divide the class into six groups. Assign each group one of the following great world leaders to analyze: Nelson Mandela of Africa, Martin Luther King of the United States, George Washington of the United States, Rosa Parks of the United States, Mother Teresa of India, Shirin Ebadi of Iran.
- Give students the Case Study of a World Leader worksheet. Point out that the worksheet employs the 5 Ws and 1 H model: Who, What, When, Where, Why, and How. Reinforce that the model is a great tool to use anytime students want to get core information about something. Tell students to use this worksheet to document basic facts about their great leader.
- As students delve into their research, they will undoubtedly have questions they want and need to pursue for more information. Give them the Key Research Questions worksheet so they can keep track of their questions.
- Encourage students to find specific examples of how their research subject used the Habits of Mind. To help with this process, give students the Habits of Mind Research worksheet (note that it is two pages in length).
- When students have finished their reports, have them present their findings to the class.

Increasing Alertness

3. Core Activity 2: Independent Research Project

- Have students work independently to complete a similar research project. This time, ask them to pick a famous person from any walk of life—a political figure, a movie star, a journalist, a stage or TV actor, a model or designer, a sports hero, an astronaut, or any other public figure who fascinates them.

- Give students the Case Study of a Famous Person worksheet and tell them to now do individually exactly what they did in their group research project. Say that this time you would like them to zero in on things about the person that they especially admire or appreciate—perhaps the person's accomplishments or attitude. Tell them to find out how the person became successful and which Habits of Mind he or she regularly used or uses.

- Give students the Key Research Questions and Habits of Mind Research worksheets to use while conducting their research.

- When students have finished their reports, have them form a group with one or two other students to discuss what they learned about their famous people and how the people used or use the Habits of Mind.

4. Core Activity 3: Partner Interviews

- Have students choose a partner. Tell them they are going to use the same model again, this time to investigate a local person they respect. Give them the Case Study of a Local Leader worksheet as a guide.

- Tell students to pick a person in the local area they really respect—for example, a neighbor, local politician, local comedian, teacher, business leader, or professional in a career they aspire to. If students don't immediately have an idea of whom to research, suggest they ask a librarian about getting lists of people in the community who have received awards such as "volunteer of the year" or "teacher of the year."

- Have students contact their chosen individual by phone or e-mail to set up a 30-minute interview. Students could make arrangements to meet the person at school, a local coffee house, a restaurant, or a public area such as a park. Students can use their worksheet to guide the interview, come up with a few questions specific to their own interests about the person, and spend some time simply getting to know the individual on a personal level.

Note: Students are often nervous about doing an interview. Reassure them that the experience is usually far more rewarding than they anticipate.

Increasing Alertness

- When students have finished their reports, have the partners form a group with another duo and share their findings.

5. Reflection Activity

- Lead a class discussion about the experience of looking for Habits of Mind in other people. Ask questions such as the following: Do you see any similarities between great national leaders, the famous person you admire, and the local person you respect? Do any of these people use similar Habits of Mind? Did you learn anything from them?
- Encourage students to elaborate as they respond to the questions and to one another's comments.

6. Extension Activity

- Give students the Obstacles on the Path worksheet and ask them to pick one or more of the people they researched and describe how the person or persons overcame obstacles.
- Encourage volunteers to share their responses aloud. Use these responses as a springboard to class discussion.

Name _____ Class _____ Date _____

Case Study of a World Leader

Ask a variety of questions, and then record your answers.

Questions	Answers
Who?	
Where?	
When?	
Why?	
What?	
How? (Which Habits of Mind?)	

Name _____ Class _____ Date _____

Case Study of a World Leader

Ask a variety of questions, and then record your answers.

> Share the following sample answers with students to help them get started.

Questions	Answers
Who?	*Mother Teresa*
Where?	*India*
When?	*Born 1910, died 1997*
Why?	*Winner of the Nobel Peace Prize in 1979, great humanitarian*
What?	*She ministered to the poor, sick, orphaned, and dying for over 40 years. She established and led missionaries throughout India and then in other countries. A documentary and book about her called* Something Beautiful for God, *by Malcolm Muggeridge, helped her garner international fame by the 1970s. She is known as a great humanitarian and advocate for the poor and helpless. Her Missionaries of Charity had expanded to 610 missions in 123 countries at the time of her death.*
How? (Which Habits of Mind?)	*Listening with Understanding and Empathy, Persisting, Responding with Wonderment and Awe, Questioning and Posing Problems*

Increasing Alertness

Name _____ Class _____ Date _____

Key Research Questions

As you do your research, brainstorm questions that will help you learn more. The following are a few examples:

- Why was _____ famous?
- Why did many people respect him or her?
- What did _____ achieve in his or her lifetime?
- What lessons does _____ teach us?

Your Research Topic:

Questions:

Name _____ Class _____ Date _____

Habits of Mind Research

As you do your research, record notes on the Habits of Mind as you see them exemplified and put into practice.

Research Topic: _____

Habits of Mind: Part 1

Habit of Mind	Example	What did using this Habit of Mind achieve?
Persisting		
Managing Impulsivity		
Listening with Understanding and Empathy		
Thinking Flexibly		
Thinking About Thinking (Metacognition)		
Striving for Accuracy and Precision		
Questioning and Posing Problems		
Applying Past Knowledge to New Situations		

Name _____ Class _____ Date _____

Habits of Mind Research, *continued*

Research Topic: _____

Habits of Mind: Part 2

Habit of Mind	Example	What did using this Habit of Mind achieve?
Thinking and Communicating with Clarity and Precision		
Gathering Data Through All Senses		
Creating, Imagining, and Innovating		
Responding with Wonderment and Awe		
Taking Responsible Risks		
Finding Humor		
Thinking Interdependently		
Learning Continuously		

Increasing Alertness

Name _____ Class _____ Date _____

Habits of Mind Research

As you do your research, record notes on the Habits of Mind as you see them exemplified and put into practice.

> Share the following sample answers with students to help them get started.

Research Topic: *Mother Teresa*

Habits of Mind: Part 1

Habit of Mind	Example	What did using this Habit of Mind achieve?
Persisting	*Many people thought she was crazy helping the outcast, miserable, and poor people, because there were too many and their lives were of questionable value.*	*Her ability to persist despite a lot of doubt and prejudice allowed people to see that everyone has value and everyone deserves food, shelter, and a safe environment.*
Managing Impulsivity		
Listening with Understanding and Empathy	*She ministered to the poor and won the Nobel Peace Prize for her efforts.*	*Her ability to see everyone as important and empathize with everyone's struggle helped her bring great relief and inspired thousands of other humanitarians.*

Increasing Alertness

Habits of Mind: Part 1 (*continued*)

Habit of Mind	Example	What did using this Habit of Mind achieve?
Thinking Flexibly	*She identified problems and found new ways of solving them.*	*She found a way through the many obstacles to achieve her goal.*
Thinking About Thinking (Metacognition)		
Striving for Accuracy and Precision		
Questioning and Posing Problems		
Applying Past Knowledge to New Situations		

Name _____ Class _____ Date _____

Case Study of a Famous Person

Ask a variety of questions, and then record your answers.

Questions	Answers
Who?	
Where?	
When?	
Why?	
What?	
How? (Which Habits of Mind?)	

Name _____ Class _____ Date _____

Case Study of a Famous Person

This is an example only. Students will have chosen their own topic.

Ask a variety of questions, and then record your answers.

Questions	Answers
Who?	*Mohammed Ali, previously known as Cassius Clay*
Where?	*Louisville, Kentucky, USA*
When?	*Born in 1942; won Olympic gold medal in 1960; throughout the 1960s and 1970s earned the title of WBA heavyweight boxing champion many times.*
Why?	*He was an amazing boxer with a unique "dancing" style and a fierce belief in his capabilities.*
What?	*Muhammad Ali won 56 matches and lost only 5; he was the three-time world heavyweight champion; he beat almost every top heavyweight in his era; he is an inductee into the International Boxing Hall of Fame and has beaten seven other Hall of Fame inductees; he is one of only three boxers to be named Sportsman of the Year by* Sports Illustrated; *he was awarded the Arthur Ashe Courage Award; he continues to contribute to society despite suffering from Parkinson's disease.*
How? (Which Habits of Mind?)	*Persisting; Thinking and Communicating with Clarity and Precision; Creating, Imagining, Innovating; Striving for Accuracy and Precision*

Increasing Alertness

Name _____ Class _____ Date _____

Case Study of a Local Leader

Ask a variety of questions, and then record your answers.

Questions	Answers
Who?	
Where?	
When?	
Why?	
What?	
How? (Which Habits of Mind?)	

Increasing Alertness

Name _____ Class _____ Date _____

Case Study of a Local Leader

This is an example only. Students will have chosen their own topic.

Ask a variety of questions, and then record your answers.

Questions	Answers
Who?	*Janie Smith*
Where?	*Austin, Texas, USA*
When?	*2009 Volunteer of the Year*
Why?	*She is determined to help people have adequate housing.*
What?	*Janie won the 2009 Volunteer of the Year award for her work with Habitat for Humanity. She helped build more than 35 houses last year. As a retired architect, Janie donated the plans for each home and logged countless hours hammering, sawing, lifting, painting, and gardening to make the homes special. Her efforts helped the Habitat program build twice as many homes this year as last. These homes now provide a safe place for 140 people to live. Janie is 75 years old.*
How? (Which Habits of Mind?)	*Persisting; Applying Past Knowledge to New Situations; Thinking and Communicating with Clarity and Precision; Creating, Imagining, and Innovating; Taking Responsible Risks; Thinking Interdependently; Learning Continuously; Listening to Others with Understanding and Empathy; Striving for Accuracy and Precision*

Increasing Alertness

Name _____ Class _____ Date _____

Obstacles on the Path

Complete the following tree map to show successes, failures, and obstacles the subject of your research experienced on his or her path to success.

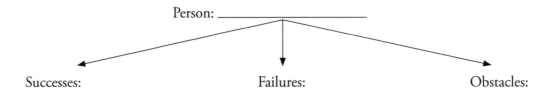

Person: _____

Successes: Failures: Obstacles:

Which Habits of Mind helped this person overcome obstacles?	How did the Habits of Mind help this person?	What evidence supports your claim?

Professional Applications

PURPOSE OF THIS TOOL

This tool helps students focus on how Habits of Mind are applied in the workplace. In groups, students analyze a number of professions to determine which habits are most relevant and why. They also examine possible consequences if those habits are not used regularly. Then students work independently to explore and compare professions of personal interest. They analyze the Habits of Mind most relevant to those careers and see how they match up with the students' own personal strengths. Then students target areas for improvement and create an action plan to develop useful Habits of Mind.

As they go through these exercises and think about their futures, students will increasingly recognize, without prompting, when to apply the habits. Students will also become more astute at observing people around them who are using Habits of Mind.

The resources in this tool will enable students to

- Explore how Habits of Mind are used in the workplace.
- Target a couple of professions of personal interest and analyze the most relevant Habits of Mind.
- Compare Habits of Mind needed for professions of interest to their own personal aptitudes.
- Create an action plan to improve a Habit of Mind.

HOW TO USE THIS TOOL

This tool will support student understanding of how Habits of Mind can contribute to their career success. The following is the suggested sequence for exploring this habit:

- Profession Cards (Advance Preparation)
- Profession Analysis worksheet (Motivating Activity)
- Summary of 16 Habits of Mind (Motivating Activity)
- Two Professions worksheet (Core Activity)
- Career Action Plan worksheet (Core Activity)
- Thinking Forward discussion (Reflection Activity)

Note: The Summary of 16 Habits of Mind worksheet is available in Appendix B.

The activities and tasks included in this tool should take about 60 minutes plus extra-curricular time for interested students to complete their career exploration. Some advance preparation is needed.

Increasing Alertness

Note: To use this tool with students in primary grades, see the suggestions provided for adapting it for younger students.

TIPS AND VARIATIONS

1. Advance Preparation

- Copy and cut out the items on the Profession Cards worksheet. If possible, use card stock.

2. Motivating Activity

- Divide the class into groups of two or three. Randomly distribute three or four Profession Cards so that each student has one. Give each group one copy of the Profession Analysis worksheet and the Summary of 16 Habits of Mind worksheet (Appendix B).
- Tell the groups to discuss each profession and fill in the analysis sheet. Encourage students to clearly describe all relevant Habits of Mind. Have additional copies of this form available in case students need it, or you may want to recreate the form on larger paper to allow students more room for description.
- Ask the groups to add two or three more professions to the Profession Analysis worksheet and analyze them.

3. Core Activity

- Once students have finished analyzing professions, instruct them to leave their completed worksheets at their group stations and then get up and move through all other group stations to see the range of careers their classmates have explored. Encourage them to pay special attention to professions that look interesting to them.
- Have students return to their own desks. Give them the Two Professions worksheet and ask them to compare and contrast two professions. Students can use professions their group or another group analyzed, or they can come up with two new professions that interest them. Allow students to do Internet or library research on these professions.
- Point out to students that the Two Professions worksheet can serves as a good starting place to explore careers of interest. To extend the activity, suggest that students visit a career counselor or interview persons in the professions. As students explore, encourage them to look for Habits of Mind relevant to each profession.
- Have students consider how well they themselves apply the Habits of Mind that are most relevant to their preferred careers. Give students the Career Action Plan

Increasing Alertness

worksheet as a guide. Help students analyze and reflect on the best Habits of Mind for their career aspirations, and help them create a good plan for monitoring and improving those habits.

4. Reflection Activity

- Have students work in small groups to discuss the following questions:

  Suppose you are in charge of training new police recruits. Which three Habits of Mind would you train them in, and why?

  Which Habits of Mind are most relevant to a career of interest to you?

  Think about up-and-coming jobs of the future, or jobs that have increasing demand every year. Which Habits of Mind are likely to be most useful for these jobs?

- Ask the groups to share some of their discussion highlights with the whole class.

ADAPTATIONS FOR YOUNGER CHILDREN

1. Advance Preparation

- If your students are in primary grades, you may wish to create several sets of the 16 Habits of Mind on labels so they can attach them to appropriate cards. You could make the cards with names and pictures so students can make clear associations.

2. Core Activity

- Have students work in small groups. Give them two or three Profession Cards and ask them to decide which Habit of Mind label is best for each profession. If students are older elementary students, simply have them write the Habits of Mind on appropriate cards.
- Hold a class discussion to review two or three careers.
- Ask volunteers to suggest a profession the class can analyze together.

3. Reflection Activity

- Have students work in small groups to discuss which careers are the most interesting to them.
- Ask the groups to share highlights of their discussion with the whole class.

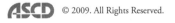

Profession Cards

Copy and cut out the following cards to distribute to students. If possible, use card stock. Several blank cards are included for you to add professions you think will interest your students. If necessary, create more class-specific cards.

Increasing Alertness

Doctor	Nurse	Firefighter	Scientist
Museum Director	Teacher	Writer	Actor
King or Queen	Banker	Librarian	Carpenter
Dentist	Chef	Bridge Builder	Soldier
Referee	Minister	Nanny	Musician
Comedian	Inventor	Painter	Mechanic

Name _____ Class _____ Date _____

Profession Analysis

The profession I am analyzing is: _____

Habits of Mind a person in this profession regularly uses	How this Habit of Mind relates to this job	Consequences if the Habit of Mind is not used

Increasing Alertness

Name _____ Class _____ Date _____

Two Professions

Use this worksheet to compare two professions that interest you.

The two professions I am comparing are

The similarities between Habits of Mind used in these professions are

The differences between Habits of Mind used in these professions are

Other similarities between these professions are

Other differences between these professions are

To better compare these professions, I would like to know more about

Name _____ Class _____ Date _____

Career Action Plan

List Habits of Mind most relevant to careers of interest to you. Then complete this action plan to help you develop those habits.

Habits of Mind I Can Develop to Prepare for These Careers

1.

2.

3.

My Action Plan to Improve These Habits of Mind in One Month

I will do these specific things:

I can seek assistance from these sources:

I can monitor my improvement in these ways:

Important Issues

PURPOSE OF THIS TOOL

Through this tool, students learn about a pressing global issue. They explore how Habits of Mind relate to the issue and how people are using Habits of Mind to address the issue today. Students explore the scope of global issues and particularly the relevance of the Thinking Interdependently Habit of Mind in resolving issues that cross international borders.

Students then brainstorm issues of concern in their local area. They work in groups to pick one issue and research it. They also explore relevant Habits of Mind and consequences related to not using the habits to resolve the issue. Finally, students are encouraged to interview someone working on the issue to see firsthand which Habits of Mind are being applied.

The resources in this tool will enable students to

- Explore a global issue.
- Determine how Habits of Mind relate to a global issue.
- Brainstorm local issues.
- Research a local issue.
- Determine how Habits of Mind relate to a local issue.
- Interview someone who is working on a local issue.

HOW TO USE THIS TOOL

This tool extends students' exploration of authentic, real-world applications of Habits of Mind in the world of international relations and global interdependence, as well as in their local area. The following set of resources is especially useful in helping students to expand their research and investigation competencies while considering a relevant global or local issue of concern to them.

- Issue Analysis worksheet (Introductory Activity)
- Summary of 16 Habits of Mind (Introductory Activity)
- Case Study of a Local Issue worksheet (Core Activity)
- Issue Analysis worksheet (Core Activity)
- Key Research Questions worksheet (Core Activity)
- Case Study of a Local Leader worksheet (Synthesis Activity)
- Obstacles on the Path worksheet (Synthesis Activity)

Increasing Alertness

Note: The Summary of 16 Habits of Mind, Case Study, and Obstacles on the Path worksheets can be found in Appendix B.

The activities and tasks included in this tool should take 1–2 weeks to complete, including research time.

TIPS AND VARIATIONS

1. Introductory Activity

- Tell students that the Secretary-General of the United Nations, Ban Ki-moon, has called climate change the "defining issue of our era" and has said that "how we address it will define us, our era, and ultimately the global legacy we leave for future generations."
- Explain that you would like to explore this issue as a class. Then show students all or part of a film or TV program that chronicles the issue of climate change. Suggestions:

    An Inconvenient Truth, Al Gore's 2007 documentary

    Global Warming: Too Hot Not to Handle, HBO 2008 documentary

    The 11th Hour, Leonardo di Caprio's 2007 documentary

    Global Warming: The Signs and the Science, PBS Home Video

    Earth to America! short features at www.stopglobalwarming.com

- After the film, give students the Issue Analysis worksheet and the Summary of 16 Habits of Mind worksheet (Appendix B). Ask them to pick five Habits of Mind that are related in some way to this issue and then complete the chart.
- Have a class discussion about the issue. Ask: What Habits of Mind might have prevented this situation? Why didn't nations do something about the global climate issue sooner? What Habits of Mind, had they been applied, might have helped prevent the current problem? What habits can be used now to help solve the problem? Predict what might happen if Habits of Mind were never used.
- Read another quote from the Secretary-General of the United Nations, Ban Ki-moon:

    We must … leave this conference with a sense of purpose and mission, knowing that we are allied in our determination to make a difference. Only by acting together, in partnership, can we overcome this crisis, today and for tomorrow. Hundreds of millions of the world's people expect no less. (Presentation at the High-Level Conference on World Food Security: The Challenges of Climate Change and Bioenergy, Rome, June 2008)

Increasing Alertness

- Ask: Which Habit of Mind does this quote exemplify? (Thinking Interdependently.) Point out that this statement was not made in relation to climate change but at a conference on world food security. Having enough food to feed the world's people is another global issue.

- Ask: What are some other global issues? Have students brainstorm in small groups. (Examples: endangered species, international peace, human rights, energy development, space travel, sustainable development, and disaster relief.)

2. Core Activity

- Write the following quotation on the board:

  Think globally, act locally.
  —David Brower

- Ask students what they think this statement might mean. (Having a global perspective is important. Everyone should realize that his or her actions affect the health of our global environment.) Because that scale is so large that it's difficult to fathom, ask: How can you—one little person—possibly save or prevent global crises? (By acting locally.) Point out that that if everyone improves his or her own relationship with the environment, the positive effects would spread across the globe.
- Have students work in small groups to discuss major social or environmental issues in your local area. Ask them to brainstorm a list of current, pressing issues. (Examples: protection of local water resources or species, suburban sprawl, farm support, pollution, waste management, energy resources, health care, homelessness, child protection and safety, and human rights.)
- Ask students to choose one of these issues to research. Allow them to work either individually or in small groups for this project. Give them the following worksheets to direct their research: Case Study of a Local Issue, Key Research Questions, and Issue Analysis.
- Have students create a presentation on their chosen topic to educate the class. Remind them to emphasize the relevance of Habits of Mind throughout their presentations.

3. Synthesis Activity

- Encourage students to interview someone who works or volunteers for a local organization working on the issue they studied. Afterward, have students use the Case

Increasing Alertness

Study of a Local Leader and Obstacles on the Path worksheets to analyze and summarize the experience.

• Have students share their findings with the class.

Increasing Alertness

Name _____ Class _____ Date _____

Issue Analysis

The issue I am analyzing is _____

Related Habits of Mind	Relevance of Habits of Mind	Consequences of Not Using Habits of Mind

Increasing Alertness

Name _____ Class _____ Date _____

Issue Analysis

The issue I am analyzing is _____ *Global Climate Change* _____

Related Habits of Mind	Relevance of Habits of Mind	Consequences of Not Using Habits of Mind
Gathering Data Through All Senses	*The more scientific data we can get on this issue, the better off we will be. We need to monitor physical changes to the climate and document changes over time.*	*For years, people have ignored the reality of global climate problems. As more data are gathered and made public, it becomes more difficult to ignore the evidence.*
Thinking Interdependently	*Solving the global climate issue requires that the governments of many nations work together, think together, and brainstorm together.*	*This is a global problem; without support from nations all over the globe, it is going to be difficult to resolve.*
Questioning and Posing Problems	*We need to do a better job of questioning whether the things we do today are harming our environment now or may in the future.*	*If we continue to serve our interests without consideration of the future, we could seriously harm our environment and handicap future generations.*
Learning Continuously	*We need to continuously monitor and study. By looking at the situation in new and more detailed ways and continuously gathering data, we will be better equipped to solve the problem.*	*This is a dynamic issue. The environment is constantly changing and so are human technologies. We need to continue to learn about our effects on the climate and new ways to reduce harm.*
Thinking and Communicating with Clarity and Precision	*Solving this issue is highly dependent upon scientists, politicians, and others thinking carefully about the issue and then communicating evidence and future predictions with clarity and precision.*	*One of the reasons this is a global problem is that we did not have enough people communicating well about it. We need constant, clear, and convincing communication and thoughtful reflection.*

Increasing Alertness

Name _____ Class _____ Date _____

Case Study of a Local Issue

Share the following sample answers with students to help them get started.

Ask a variety of questions and then record your answers.

Questions	Answers
What?	
Where?	
When?	
Why?	
Who?	
How?	

Name _____ Class _____ Date _____

Case Study of a Local Issue

Ask a variety of questions and then record your answers.

Questions	Answers
What?	Here students should describe the local issue.
Where?	What part or how much of the local area suffers from this issue?
When?	How long has this been an issue?
Why?	How did this issue come to be a problem?
Who?	What organizations or individuals are working to resolve this issue? Who contributes to the issue?
How?	How can this issue be resolved? What Habits of Mind could help?

Increasing Alertness

Name _____ Class _____ Date _____

Key Research Questions

As you do your research, brainstorm questions you would like to get answered in order to learn more. The following are a few examples:

- Why is this a problem?
- What are the short- and long-term consequences of this problem?
- What can be done to resolve this problem?
- Who is working on this issue?
- How widespread is the problem?

Your research topic:

Questions:

Evaluating Progress

PURPOSE OF THIS TOOL

This tool provides an opportunity to evaluate how students are progressing in relation to their understanding of the Habits of Mind. In addition, students will conduct self-evaluations, then use their results to create an action plan for continued and future development of the Habits of Mind.

The resources in this tool will enable students to

- Self-evaluate their competence in using the Habits of Mind.
- Review a teacher evaluation of their competence in using the Habits of Mind and compare it to their own evaluation.
- Create an action plan to improve one area of competence.

HOW TO USE THIS TOOL

Striving for Accuracy and Precision and Metacognition are extremely important Habits of Mind for students to internalize and apply on a regular basis both in the classroom and in the world beyond it. This tool contains the following resources, each of which will help students evaluate their own progress toward understanding and applying the 16 Habits of Mind:

- Teacher Evaluation of Student checklist (Teacher Activity)
- Student Self-Evaluation checklist (Core Activity)
- Action Plan for Habits of Mind Development worksheet (Synthesis Activity)

The activities and tasks included in this tool should take 60–90 minutes to complete.

TIPS AND VARIATIONS

1. Teacher Activity

- By this stage, students should be alert to the use of Habits of Mind on a global level, in your local area, and in their personal lives.
- Take a moment to evaluate how competent each student is in using the Habits of Mind. Use the Teacher Evaluation of Student Checklist to assist you in this process. Include additional items in the blank spaces as necessary.

Increasing Alertness

2. Core Activity

• Point out to students that by this stage they have become more alert to the use and potential of the Habits of Mind. Then ask: How can you know when you've mastered these skills? How will you know when you're ready to move on to the next stage in your learning journey?

• Say to students that you have a wonderful tool to help them keep track of their personal progress. Hand out the Student Self-Evaluation Checklist. Ask students to complete the checklist to gauge their understanding of the Habits of Mind right now. Tell them to be honest about their abilities. Encourage everyone to find a partner who can check their answers and give them honest feedback.

3. Synthesis Activity

• Give students your evaluation of their competence. Have them compare their own evaluation to yours. Encourage students to confer with you if they have any questions.

• Give students the Action Plan for Habits of Mind Development worksheet. Ask them to pick one area from their evaluations that requires improvement and develop a plan for improvement using this worksheet. You may wish to help students evaluate the best competency to target. Then work with them to create a good plan for monitoring and improving that competency.

Name _____ Class _____ Date _____

Teacher Evaluation of Student Checklist

This student is able to	Seldom	Sometimes	Usually	Consistently
Recognize increasingly diverse, complex, and novel situations in which to apply the Habits of Mind.				
Spontaneously draw forth appropriate Habits of Mind when confronted with ambiguous and perplexing situations.				
Recognize a wide range of situations in which to apply the Habits of Mind.				
Recognize, without assistance, novel and complex situations in which to apply the Habits of Mind.				
Articulate the criteria upon which the decisions reflected in this review were made.				

Increasing Alertness

Name _____ Class _____ Date _____

Student Self-Evaluation Checklist

Complete this checklist to evaluate your progress in applying the Habits of Mind. In the blank rows, you can add areas you would like to be aware of and improve. Be honest with yourself!

I am able to	Seldom	Sometimes	Usually	Consistently
Recognize different and complex situations in which to use the Habits of Mind.				
Suggest which Habits of Mind are useful or relevant when looking at new situations.				
Recognize a wide range of situations in which to apply the Habits of Mind.				
Recognize, without assistance, new and complex situations in which to apply the Habits of Mind.				
Explain why I would use certain Habits of Mind in a situation.				

Increasing Alertness

Name _____ Class _____ Date _____

Action Plan for Habits of Mind Development

Pick one Habit of Mind competency that you would like to improve. Then create an action plan for improvement using the following form.

The competency I would like to improve is: _____

Action Plan to Improve This Competency in One Month

In order to improve, I will do these specific things:

I can seek assistance from these sources:

I can monitor my improvement in these ways:

ASCD © 2009. All Rights Reserved.

Increasing Alertness

Extending Values

Individually, we are one drop. Together, we are an ocean.

—Ryunosuke Satoro

This section explores the concept of extending values by suggesting strategies for creating a "school as a home for the mind" (Costa, 2007). This theme is central to Costa and Kallick's belief that the full potential of the Habits of Mind cannot be realized unless the program is employed schoolwide and in all aspects of school culture. Having teachers promote Habits of Mind in their own classrooms is a great start, but when they are applied on a larger scale, students are more likely to realize the full potential of the habits. The following activation model illustrates how a schoolwide, all-embracing adoption of the habits extends them beyond the classroom. The model outlines the different levels and responsibilities involved in creating a school that is truly a home for the mind. Its premise is that sustainable change happens from the center, or the leaders of an organization, and moves outward.

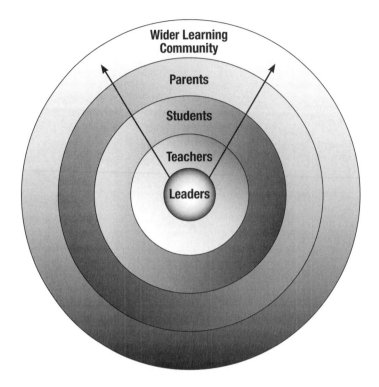

When a schoolwide, all-embracing adoption of the habits is complete, students, teachers, and school leaders see the habits as being of great value in everything that takes place across the school. As new developments, projects, and challenges arise in the school, the habits are automatically valued as part of the solution.

HOW TO USE THE ACTIVATION MODEL

The model shows an ideal method for implementing a Habits of Mind program so that it achieves the greatest impact. Leaders introduce the model to teachers. Then a schoolwide program teaches the habits to students. Parents learn from their children and from visits to the school. Leaders, teachers, students, and parents take the message to the community by modeling it.

This section includes a number of methods for setting up a schoolwide program. In addition, it provides teaching strategies, examples, and ideas from actual schools and students—some from elementary school experiences, others from secondary schools. Most, however, apply to both. Additional samples and ideas can be found in the Building Commitment section.

TIPS AND VARIATIONS FOR USING THE ACTIVATION MODEL

This section consists of a variety of individual tools to support your implementation of the activation model. The tools are grouped into two overall categories: ideas to promote high levels of schoolwide implementation and specific teaching strategies that can become a regular part of classroom practice, including ideas for teacher observation and walk-through processes. Through both types of tools, students are led to eventually take charge of their own mastery of the Habits of Mind.

CONTENTS

TITLE OF TOOL

Extending Values

Ideas for Schoolwide Implementation

The Habits of Mind offer the greatest potential when they are seen, heard, and felt across every aspect of school life. Achieving this goal requires strategic leadership. Suggestions for implementation approaches are described in this tool.

1. Outlining a Skills Vision for the School

Work with other school leaders to create a plan for widespread integration. Gather other school leaders together and begin by analyzing where you are and what you are hoping to achieve, using questions such as the following:

> Step 1: What skills and dispositions do lifelong learners in the 21st century need?
>
> Step 2: What skills and dispositions do you want your learners to have before graduating from your school?
>
> Step 3: To what extent do you achieve this already? Where are the gaps?
>
> Step 4: How could you fill in the gaps?

Then discuss whether and how a Habits of Mind program might help fill the gaps.

2. Having Schoolwide Thematic Assemblies

A great way of heralding the Habits of Mind across a school is to have a school assembly centered on one habit at a time. You could take a current event, a news story, a fairy tale, a parable, or an issue within the school and use it to outline the appropriate habit.

Example: Several years ago a principal introduced the Habit of Mind of Persisting in a whole-school assembly. The audience consisted of girls ages 11–18. The principal told the girls a story of a young French woman who had recently climbed to the top of Mt. Blanc. The principal described the incredible obstacles the girl faced during her climb. Despite these difficulties, the girl persevered and pushed forward, determined to reach her goal—and she was successful. The principal concluded the story by asking the girls to consider the "mountains" they themselves had climbed in the past and might climb in the future and by assuring them that if they persisted in their efforts they would reach their personal summits.

3. Using Other Methods to Deliver Consistent Messages

Look for opportunities to deliver consistent schoolwide messages both to students and staff. For example, discuss a Habit of Mind at every pep rally, or at regular times (e.g.,

Extending Values

once a week or once a month) via the school announcement system. Ask teachers to display Habits of Mind materials at school open house events for parents; highlighting different habits in different classrooms would allow parents to learn about several Habits of Mind. School newsletters, other school publications, the school Web site, and award certificates are also useful ways to reinforce the message of the habits.

Example: The principal of a private school introduces or reinforces the Habits of Mind during chapel time. She links the topic of Managing Impulsivity to a suitable illustrative story and discusses the importance of this habit in today's world. On appropriate occasions, this creative school principal also links songs and actions to illustrate her point.

4. Sharing a Common Language

One important method for applying the Habits of Mind in a meaningful way is to have all teachers use similar words to describe concepts, make assignments, and communicate with students. Teachers and administrators use many Habits of Mind on a daily basis. Encourage them to make that process transparent for students by using language that identifies the habits. Leaders can model the use of this language for other teachers, who can then model it for students.

Examples: The following methods are particularly useful for teachers to use in the classroom.

- Create word splashes to "unpack" each habit. Word splashes generate multiple ways of defining a concept so that it has meaning for students. For example, "Think before you act" is another way to say Managing Impulsivity.
- Use thinking words to create a new type of literacy—literacy in the communication of *thinking*. Using specific, cognitive terminology—or mindful language—during instruction will increase the likelihood that students will use mindful language in their communications.

Rather than ...	Use mindful language by saying ...
"Let's look at these two pictures."	"Let's compare these two pictures."
"What do you think will happen when ..."	"What do you predict will happen when ..."

Extending Values

- Reinforce terminology by recognizing, identifying, and labeling student uses of the Habits of Mind.

    "You really *persisted* on that problem."

    "That is an intriguing *problem* you are *posing*."

- Use mindful discipline. Discourage and reinforce behaviors at once.

Rather than ...	Use mindful discipline by saying ...
"Sarah, get away from Kathryn."	"Sarah could you find someplace better to do your best work?"
"Stop running."	"Why do we have a rule about always walking in the hall?"

- Provide data, not solutions. Allow students to become more autonomous by providing them with data to aid their decision making rather than making their decisions for them.

When a student ...	Use mindful language by saying ...
Repeatedly taps his pencils on the desk ...	"I want you to know that your pencil tapping is disturbing me."
Interrupts other students ...	"I like it when you take turns to speak."

- Promote autonomous learning. Avoid treating students like robots, feeding them information and getting a specific action in return. Instead, lead them to analyze a task, decide what is needed, and then act autonomously.

Extending Values

Rather than …	Use mindful language by saying …
"Remember to write your name in the top left corner."	"What must you remember to do for me to know whom the test belongs to?"
"The bell is about to ring. Pack up your desk, put up your chairs, and line up at the door."	"The bell is about to ring. What do we need to do before we leave?"

• Apply metacognitive strategies. The Thinking About Thinking Habit of Mind begets more thinking. Discussing the thinking process can cause that process to become more overt.

When a student says …	Use mindful language by saying …
"I don't know how to solve this problem."	"What can you do to get started?"
"I'm finished."	"How do you know you are correct?"

• Avoid negative presuppositions. Many times, teacher comments to students carry implicit meaning involving negative presuppositions. Over time, such remarks can damage students' self-esteem and their self-concept as thinkers and lead to negative behaviors.

Rather than …	Use mindful language by saying …
"Why did you forget your assignment?"	"As you plan for your assignment, what materials do you need and what is your time line?"
"When will you grow up?"	"As we grow older, we learn how to solve these problems from experiences such as these."

282 ☐

Extending Values

5. Displaying Posters Around the School

Displaying Habits of Mind posters around the school is a great way to increase student consciousness of the habits and extend their value. You may want to use purchased posters, or you may prefer to have teachers or students design their own posters to further increase their sense of ownership of the habits.

Examples:

Design a poster that includes pictures of students or teachers demonstrating a particular habit via an activity.

Have students design their own posters, including their own icon or logo to represent the habit.

After a field trip, design a poster that includes photographs of different activities that highlight a particular habit. Students could create posters like these in groups or as a class.

6. Coaching Teachers to Be Coaches

Support and nurture teachers who are enthusiastic in their adoption of the Habits of Mind and who consistently model the habits. Invest in professional development for these passionate teachers. Showcase their achievements and encourage them to share their experiences. They will then serve as valuable models for schoolwide implementation and become the core of a network of inspired teachers. When other teachers see that these early adopters of the program are valued, they understand that school leadership is serious about implementing the habits and developing the school as a home for the mind.

Example: When reviewing teaching practice, the curriculum, or the success of a school event with colleagues, employ the language of the habits in your discussions.

The strategies and examples provided here are just a few of many ways to teach and instill Habits of Mind schoolwide. Keep in regular communication with other leaders to share ideas.

You may also choose to use activities described in other sections of this ASCD Action Tool as springboards for developing additional strategies for schoolwide implementation. The next tool in this section offers even more strategies for consideration.

Extending Values

ACTION TOOL

Specific Teaching Strategies

Here you will find numerous specific teaching strategies and examples to inspire the schoolwide integration of the Habits of Mind.

1. Solving Problems with Specific Habits of Mind

The following is a powerful example of what can happen when teachers get together to discuss a learning issue and use the Habits of Mind to problem-solve.

> Teachers in a high school mathematics department were hoping that Habits of Mind could help their students think and behave more like mathematicians. At a department meeting, they discussed exactly what aspects of student behavior they wanted to improve. They asked: If students were to behave more like mathematicians and less like students doing math, how would their behavior change?
>
> The teachers quickly and unanimously realized that the students' behavior would be less risk-adverse. They noted that their students were inclined to ask for help the moment they got stuck, rather than to look for strategies to solve a problem themselves; they were too dependent on teachers to find ways they could complete their work.
>
> To encourage the students to act like mathematicians and find ways around being stuck, the teachers focused on the Taking Responsible Risks Habit of Mind. In every math class, they asked students to write the capital letters RR in the margins of their tests or Habits of Mind assignments to indicate a place when they got stuck. They would then take a responsible risk (RR) and do their best to answer the question.
>
> The teachers praised and rewarded students for taking a responsible risk even if their work was not accurate. The independent strategizing behavior was more important than the final answer, which students would learn later. In this way, students began thinking and behaving like mathematicians.

Another idea, useful at the elementary level, is to use a "Success-o-Meter" as a rubric. The example shown on page 289 is designed to help students who are working on a writing assignment. It helps them analyze their work, think about their thinking, and see exactly what they need to do to improve. A Success-o-Meter or other symbol of progress toward a goal (e.g., a large mountain to be climbed) can be used in other content areas as well.

2. Adjusting Wait Time

Focusing on wait time (or think time) is a powerful strategy for managing impulsivity. According to a study by Mary Budd Rowe in the *Journal of Teacher Education* (1986, January/February), after asking a question, the average teacher waits one second before either calling on a student, asking another question, or answering the question herself. As a result, students do not have time to think. It is unrealistic to expect anyone to provide an informed answer in one second. Instead, Rowe recommends that teachers wait at least 7–10 seconds before calling on a student. That way, students have adequate time to think.

The following are three waiting strategies:

Wait Time I: Pause at least 7–10 seconds after asking a question.
Wait Time II: After a student replies or asks a related question, pause at least 3 seconds for a basic question and at least 5 seconds for a higher-order question.
Wait Time III: After a student asks a question, pause and model thoughtfulness.

As students benefit from seeing wait time modeled, they will learn to be better listeners and to better manage their impulsive urges.

3. Using the Think-Pair-Share Model

The Think-Pair-Share model provides an excellent strategy for helping students develop thinking skills. With this model, students start with a problem or task. They begin by thinking alone for a specified period of time. Then they form pairs to discuss the question or task. Finally, students share their thoughts and ideas with the whole class.

4. Employing Paired Verbal Fluency

This strategy encourages active listening. Students work as partners, facing each other; they are designated as Partner A and Partner B. At the signal "Go," Partner A brainstorms for one minute; Partner B must sit and quietly listen. At the end of one minute, Partner B brainstorms for one minute without repeating any of Partner A's ideas. Then Partner A brainstorms again, this time for 45 seconds and not repeating anything that has been said so far. Partner B does the same. In the final round, each partner has a turn for 30 seconds, again with neither partner repeating anything that has been said so far. Students must be good listeners to master this activity.

5. Creating a Human Graph or Continuum Graph

This activity is a powerful tool for reflecting on experiences and opinions and for learning from others. One excellent application for beginning a course of study on a Habit of

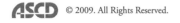

Extending Values

Mind is as follows: Choose a Habit of Mind. Have students line up along one wall. Ask if they have ever experienced this habit. Direct those who have experienced the habit to one end of the line and those who haven't to the other end. Have those who aren't sure or who don't want to commit position themselves anywhere along the continuum. Ask those students who are at the "expert" end of the graph to become group leaders, then divide the rest of the class into groups and allocate one "expert" to each group. Have each group leader describe his or her experience of the habit to the group. Then encourage other group members to think about whether they might have experienced the habit without realizing it. After hearing from a peer, students usually realize that they have indeed experienced the habit for themselves in some way.

6. Sharing Stories

Many teachers are accustomed to reading stories to or with their classes. Many rich and exciting varieties of stories from numerous cultures exemplify the Habits of Mind in different contexts. A powerful way of motivating students to value the habits is to highlight one or more habits relevant to the story. For example, introduce a tale as a story about the Habit of Mind of Persisting and, later, encourage students to identify additional relevant habits. Or read the story to the class and then ask students to identify the habits they believe are involved. To extend this exercise, ask students to analyze which habits might have prevented a problem from arising or might have helped solve a difficult issue. In this way, students can see the habits valued in a variety of ways and in many different contexts.

7. Considering Frame of Reference

The frequent infusion of the Habits of Mind into all aspects of learning, rather than isolating them into specific lessons, sends a clear message to students that the habits are valuable. If the habits are used as a frame of reference across the curriculum, students learn to analyze new situations in terms of the habits and become more adept at personally cultivating the habits.

8. Using Bookmarks

A teacher in Christchurch, New Zealand, uses Habits of Mind bookmarks to encourage students to set goals and focus on developing each habit. At the beginning of the term, the teacher has each student choose a habit he would like to develop, then gives students bookmarks that display information about their chosen habit. Students can write personal goals on the reverse of the bookmark and laminate it. They keep the bookmark in

Extending Values

their reading book to refer to every day. This is a simple but highly effective way of helping children maintain focus on Habits of Mind.

9. Modeling the Habits

An excellent example of modeling occurred when one teacher was instructing students on writing. As the teacher was writing a story on the board, she openly discussed and challenged her own thinking. She wrote: "'Oh no!' said John" on the board and then she said, "Oh! I already used *said John* in the last sentence. This time I want to use *exclaimed* instead because John is shocked and upset, so *exclaimed* is a more accurate word and it prevents my saying the same thing over again." With just these few words, the teacher modeled her thinking process and enabled students to become more aware of their own thinking processes when writing. When teachers show that they value the habits, students will respond to teachers' cues and find their own value in the habits.

10. Using Thinking Verbs

If your goal is to encourage students to think, explicitly use thinking words such as those below. Students will then become better adept at understanding and using them.

Examples of Thinking Verbs

analyze	observe
apply	organize
classify	paraphrase
compare	predict
connect	respond
contrast	support
describe	represent
discuss	visualize
elaborate	reason
explore	verify
diagram	solve
identify	summarize
interpret	simplify
judge	determine

Extending Values

These key thinking words are of universal application across subject areas. Investing time to teach these terms to students can have a significant impact on skillful thinking across a school.

11. Using Checklists, Rubrics, Action Plans, and Other Evaluation Tools

Evaluation is an important part of the Habits of Mind program. A Success-o-Meter and a Group Work Evaluation are provided as examples. Other assessment tools are incorporated throughout this action tool. Appendix B includes both specific and generic evaluation tools.

You can also encourage students to take charge of their own mastery of the Habits of Mind. For example, they can design their own rubrics, table tops, desk liners, and games. They can employ self-management tools such as variations of the Before-During-After model to chronicle what they knew before, learned during, and knew after studying a topic.

Journal writing is another highly effective method of promoting evaluation. As students record their thoughts in an ongoing manner, they practice the metacognitive process and can track their growth over time, gaining skills in self-assessment and self-regulation. Introduce students to journal writing with simple idea starters, or ask them to describe the thinking, steps, and sequences related to a task (before, during, and after), with an emphasis on a particular Habit of Mind.

12. Managing Student Behavior

In addition to their value as a framework for learning and teaching, the Habits of Mind can be valuable in classroom management and issues of student behavior. For example, students who have been involved in behavior problems or incidents with other students can be asked to sit down and write a "think paper" in which they reflect upon their thinking and behaviors in response to prompts such as those provided on page 291.

Success-o-Meter

This is an example of a type of rubric students can use to evaluate one another's writing skills.

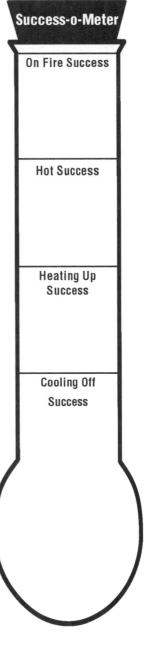

Excellent description.
Mixture of short, medium, and long sentences with interesting words to start each sentence.

Good description.
Some long, medium, and short sentences.
Start sentences with different words. Great punctuation.

No description.
Simple, short sentences. Some punctuation.

No description.
Only one long sentence. No punctuation—
needs capital letter at beginning and period at end.

Success-o-Meter

On Fire Success

Hot Success

Heating Up Success

Cooling Off Success

Name _____ Class _____ Date _____

Group Work Evaluation

1. When I knew an idea I shared it with my group. ☺ ☹

2. I encouraged others in my group. ☺ ☹

3. I used people's names. ☺ ☹

4. When I did not understand, I asked my partner. ☺ ☹

5. When my partner did not understand, I helped. ☺ ☹

Goal Setting:

What could you do to improve your group work?

Extending Values

Suggested Prompts for a Student "Think Paper"

What was the incident in which you were involved?

What caused this incident?

Which Habits of Mind should you have used to avoid this situation?

What are the consequences of this situation for you, the other person, and others in the school?

Which Habits of Mind are you going to put into play to repair the situation with the others involved?

Which Habits of Mind would you like to see the other people use to help you repair the situation?

Which Habits of Mind would help prevent another situation like this from happening again?

How will you incorporate these Habits of Mind into your behavior from now on?

Building Commitment

Excellence is not a singular act but a habit. You are what you repeatedly do.

—Shaquille O'Neal

This section relates to the final goal of the Habits of Mind program: making the habits automatic. The tools provided here take learners from thinking consciously about using a habit to internalizing the habit to such a degree that it is a regular part of how the learners think, learn, and live. In other words, the habits become a part of a learner's being such that they naturally and unconsciously direct the person's behavior.

This process, which is called habituation, is the ultimate goal for any mindful, independent learner. However, we cannot become complacent as we habituate the Habits of Mind. We must find ways of continuously growing and improving. The model on the next page demonstrates how the Habits of Mind provide a continuous disposition for lifelong learning.

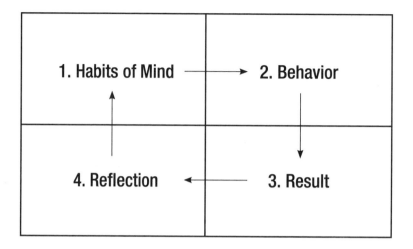

As the diagram shows, the Habits of Mind unconsciously give form to learners' thinking and shape their behaviors. Their behaviors then lead to results, or outcomes, which may be positive or negative. Learners then take time to reflect on the results and the processes.

By the time learners have reached the habituation stage, this self-reflection is an automatic process if they intend to change results or outcomes. Two key components of the reflection stage are to evaluate how the habits were used and to consider how to refine their use to achieve the desired change.

CONTENTS

TITLE OF TOOL

School Leaders Building Commitment

Watch your thoughts for they become words,
watch your words for they become actions,
watch your actions for they become habits,
watch your habits for they become character,
watch your character for it becomes your destiny.

—Ralph Waldo Emerson

PURPOSE OF THIS TOOL

This tool provides a series of recommendations and strategies for helping school leaders—especially administrators and teacher leaders—to promote the growth and sustain the use of Habits of Mind within the school as a learning organization. It provides an overview of suggestions proven effective in schools that have been successful in making the 16 Habits of Mind a clear and continuous part of the school's climate, culture, policies, and practices.

HOW TO USE THIS TOOL

School leaders may elect to incorporate the materials in this tool into school improvement planning sessions as well as faculty meetings devoted to Habits of Mind. Specifically, study groups responsible for introducing and sustaining the use of Habits of Mind as part of ongoing school improvement planning and professional development will find these recommendations both practical and immediately applicable. Leaders may elect to have members of a Habits of Mind study group discuss and debate which of the recommendations presented here have the most immediate relevance.

TIPS AND VARIATIONS

This tool addresses six topics related to integrating Habits of Mind into key aspects of organizational change and strategic planning processes. School leaders may choose whichever topics are most appropriate for their particular circumstances.

1. Revisiting Strategic Plans

When the Habits of Mind are an integral part of a school's strategic plan, building commitment is inherent in school goals. The Boyes-Watts Model of Activation can help you create strategic purpose. Use of the model to increase alertness is described in the previous

section (Extending Values) of this action tool. By revisiting your strategic plan every year to review and reflect on goals and current practices, you can change your use of the Habits of Mind as necessary to build commitment and improve your program. It is all too easy for any initiative to be sidelined as new initiatives are implemented. By committing to annual strategic planning, your program will improve with time.

The following are three sets of sample questions for reviewing the effectiveness of current Habits of Mind implementation. Make sure school leaders, teachers, and students are all involved in the review process. This way, you have a shared understanding and a common sense of purpose and direction.

- Strategic Planning Questions for School Leaders

    Are you displaying the leadership qualities required to sustain the Habits of Mind?

    Are you using mindful language in your conversations?

    Are you investing in the ongoing development of your school as a home for the mind?

- Strategic Planning Questions for Teachers

    Are you using mindful language?

    Do you model your own thinking for students?

    Do you allow wait time for students to answer questions?

    Do you allow opportunities for the development of the Habits of Mind in your teaching?

- Strategic Planning Questions for Students

    Are you improving your use of the Habits of Mind?

    Have you set targets to further develop the habits?

    Are you transferring Habits of Mind from one situation to another?

    Are you using the habits in your life outside the classroom?

2. Supporting Ongoing Professional Development

Support and nurture the enthusiasm of teachers who are using Habits of Mind and modeling the habits. When teachers get regular opportunities to grow their personal skills, they understand that school leadership is serious about an ongoing, continued implementation of the habits to keep the school as a "home for the mind." With regular professional development, teachers can continue to build and maintain their commitment to teaching and modeling Habits of Mind.

3. Inducting New Staff and Students

Introduce new students and teachers to the Habits of Mind and their role at your school as soon as possible. Induction may take the form of an information booklet, a training DVD, staff meetings, parent evenings, or assemblies. The sooner those new to the school are familiar with the habits, the sooner they can grow their understanding and build commitment.

4. Maintaining a Universal, Mindful Language

The importance of maintaining a shared language cannot be overemphasized. When school leaders, teachers, students, and parents all understand and use a shared vocabulary of learning, they can build on common ground. The previous section of this action tool (Extending Values) discusses the importance of mindful language and the need for school leaders, teachers, and parents to consciously use mindful language every day to support student learning. To build commitment, the Habits of Mind must become the fabric of learning that weaves through the school community and beyond. In other words, the habits must become "the way we do it around here."

5. Creating School Newsletters

Newsletters are a great tool for facilitating communication between school and home. With this tool, you can explain the function and role of the Habits of Mind. You can also include articles that focus on a particular habit relevant at that time or explain how the habits are preparing students to be lifelong learners. Remember that the habits are of service to the parents since they are the students' teachers and guides at home; parents who adopt the habits find them to be a powerful tool in parenting. So newsletters not only let parents know what is happening at the school but also give them a useful tool to help them help their children learn and build commitment.

6. Routinely Allowing Time for Thinking

If students have time to think and reflect, they can apply the Habits of Mind to new situations and in their own ways. So if you want students to think, give them the time they need. The following are three strategies for providing sufficient time for thinking:

- Pause at least 7–10 seconds after asking a question.
- After a student replies or asks a related question, pause at least 3 seconds for a basic question and at least 5 seconds for a higher-order question.
- After a student asks you a question, pause and model thoughtfulness.

Building Commitment

Teachers Building Commitment

The only limit to your impact is your imagination and commitment.

—Anthony Robbins

PURPOSE OF THIS TOOL

Teachers who are embarking on teaching the Habits of Mind or who have been involved in the program for some time may ask questions such as these: How do you know if you are building commitment? What is internalizing the Habits of Mind like? To answer these questions, a good starting place and invaluable ongoing resource is self-reflection. In teacher training sessions, you can give teachers a tool for self-reflection and then discuss how teachers might target specific areas to improve. Teachers can then periodically use the tool to check their personal progress. The resources in this tool will support instructional leaders and other educators in this process.

HOW TO USE THIS TOOL

One Teacher Self-Reflection tool is provided on page 302. On this form, teachers can score their current level of mastery of each Habit of Mind on a scale of 1–10. (For additional reflection tools, see Appendix B.) In addition to using data from the implementation of this tool, leaders may wish to share examples of how they can work with staff members to create Habits of Mind signals within the school environment.

TIPS AND VARIATIONS

1. Encourage teachers to reflect frequently on their own use of the Habits of Mind. The Teacher Self-Reflection provided on page 302 is an example of one instrument you might use.

2. Display the Habits of Mind throughout the school to demonstrate the program's value and your commitment to it. Ideas for displays can come from teachers, students, and administrators. You can create songs, posters, plaques, acronyms, or a school motto to broadcast the habits and create cues for learning, remembering, and integrating the habits. See the examples on the following pages to help you get started.

Building Commitment

3. Provide awards to students and teachers for demonstrating use of various habits or for creating artwork or some other instrument for publicizing the habits and helping students learn and use them.

4. Review the previous section (Extending Values) for specific teaching strategies and samples.

Teacher Self-Reflection Tool

Habit of Mind	I am a teacher who ...
Persisting	Perseveres with challenging students and ensures all students have a depth of understanding and skills as a learner. *Rate yourself: 1 2 3 4 5 6 7 8 9 10*
Managing Impulsivity	Uses wait time and the techniques of pausing, paraphrasing, and probing; I demonstrate thoughtfulness. *Rate yourself: 1 2 3 4 5 6 7 8 9 10*
Listening with Understanding and Empathy	*Actively listens to others; I make genuine attempts to understand where others are coming from and to perceive their points of view.* *Rate yourself: 1 2 3 4 5 6 7 8 9 10*
Thinking Flexibly	Is open to the points of view of others; changes plans and strategies when needed to better meet groups' needs; grasps the teachable moment to foster interest and achievement. *Rate yourself: 1 2 3 4 5 6 7 8 9 10*
Thinking About Thinking (Metacognition)	Is aware of my own thinking processes; I invest time in reflection; I model my thinking processes to those around me. *Rate yourself: 1 2 3 4 5 6 7 8 9 10*
Striving for Accuracy and Precision	Sets high standards in the things I do and in relations with others. I check for accuracy in written documents and communications. *Rate yourself: 1 2 3 4 5 6 7 8 9 10*
Questioning and Posing Problems	Is skilled in composing and asking complex questions. *Rate yourself: 1 2 3 4 5 6 7 8 9 10*
Applying Past Knowledge to New Situations	Uses past experiences, resources, and knowledge to ensure good practice. I offer wide knowledge to support student learning. *Rate yourself: 1 2 3 4 5 6 7 8 9 10*
Thinking and Communicating with Clarity and Precision	Strives to be accurate in all communications. I use thinking verbs when giving instructions. *Rate yourself: 1 2 3 4 5 6 7 8 9 10*
Gathering Data Through All Senses	Stays alert to people and situations by gathering data through my senses. *Rate yourself: 1 2 3 4 5 6 7 8 9 10*

Teacher Self-Reflection Tool

Habit of Mind	I am a teacher who ...
Creating, Imagining, and Innovating	Is creative and innovative in finding new ways and alternatives. *Rate yourself:* 1 2 3 4 5 6 7 8 9 10
Responding with Wonderment and Awe	Is enthusiastic about my teaching, my students' learning, and new discoveries. *Rate yourself:* 1 2 3 4 5 6 7 8 9 10
Taking Responsible Risks	Moves outside my comfort zone and becomes adventurous after thoughtful consideration. *Rate yourself:* 1 2 3 4 5 6 7 8 9 10
Finding Humor	Can laugh with others and at myself; I do not take myself too seriously. *Rate yourself:* 1 2 3 4 5 6 7 8 9 10
Thinking Interdependently	Works collaboratively with others; I can learn from those around me. *Rate yourself:* 1 2 3 4 5 6 7 8 9 10
Learning Continuously	Has the humility and pride to admit when I don't know something; I resist complacency. *Rate yourself:* 1 2 3 4 5 6 7 8 9 10

Building Commitment

Examples and Ideas for Building Commitment

FOCUSING ON ONE HABIT OF MIND PER WEEK

- Refer to the habit of the week whenever possible during content instruction and class activities. Examples:

    Introduce words related to the habit during vocabulary lessons.
    Discuss characters' use (or lack of use) of the habit during literature lessons.
    Assign homework that will assure students practice or focus on the habit at
        home in some way.

- Have students create posters, artworks, poems, songs, or other products that demonstrate the habit. Allow students to display their work in the classroom or hallway for other students to see and enjoy.
- Create a class mural depicting aspects or examples of the habit of the week.
- Award a small prize or certificate at the end of the week to students who most frequently exhibited the habit in class or to students who showed the most improvement in the habit during the week.

CREATING SLOGANS

- Write a catchy phrase that can become a tag line on school stationery, the school's Web site, the masthead of the school newspaper, or elsewhere. Examples:

    Berkshire Elementary: A Habits of Mind Learning Community
    Amherst Academy: Specializing in Habits of Mind for Lifelong Learning
    Brentford School: Where learning is Habit (of Mind)-forming
    Canterbury School: Habits of Mind, tales of success

- Use a familiar advertising slogan for an organization, an industry, or a product—but give it a twist. Examples:

    For Thinking Flexibly: Better living through better thinking.
    For Striving for Accuracy: Because it absolutely, positively should be right!
    For Creating, Imagining, and Innovating: Let your imagination do the walking.

- Incorporate the school mascot in a slogan. Examples:

    For Thinking and Communicating with Clarity and Precision: Taylor School
        Tigers "paws" to think.

Building Commitment

For Learning Continuously: Braddock High School—Where Bruin power is brain power; Braddock High School—Where Bruins use their brains; Braddock High School—Our Bruins have powerful brains.

For Taking Responsible Risks: Whittier Wildcats take responsible risks.

For Learning Continuously: Lakewood Lions take "pride" in learning.

For Thinking Flexibly: At Edgar Allan Poe School, we're "raven"ous about learning with Habits of Mind.

USING ACRONYMS

• Use the school name to create an acronym. Examples:

Burke Middle School: **B**uilding **U**nderstanding, **R**esponsibility, and **K**nowledge to achieve **E**xcellence

Holmes Elementary School: Our **H**abit **O**f **L**earning **M**akes **E**xcellent **S**tudents

Dunleigh Academy: **D**eep **UN**derstanding and **L**earning, **E**xciting **I**nnovation, **G**reat **H**abits

DESIGNING POSTERS AND OTHER MESSAGES

• Place posters throughout the school to inspire students to make the habits their own.

• Sponsor a contest in which classes compete to design a unique way to foster the habits schoolwide. Reward the winning class with a pizza party or other suitable celebration. This could be a monthly event with different requirements each month—for example, one month all entries must be rap song lyrics, another month posters, another cheers ("Two-four-six-eight; come see how we innovate!"), and so on.

• If the school has a Web site, feature the Habits of Mind on the home page, perhaps with a link to information about the habits, reports of how students are learning them, photographs of student creations that illustrate them, and so on.

• Coordinate a schoolwide art show of student and teacher artifacts that illustrate or demonstrate various Habits of Mind. Suggest that the PTA hold one of its meetings at the time the art show is set up, so parents can tour it. Invite a panel of judges to view all works and award ribbons of excellence to deserving pieces.

• Put a Habit of Mind of the Month bulletin board in a prominent place in the school—for example, the lobby or cafeteria.

- Institute a Habits of Mind column for the school newspaper or newsletter. Teachers or students could be the writers, describing how their class has learned about and used each featured habit.
- Plan a schoolwide or grade-level assembly in which parents or community volunteers are invited to participate in a panel. Have student representatives ask questions about how the panelists use different Habits of Mind in their work or at home. Afterward, have students write a summary of the event in a form of their choosing (a descriptive paragraph, a review for the newspaper, an editorial commentary, and so on).
- Think about other creative ways to show commitment to the Habits of Mind philosophy. For example, one school symbolized growing the habits by planting a tree on school property for each habit and placing a marker for each habit at the tree's base.

Students Building Commitment

Effort only fully releases its reward after a person refuses to quit.

—Napoleon Hill

PURPOSE OF THIS TOOL

Like the rest of us, students build commitment progressively. Periodically take a moment to stop and reflect on their progress with questions such as these: How have the Habits of Mind influenced student decision making about learning? What were some effects of a particular habit on a student or students? As students reflect on their work, which habits do they feel have served them most?

HOW TO USE THIS TOOL

The strategies in this tool will help you and your students keep track of student progress and build upon what they are learning. The central impetus of the models, strategies, and suggestions included here is to create classrooms as learning communities in which Habits of Mind are discussed, revisited, and used as catalysts for promoting high levels of student metacognition, self-regulation, and self-assessment. Additional strategies can be found in the previous section (Extending Values).

TIPS AND VARIATIONS

Share the ideas and strategies included with this tool as samples and models for staff members to identify and implement ways to help students build momentum, ownership, and sustained use of the Habits of Mind.

1. Building Portfolios

Portfolios are a wonderful resource. They allow students to keep track of their work, and they allow both you and the student to see growth over time. The following is one method you can use for building a portfolio. It can be summed up in four steps as follows:

- Collect: Deposit class work and other materials in a central area such as a folder or binder.
- Select: Pick work samples that show learning and growth.
- Reflect: Think about the learning the items show, and identify evidence of growth.

- Connect: Build links across classes, disciplines, and semesters. Strengthen connections between school, community, and work.

A typical Habits of Mind portfolio includes work samples, journal writings, self-assessments and other reflection tools, information and ideas, and action plans. Stress that students do some reflection and attach a description of why each piece is included in a portfolio. The following are a few sample starters:

- I chose this piece of work because . . .
- My parents liked this piece of work because . . .
- I will remember this piece of work in 20 years because . . .
- The Habit of Mind called . . . was useful with this piece of work because . . .
- This piece of work would have been better if I had focused on the Habit of Mind called . . . because . . .
- The Habit of Mind I have improved the most is . . . because . . .
- The Habit of Mind that will add the most to my work in the future is . . . because . . .

2. Earning Rewards

Certificates, stickers, ribbons, calendars, and other items make great rewards. Students can take these items home to develop a link between the Habits of Mind taught at school and principles taught at home. For example, early in the year, a teacher could introduce parents to a habit the class will study, then periodically send home a certificate with blank spaces for students and parents to complete together. Many students are eager to complete the certificates, so they look for opportunities to practice the habit. Parents also learn about the Habits of Mind and are able to support their children's learning at home.

3. Reading Relevant Literature

Why not have a display of books, both fiction and nonfiction, to help build awareness and commitment to a particular Habit of Mind? Give your library staff sufficient notice and ask them to select books that illustrate a particular habit. Then put together a display of books and posters to help attract students to learn more about the habit. Suggest that students who read the books write a review for the school newspaper or write a letter to a story character congratulating him or her on use of a habit.

Building Commitment

4. Using Learning Ladders

Using learning ladders helps students become competent and proficient with the Habits of Mind. The ladders allow students to reflect on how they use a habit on a regular basis. The bottom rung of a learning ladder lists beginning skills. The next rungs show developing, proficient, and expert skills, respectively. Students can define each step for clarity. Then they can regularly return to the ladder to reflect on their current level of development. The ladder might be in a student's notebook, on a wall, on a table, or inside a desk. You could post one ladder if you are focusing on a specific habit, or display several ladders to focus on habits that are key to your students' learning at a particular time. If you have enough time and space, have students create a ladder for each of the 16 habits. Another possibility is to have them create digital resources to represent the ladders.

5. Creating Wall Charts or Posters

Students can make colorful and creative reminders of the Habits of Mind to post in the classroom and around the school. You might like to have students compete to create sets or summaries of the habits. Suggest that students use the Summary of 16 Habits of Mind (Appendix B) as a resource. Help students compile their products into a personalized book that they can keep.

6. Designing New Logos

As you have seen throughout this ASCD Action Tool, each Habit of Mind has a thoughtful and interesting logo; these can be excellent tools for teaching. You can help students integrate a personal understanding of the habits by asking them to design their own logos. By collecting and keeping these student artworks over the years, you can build a unique set. You could take the idea one step further and have students create objects, sculptures, toys, or other items to represent the habits. For example, they might produce posters, toys, or stories with titles such as *Mount Persistence*, *The Wiggly Worm of Thinking Flexibly*, the *Dart Board of Accuracy*, the *Lightbulb of Creating*, or the *Happy Face of Finding Humor*. Students are often the best resources for finding creative new ways to signify and symbolize the habits; their products often create lasting impressions and help students internalize.

7. Extending Beyond the Classroom

Students who are involved in extracurricular activities both in school and outside of school can practice, appreciate, and extend the Habits of Mind in a variety of ways.

Building Commitment

Examples:

• Athletes in both individual and team sports take responsible risks, apply past knowledge to new situations, gather data through all senses, and think interdependently. These students can share their use of and reflections on such habits with classmates, coaches, sponsors, and fans.

• After-school special-interest clubs and organizations can focus on various habits as part of their activities and assessment of their events (chess team members use metacognition, science club members learn continuously, student office assistants strive for accuracy, and so on).

• Cheerleaders can publicize Habits of Mind by composing cheers about them. They can then choreograph motions to accompany the cheers and perform them at assemblies, rallies, and even athletic events.

• The student council could organize a Habits of Mind parade as part of a schoolwide event such as the annual carnival, family fun fair, field day, spirit week, or homecoming activities. Various teams or classes could make a festive float or other parade entry about a chosen habit. Students might enjoy competing for various awards (best design, most unusual, etc.) for their creations.

8. Extending Beyond the School

Students can look for opportunities to extend the Habits of Mind beyond the school grounds. For example, students can

• Participate in the school's hosting of a training session for parents to teach them to model the habits and use mindful language.

• Encourage their parents and families to use the habits at home.

• Encourage their friends and classmates to use the habits in making decisions that affect their personal life, such as what kinds of friends to choose, how to handle conflicts with siblings, how to spend their money wisely, and so on.

• Request that the PTA sponsor a special event to highlight the habits, such as a Habits of Mind fair, or that the PTA work the habits into a regular event such as Back-to-School Night.

• Assume responsibility for the Habits of Mind portion of the school's Web site, designing it and keeping it fresh with ideas and information submitted by all classes.

• Volunteer to be Habits of Mind columnists for the school newsletter or newspaper.

• Create a video of skits depicting each Habit of Mind and then show the video to younger classes and to parents.

Building Commitment

9. Regularly Reflecting and Assessing

Ongoing assessment is an important part of integration. Tools and activities throughout this ASCD Action Tool incorporate ways for students to analyze specific growth at a point in time. A sample self-assessment tool for students is available on the next page. Additional resources are available in Appendix B.

Student Self-Assessment: Assess Your Persisting Skills

Rate your skills by circling a number from 1 to 10, with 1 representing the lowest level and 10 the highest level of development.

I can ...	Rating
stay on task.	1 2 3 4 5 6 7 8 9 10
use a broad range of strategies to solve a problem.	1 2 3 4 5 6 7 8 9 10
keep going until the solution is found.	1 2 3 4 5 6 7 8 9 10
keep going until the assignment is finished.	1 2 3 4 5 6 7 8 9 10
keep attempting new ways to solve a problem.	1 2 3 4 5 6 7 8 9 10
put up with frustration and confusion to achieve my goals.	1 2 3 4 5 6 7 8 9 10
refuse to quit even when it gets tough.	1 2 3 4 5 6 7 8 9 10
persevere even when answers or solutions are not immediately apparent.	1 2 3 4 5 6 7 8 9 10
enjoy the satisfaction of succeeding in a challenging new task.	1 2 3 4 5 6 7 8 9 10
keep trying even if something gets difficult.	1 2 3 4 5 6 7 8 9 10

Internalization

All of a sudden these new concepts stopped churning within you, and a new reality is born: You and the concepts are one. They have literally become you. You have become them.

—Tom Hopkins

PURPOSE OF THIS TOOL

This tool provides a brief but powerful summary of ideas and conclusions about how students can be supported toward the act of internalization—that is, making their use of Habits of Mind an automatic and spontaneous part of their lifelong learning process. Perhaps most significant, the ideas presented here reinforce the idea that internalization is always a work in progress, never an end point.

HOW TO USE THIS TOOL

Share ideas presented on the previous pages of this section with staff members, parents, and community members as part of outreach and development efforts to reinforce the significance and power of the 16 Habits of Mind. Consider with participants the following essential question: How do we make Habits of Mind a significant, sustainable, and powerful part of our organizational culture and commitment to lifelong learning for every student?

TIPS AND VARIATIONS

An ideal format for reviewing and discussing the ideas presented throughout this Building Commitment section is a cooperative learning jigsaw activity. Participants can select a partner or a small group to process one or more of the ideas presented in this tool. The ideas are also good starting points for follow-up study groups and inquiry teams.

1. Adopting a New Way of Being

Building commitment refers not just to learning within school but to life outside of and after school. A teacher in New Zealand commented that "the Habits of Mind have made me a better father." This recognition that the habits are not just for students in the classroom but are also for all teachers to live by is significant. To fully benefit from the Habits of Mind, we need to understand they are a way of being. They are not something teachers turn on when they arrive at school in the morning and turn off when they leave.

Building Commitment

The habits offer service to professional practice and enhance teachers' participation in the wider world.

2. Reinforcing That No Internalization Is Final

So what is meant by *internalization*? Costa and Kallick suggest that the Habits of Mind can never be fully mastered. As continuous learners, we must continually practice, modify, and refine them. When we are truly habituated to a Habit of Mind, we demonstrate that habit automatically, spontaneously, and without prompting. When confronted with complex decisions, ambiguous tasks, challenging problems, or perplexing dilemmas, we ask ourselves questions such as these: What is the most flexible thing I can do right now? What questions do I need to ask myself and others? Who else do I need to think about? How can I refine the problem to make it clearer? What intrigues me about this problem? Realizing that we are all works in progress, we can be metacognitive about how the habits serve us and how they can serve others. Suppose, for example, that you are in a group in which problem solving is not going well and one group member says, "This is too hard. Let's quit." The person with commitment might advocate for the Habit of Mind of Persisting by saying, "C'mon. Problems are hard to solve but if we stay with it, I bet we can do it! Imagine how great we will all feel if we actually come up with a solution rather than living with this frustration." At this point, the habit has become internalized as a way of life.

3. Determining How We Can Truly Internalize the Habits of Mind

You cannot hope to build a better world without first improving the individuals. To that end, each of us must work for our own improvement and, at the same time, share a general responsibility for all humanity.

—Marie Curie

Begin by clarifying goals and purposes. For example, ask yourself: What do you want to achieve? Then make a plan of action, take action, experiment, gather evidence and become aware, monitor growth, and reflect on the successes of your strategies. Ask yourself: What did I achieve? Is this the best way of doing it? Then use the answers to those questions to modify your plans as needed to get better results. Next, revisit your goals and purposes to ensure you are on track. At this point, start over again. Thus, as the figure on the next page shows, the spiral continues ever onward.

Building Commitment

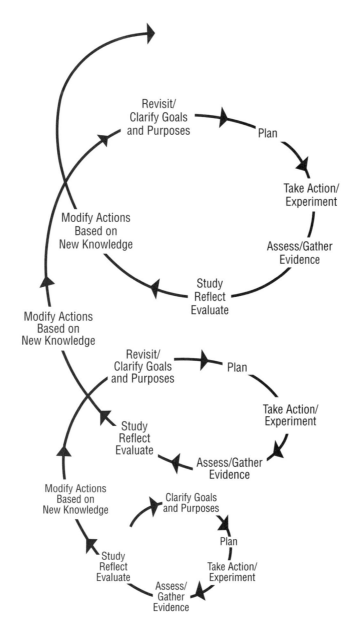

Source: From *Assessment in the Learning Organization: Shifting the Paradigm* (p. 27), by A. L. Costa and B. Kallick, 1995, Alexandria, VA: ASCD. Copyright 1995 by ASCD.

Building Commitment

Appendix A

WHAT ARE HABITS OF MIND?

This appendix provides a brief background of the Habits of Mind for those who are new to the program. Habits of Mind are behaviors associated with effective learning. When faced with new challenges or problems to solve, these behaviors can be used to effectively manage a learning situation. The Habits of Mind are long-range, enduring skills that allow us to cope with a rapidly changing world. The behaviors promote powerful thinking skills for intelligently navigating moral, ethical, and spiritual challenges.

GUIDING PRINCIPLES

Habits of Mind serve as guiding principles for learning in the classroom and outside the school walls throughout students' life experiences. The habits are powerful tools for

- Establishing and maintaining positive relationships.
- Developing effective communication techniques.
- Applying flexible-thinking strategies in complex situations.
- Learning powerful character traits such as self-reflection and resilience.

Resources and References

RELEVANCE TO ALL

Habits of Mind are as useful for adults as they are for students. When teachers internalize these dispositions themselves, they can better model desirable behavior in their students. In addition, Habits of Mind are relevant to students of all ages and in all subject areas. In fact, Habits of Mind can extend beyond a single classroom to create a whole-school learning culture.

Noted educators Arthur L. Costa and Bena Kallick identify and describe 16 types of intelligent behavior in several of their publications. Their recent book, *Learning and Leading with Habits of Mind: 16 Essential Characteristics for Success* (ASCD, 2008), defines and summarizes the habits on pages 15–38.

Describing 16 Habits of Mind

By Arthur L. Costa and Bena Kallick

By definition, a problem is any stimulus, question, task, phenomenon, or discrepancy, the explanation for which is not immediately known. Thus, we are interested in focusing on student performance under those challenging conditions that demand strategic reasoning, insightfulness, perseverance, creativity, and craftsmanship to resolve a complex problem. We are interested not only in how many answers students know but also in how they behave when they *don't* know. We are interested in observing how students produce knowledge rather than how they merely reproduce it. The critical attribute of intelligent human beings is not only having information but also knowing how to act on it.

A Habit of Mind is a disposition toward behaving intelligently when confronted with problems that do not have immediately known answers. When humans experience dichotomies, are confused by dilemmas, or come face to face with uncertainties, our most effective actions require drawing forth certain patterns of intellectual behavior. When we draw upon these intellectual resources, the results that are produced are more powerful, of higher quality, and of greater significance than if we fail to employ those patterns of intellectual behaviors.

Employing Habits of Mind requires a composite of many skills, attitudes, cues, past experiences, and proclivities. It means that we value one pattern of thinking over another; therefore, it implies choice making about which pattern should be employed at which time. It includes sensitivity to the contextual cues in a situation that signal an appropriate time and circumstance in which the employment of a pattern would be useful. It requires a level of skillfulness to employ and carry through the behaviors effectively over time. It suggests that as a result of each experience in which the behaviors were employed, the effects of their use are reflected upon, evaluated, modified, and carried forth to future applications.

Habits of Mind attend to

- Value: Choosing to employ a pattern of intellectual behaviors rather than other, less productive patterns.
- Inclination: Feeling the tendency toward employing a pattern of intellectual behaviors.
- Sensitivity: Perceiving opportunities for and appropriateness of employing the pattern of behaviors.

Resources and References

• Capability: Possessing the basic skills and capacities to carry through with the behaviors.
• Commitment: Constantly striving to reflect on and improve performance of the behaviors.

DESCRIBING HABITS OF MIND

> *When we no longer know what to do we have come to our real work and when we no longer know which way to go we have begun our real journey. The mind that is not baffled is not employed. The impeded stream is the one that sings.*
>
> —Wendell Berry

What behaviors are indicative of the efficient, effective problem solver? Just what do human beings do when they behave intelligently? Research in effective thinking and intelligent behavior by Feuerstein (1980), Glatthorn and Baron (1985), Sternberg (1985), Perkins (1985), and Ennis (1985) indicates that there are some identifiable characteristics of effective thinkers. These are not necessarily scientists, artists, mathematicians, or the wealthy who demonstrate these behaviors. These characteristics have been identified in successful mechanics, teachers, entrepreneurs, salespeople, and parents—people in all walks of life.

Following are descriptions and an elaboration of 16 attributes of what human beings do when they behave intelligently. We choose to refer to them as Habits of Mind. They are the characteristics of what intelligent people do when they are confronted with problems that do not have immediately apparent resolutions.

These behaviors are seldom performed in isolation. Rather, clusters of such behaviors are drawn forth and employed in various situations. When listening intently, for example, one employs flexibility, metacognition, precise language, and perhaps questioning.

These are not the only 16 ways in which humans display their intelligence. It should be understood that this list is not meant to be complete. It should serve to initiate the collection of additional attributes. Although 16 Habits of Mind are described here, you, your colleagues, and your students will want to continue the search for additional Habits of Mind by adding to and elaborating on this list and the descriptions.

1. Persisting

> *Persistence is the twin sister of excellence.*
> *One is a matter of quality; the other, a matter of time.*
>
> —Marabel Morgan
> *The Electric Woman*

Efficacious people stick to a task until it is completed. They don't give up easily. They are able to analyze a problem and to develop a system, structure, or strategy to attack it. They employ a range and have a repertoire of alternative strategies for problem solving. They collect evidence to indicate their problem-solving strategy is working, and if one strategy doesn't work, they know how to back up and try another. They recognize when a theory or idea must be rejected and another employed. They have systematic methods of analyzing a problem, which include knowing how to begin, knowing what steps must be performed, and knowing what data need to be generated or collected. Because they are able to sustain a problem-solving process over time, they are comfortable with ambiguous situations.

Students often give up in despair when the answer to a problem is not immediately known. They sometimes crumple their papers and throw them away saying, "I can't do this," or "It's too hard," or they write down any answer to get the task overwith as quickly as possible. Some have attention deficits; they have difficulty staying focused for any length of time, they are easily distracted, they lack the ability to analyze a problem or to develop a system, structure, or strategy of problem attack. They may give up because they have a limited repertoire of problem-solving strategies. If their strategy doesn't work, they give up because they have no alternatives.

2. Managing Impulsivity

> *[A] goal-directed, self-imposed delay of gratification is perhaps the essence of emotional self-regulation: the ability to deny impulse in the service of a goal, whether it be building a business, solving an algebraic equation, or pursuing the Stanley cup.*
>
> Daniel Goleman
> *Emotional Intelligence* (1995, p. 83)

Effective problem solvers have a sense of deliberativeness: they think before they act. They intentionally form a vision of a product, plan of action, goal, or destination before they begin. They strive to clarify and understand directions, develop a strategy for approaching a problem, and withhold immediate value judgments about an idea before fully understanding it. Reflective individuals consider alternatives and consequences of several possible directions prior to taking action. They decrease their need for trial and error by gathering information, taking time to reflect on an answer before giving it, making sure they understand directions, and listening to alternative points of view.

Often, students blurt out the first answer that comes to mind. Sometimes they shout out an answer, start to work without fully understanding the directions, lack an organized plan or strategy for approaching a problem, or make immediate value judgments about an idea—criticizing or praising it—before fully understanding it. They may take the first suggestion given or operate on the first idea that comes to mind rather than considering alternatives and consequences of several possible directions.

3. Listening to Others with Understanding and Empathy

> *Listening is the beginning of understanding . . .*
> *Wisdom is the reward for a lifetime of listening.*
> *Let the wise listen and add to their learning and let the discerning get guidance.*
>
> Proverbs 1:5

Highly effective people spend an inordinate amount of time and energy listening (Covey, 1989). Some psychologists believe that the ability to listen to another person and to empathize with and understand their point of view is one of the highest forms of intelligent behavior. Being able to paraphrase another person's ideas, detecting indicators (cues) of feelings or emotional states in oral and body language (empathy), accurately expressing another person's concepts and emotions and problems—all are indications of listening behavior (Piaget called it "overcoming ego-centrism"). Effective listeners are able to see through the diverse perspectives of others. They gently attend to another person, demonstrating their understanding of and empathy for an idea or feeling by paraphrasing it accurately, building upon it, clarifying it, or giving an example of it.

Senge and his colleagues (1994) suggest that to listen fully means to pay close attention to what is being said beneath the words. You listen not only to the "music" but also to the essence of the person speaking. You listen not only for what someone knows but also for what he or she is trying to represent. Ears operate at the speed of sound, which is far slower than the speed of light the eyes take in. Generative listening is the art of developing deeper silences in yourself, so you can slow your mind's hearing to your ears' natural speed, and hear beneath the words to their meaning.

We spend 55 percent of our lives listening, yet it is one of the least-taught skills in schools. We often say we are listening, but in actuality we are rehearsing in our head what we are going to say next when our partner is finished. Some students ridicule, laugh at, or put down other students' ideas. They interrupt or are unable to build upon, consider the merits of, or operate on another person's ideas. We want our students to learn to devote their mental energies to another person and invest themselves in their partner's ideas.

We want students to learn to hold in abeyance their own values, judgments, opinions, and prejudices in order to listen to and entertain another person's thoughts. This is a very complex skill, requiring the ability to monitor one's own thoughts while at the same time attending to the partner's words. This does not mean that we can't disagree with someone. A good listener tries to understand what the other person is saying. In the end he may disagree sharply, but because he disagrees, he wants to know exactly what it is he is disagreeing with.

4. Thinking Flexibly

> *If you never change your mind, why have one?*
> —Edward deBono

An amazing discovery about the human brain is its plasticity—its ability to "rewire," change, and even repair itself to become smarter. Flexible people are the ones with the most control. They have the capacity to change their mind as they receive additional data. They engage in multiple and simultaneous outcomes and activities, draw upon a repertoire of problem-solving strategies, and can practice style flexibility, knowing when it is appropriate to be broad and global in their thinking and when a situation requires detailed precision. They create and seek novel approaches and have a well-developed sense of humor. They envision a range of consequences.

Flexible people can approach a problem from a new angle using a novel approach—deBono (1970) refers to this as lateral thinking. They consider alternative points of view or deal with several sources of information simultaneously. Their minds are open to change based on additional information and data or reasoning that contradicts their beliefs. Flexible people know that they have and can develop options and alternatives to consider. They understand means-ends relationships; are able to work within rules, criteria, and regulations; and can predict the consequences of flouting the rules. They not only understand immediate reactions but are also able to perceive the bigger purposes that such constraints serve. Thus, flexibility of mind is essential for working with social diversity, enabling an individual to recognize the wholeness and distinctness of other people's ways of experiencing and making meaning.

Flexible thinkers are able to shift, at will, through multiple perceptual positions. One perceptual orientation is what Jean Piaget called egocentrism—perceiving from our own point of view. By contrast, allocentrism is the position in which we perceive through another person's orientation. We operate from this second position when we empathize with others' feelings, predict how others are thinking, and anticipate potential misunderstandings.

Another perceptual position is macrocentric. It is similar to looking down from a balcony at ourselves and our interactions with others. This bird's-eye view is useful for discerning themes and patterns from assortments of information. It is intuitive, holistic, and conceptual. Since we often need to solve problems with incomplete information, we need the capacity to perceive general patterns and jump across gaps of incomplete knowledge.

Yet another perceptual orientation is microcentric—examining the individual and sometimes minute parts that make up the whole. This "worm's-eye view," without which science, technology, and any complex enterprise could not function, involves logical analytical computation searching for causality in methodical steps. It requires attention to detail, precision, and orderly progressions.

Flexible thinkers display confidence in their intuition. They tolerate confusion and ambiguity up to a point, and are willing to let go of a problem, trusting their subconscious to continue creative and productive work on it. Flexibility is the cradle of humor, creativity, and repertoire. While there are many possible perceptual positions—past, present, future, egocentric, allocentric, macrocentric, visual, auditory, kinesthetic—the flexible mind is activated by knowing when to shift perceptual positions.

Some students have difficulty in considering alternative points of view or dealing with more than one classification system simultaneously. Their way to solve a problem seems to be the only way. They perceive situations from a very ego-centered point of view: "My way or the highway!" Their mind is made up: "Don't confuse me with facts; that's it."

5. Thinking About Thinking (Metacognition)

> *When the mind is thinking it is talking to itself.*
> —Plato

Occurring in the neocortex, metacognition is our ability to know what we know and what we don't know. It is our ability to plan a strategy for producing what information is needed, to be conscious of our own steps and strategies during the act of problem solving, and to reflect on and evaluate the productiveness of our own thinking. While "inner language," thought to be a prerequisite, begins in most children around age 5, metacognition is a key attribute of formal thought flowering about age 11.

Probably the major components of metacognition are developing a plan of action, maintaining that plan in mind over a period of time, then reflecting back on and evaluating the plan upon its completion. Planning a strategy before embarking on a course of action assists us in keeping track of the steps in the sequence of planned behavior at the conscious awareness level for the duration of the activity. It facilitates making temporal and comparative judgments, assessing the readiness for more or different activities, and monitoring our interpretations, perceptions, decisions, and behaviors. An example of this would be what superior teachers do daily: developing a teaching strategy for a lesson, keeping that strategy in mind throughout the instruction, then reflecting back upon the strategy to evaluate its effectiveness in producing the desired student outcomes.

Intelligent people plan for, reflect on, and evaluate the quality of their own thinking skills and strategies. Metacognition means becoming increasingly aware of one's actions and the effect of those actions on others and on the environment; forming internal questions as one searches for information and meaning; developing mental maps or plans of action, mentally rehearsing them prior to performance, and monitoring those plans as they are employed—being conscious of the need for midcourse correction if the plan is not meeting expectations; reflecting on the plan upon completion of the implementation for the purpose of self-evaluation; and editing mental pictures for improved performance.

Interestingly, not all humans achieve the level of formal operations (Chiabetta, 1976). As Alexander Luria, the Russian psychologist, found, not all adults metacogitate (Whimbey, 1976). The most likely reason is that we do not take the time to reflect on our experiences. Students often do not take the time to wonder why we are doing what we are doing. They seldom question themselves about their own learning strategies or evaluate the efficiency of their own performance. Some children virtually have no idea of what they should do when they confront a problem and are often unable to explain their strategies of decision making (Sternberg & Wagner, 1982). When teachers ask, "How did you solve that problem? What strategies did you have in mind?" or say, "Tell us what went on in your head to come up with that conclusion," students often respond by saying, "I don't know, I just did it."

We want our students to perform well on complex cognitive tasks. A simple example of this might be drawn from a reading task. It is a common experience while reading a passage to have our minds wander from the pages. We see the words but no meaning is being produced. Suddenly we realize that we are not concentrating and that we've lost contact with the meaning of the text. We recover by returning to the passage to find our place, matching it with the last thought we can remember, and, once having found it, reading on with connectedness. This inner awareness and the strategy of recovery are components of metacognition.

6. Striving for Accuracy and Precision

> *A man who has committed a mistake and doesn't correct it is committing another mistake.*
> —Confucius

Embodied in the stamina, grace, and elegance of a ballerina or a shoemaker is the desire for craftsmanship, mastery, flawlessness, and economy of energy to produce exceptional results. People who value accuracy, precision, and craftsmanship take time to check over their products. They review the rules by which they are to abide; they review the models and visions they are to follow; and they review the criteria they are to employ and confirm that their finished product matches the criteria exactly. To be craftsmanlike means knowing that one can continually perfect one's craft by working to attain the highest possible standards and pursuing ongoing learning in order to bring a laser-like focus of energies to task accomplishment. These people take pride in their work and have a desire for accuracy as they take time to check over their work. Craftsmanship includes exactness, precision, accuracy, correctness, faithfulness, and fidelity. For some people, craftsmanship requires continuous reworking. Mario Cuomo, a great speechwriter and politician, once said that his speeches were never done—it was only a deadline that made him stop working on them.

Some students may turn in sloppy, incomplete, or uncorrected work. They are more anxious to get rid of the assignment than to check it over for accuracy and precision. They are willing to suffice with minimum effort rather than to invest their maximum. They may be more interested in expedience rather than excellence.

7. Questioning and Posing Problems

> *The formulation of a problem is often more essential than its solution, which may be merely a matter of mathematical or experimental skill. To raise new questions, new possibilities, to regard old problems from a new angle, requires creative imagination and marks real advances ....*
>
> —Albert Einstein

One of the distinguishing characteristics between humans and other forms of life is our inclination and ability to find problems to solve. Effective problem solvers know how to ask questions to fill in the gaps between what they know and what they don't know. Effective questioners are inclined to ask a range of questions. Examples:

- They request data to support others' conclusions and assumptions with such questions as

  What evidence do you have about ...?
  How do you know that's true?
  How reliable is this data source?

- They pose questions about alternative points of view:

  From whose viewpoint are we seeing, reading, or hearing?
  From what angle, what perspective, are we viewing this situation?

- They pose questions about causal connections and relationships:

  How are these people (or events or situations) related to each other?
  What produced this connection?

- They pose hypothetical problems characterized by "if" questions:

  What do you think would happen if ...?

  If that is true, then what might happen if ...?

Inquirers recognize discrepancies and phenomena in their environment and probe into their causes. Examples: Why do cats purr? How high can birds fly? Why does the hair on my head grow so fast, while the hair on my arms and legs grows so slowly? What would happen if we put the saltwater fish in a fresh water aquarium? What are some alternative solutions to international conflicts other than wars?

Some students may be unaware of the functions, classes, syntax, or intentions in questions. They may not realize that questions vary in complexity, structure, and purpose. They may pose simple questions intending to derive maximal results. When confronted with a discrepancy, they may lack an overall strategy of search and solution finding.

8. Applying Past Knowledge to New Situations

> *I've never made a mistake. I've only learned from experience.*
>
> —Thomas A. Edison

Intelligent human beings learn from experience. When confronted with a new and perplexing problem, they will often draw forth experience from their past. They can often be heard to say, "This reminds me of . . ." or "This is just like the time when I . . ." They explain what they are doing now in terms of analogies with or references to previous experiences. They call upon their store of knowledge and experience as sources of data to support, theories to explain, or processes to solve each new challenge. Furthermore, they are able to abstract meaning from one experience, carry it forth, and apply it in a new and novel situation.

Too often, students begin each new task as if it were being approached for the very first time. Teachers are often dismayed when they invite students to recall how they solved a similar problem previously and students don't remember. It's as if they never heard of it before, even though they had the same type of problem just recently. It's as if each experience is encapsulated and has no relationship to what has come before or what comes afterward. Their thinking is what psychologists refer to as an episodic grasp of reality (Feuerstein, 1980). That is, each event in life is a separate and discrete event with no connections to what may have come before or with no relation to what follows. Furthermore, their learning is so encapsulated that they seem unable to draw forth learning from one event and apply it in another context.

9. Thinking and Communicating with Clarity and Precision

> *I do not so easily think in words … after being hard at work having arrived at results that are perfectly clear …. I have to translate my thoughts in a language that does not run evenly with them.*
>
> —Francis Galton
> Geneticist

Language refinement plays a critical role in enhancing a person's cognitive maps and ability to think critically, which is the knowledge base for efficacious action. Enriching the complexity and specificity of language simultaneously produces effective thinking.

Language and thinking are closely entwined. Like either side of a coin, they are inseparable. When you hear fuzzy language, it is a reflection of fuzzy thinking. Intelligent people strive to communicate accurately in both written and oral form, taking care to use precise language, defining terms, using correct names and universal labels and analogies. They strive to avoid overgeneralizations, deletions, and distortions. Instead, they support their statements with explanations, comparisons, quantification, and evidence.

We sometimes hear students and other adults using vague and imprecise language. They describe objects or events with words like "weird," "nice," or "OK." They refer to specific objects using such nondescriptive words as "stuff," "junk," and "things." They punctuate sentences with meaningless interjections such as "ya know," "er," and "uh." They use vague or general nouns and pronouns: "They told me to do it." "Everybody has one." "Teachers don't understand me." They use nonspecific verbs: "Let's do it" and unqualified comparatives: "This soda is better; I like it more."

Resources and References

10. Gathering Data Through All Senses

> *Observe perpetually.*
> —Henry James

The brain is the ultimate reductionist. It reduces the world to its elementary parts—photons of light, molecules of smell, sound waves, vibrations of touch—which send electrochemical signals to individual brain cells that store information about lines, movements, colors, smells, and other sensory inputs.

Intelligent people know that all information gets into the brain through the sensory pathways: gustatory, olfactory, tactile, kinesthetic, auditory, visual. Most linguistic, cultural, and physical learning is derived from the environment by observing or taking in through the senses. To know a wine, it must be drunk; to know a role, it must be acted; to know a game, it must be played; to know a dance, it must be danced; to know a goal, it must be envisioned. Those whose sensory pathways are open, alert, and acute absorb more information from the environment than those whose pathways are withered, immune, and oblivious to sensory stimuli.

Furthermore, we are learning more about the impact of arts and music on improved mental functioning. Forming mental images is important in mathematics and engineering; listening to classical music seems to improve spatial reasoning.

Social scientists solve problems through scenarios and role playing; scientists build models; engineers use cad-cam; mechanics learn through hands-on experimentation; artists experiment with colors and textures; musicians experiment by producing combinations of instrumental and vocal music.

Describing 16 Habits of Mind

Some students, however, go through school and life oblivious to the textures, rhythms, patterns, sounds, and colors around them. Sometimes children are afraid to touch, get their hands dirty, or feel some object that might be "slimy" or "icky." They operate within a narrow range of sensory problem-solving strategies, wanting only to "describe it but not illustrate or act it," or "listen but not participate."

11. Creating, Imagining, and Innovating

> *The future is not some place we are going to but one we are creating. The paths are not to be found, but made, and the activity of making them changes both the maker and the destination.*
>
> —John Schaar,
> Political Scientist and Author
> *Loyalty in America*

All human beings have the capacity to generate novel, original, clever, or ingenious products, solutions, and techniques—if that capacity is developed. Creative human beings try to conceive problem solutions differently, examining alternative possibilities from many angles. They tend to project themselves into different roles using analogies, starting with a vision and working backward, imagining they are the objects being considered. Creative people take risks and frequently push the boundaries of their perceived limits (Perkins, 1985). They are intrinsically rather than extrinsically motivated, working on the task because of the aesthetic challenge rather than the material rewards. Creative people are open to criticism. They hold up their products for others to judge and seek feedback in an ever-increasing effort to refine their technique. They are uneasy with the status quo. They constantly strive for greater fluency, elaboration, novelty, parsimony, simplicity, craftsmanship, perfection, beauty, harmony, and balance.

Students, however, are often heard saying, "I can't draw," or "I was never very good at art," or "I can't sing a note," or "I'm not creative." Some people believe creative humans are just born that way in their genes and chromosomes.

12. Responding with Wonderment and Awe

> *The most beautiful experience in the world is the experience of the mysterious.*
>
> —Albert Einstein

Describing the 200 best and brightest of the All-USA College Academic Team identified by *USA Today*, Tracey Wong Briggs (1999) states, "They are creative thinkers who have a passion for what they do." Efficacious people have not only an "I can" attitude but also an "I enjoy" feeling. They seek problems to solve for themselves and to submit to others. They delight in making up problems to solve on their own and request enigmas from others. They enjoy figuring things out by themselves and continue to learn throughout their lifetime.

Some children and adults avoid problems and are turned off to learning. They make such comments as, "I was never good at these brain teasers," or "Go ask your father; he's the brain in this family," or "It's boring," or "When am I ever going to use this stuff?" or "Who cares?" or "Lighten up, teacher, thinking is hard work," or "I don't do thinking!" Many people never enrolled in another math class or other "hard" academic subjects after they didn't have to in high school or college. Many people perceive thinking as hard work and, therefore, recoil from situations that demand "too much."

We want our students, however, to be curious, to commune with the world around them, reflect on the changing formations of a cloud, feel charmed by the opening of a bud, sense the logical simplicity of mathematical order. Students can find beauty in a sunset, intrigue in the geometric design of a spider web, and exhilaration at the iridescence of a hummingbird's wings. They see the congruity and intricacies in the derivation of a mathematical formula, recognize the orderliness and adroitness of a chemical change, and commune with the serenity of a distant constellation. We want them to feel compelled, enthusiastic, and passionate about learning, inquiring, and mastering.

13. Taking Responsible Risks

> *There has been a calculated risk in every stage of American development—the pioneers who were not afraid of the wilderness, businessmen who were not afraid of failure, dreamers who were not afraid of action.*
>
> —Brooks Atkinson

Flexible people seem to have an almost uncontrollable urge to go beyond established limits. They are uneasy about comfort; they live on the edge. They seem compelled to place themselves in situations where they do not know what the outcome will be. They accept confusion, uncertainty, and the higher risks of failure as part of the normal process and they learn to view setbacks as interesting, challenging, and growth producing. However, they are not behaving impulsively. Their risks are educated. They draw on past knowledge, are thoughtful about consequences, and have a well-trained sense of what is appropriate. They know that not all risks are worth taking.

Risk taking can be considered in two categories: those who see it as a venture and those who see it as adventure. The venture part of risk taking might be described by the venture capitalist. When a person is approached to take the risk of investing in a new business, she will look at the markets, see how well organized the ideas are, and study the economic projections. If she finally decides to take the risk, it is a well-considered one.

The adventure part of risk taking might be described by the experiences from project adventure. In this situation, there is a spontaneity, a willingness to take a chance in the moment. Once again, a person will take the chance only if he either knows that there is past history that suggests that what he is doing is not going to be life threatening or believes that there is enough support in the group to protect him from harm. Ultimately, the learning from such high-risk experiences is that people are far more able to take actions than they previously believed. It is only through repeated experiences that risk taking becomes educated. It often is a cross between intuition, drawing on past knowledge, and a sense of meeting new challenges.

Bobby Jindal, Executive Director of the National Bipartisan Commission on the Future of Medicare, states, "The only way to succeed is to be brave enough to risk failure" (Briggs, 1999, p. 2A).

Those who hold back from taking risks are confronted constantly with missed opportunities. Some students seem reluctant to take risks. Some students hold back on games, new learning, and new friendships because their fear of failure is far greater than their experience of venture or adventure. They are reinforced by the mental voice that says, "If you don't try it, you won't be wrong" or "If you try it and you are wrong, you will look stupid." The other voice, which might say, "If you don't try it, you will never know," is trapped in fear and mistrust. These students are more interested in knowing whether their answer is correct or not, rather than being challenged by the process of finding the answer. They are unable to sustain a process of problem solving and finding the answer over time and, therefore, avoid ambiguous situations. They have a need for certainty rather than an inclination for doubt.

We hope that students will learn how to take intellectual as well as physical risks. Students who are capable of being different, going against the grain of the common, thinking of new ideas, and testing them with peers as well as teachers are more likely to be successful in this age of innovation and uncertainty.

14. Finding Humor

> *Where do bees wait? At the buzz stop.*
> —Andrew, Student, Age 6

Another unique attribute of human beings is our sense of humor. Laughter transcends all human beings. Its positive effects on psychological functions include a drop in the pulse rate, the secretion of endorphins, and increased oxygen in the blood. It has been found to liberate creativity and provoke such higher-level thinking skills as anticipation, finding novel relationships, visual imagery, and making analogies. People who engage in the mystery of humor have the ability to perceive situations from an original and often interesting vantage point. They tend to initiate humor more often, to place greater value on having a sense of humor, to appreciate and understand others' humor, and to be verbally playful when interacting with others. Having a whimsical frame of mind, they thrive on finding incongruity and perceiving absurdities, ironies, and satire; they find discontinuities and are able to laugh at situations and themselves. Some students find humor in all the wrong places—human differences, ineptitude, injurious behavior, vulgarity, violence and profanity. They laugh at others yet are unable to laugh at themselves.

We want our student to acquire the characteristic of creative problem solvers, so that they can distinguish between situations of human frailty and fallibility, which are in need of compassion, and those that are truly funny (Dyer, 1997).

15. Thinking Interdependently

> *Take care of each other. Share your energies with the group. No one must feel alone, cut off, for that is when you do not make it.*
>
> —Willie Unsoeld
> Mountain Climber

Human beings are social beings. We congregate in groups, find it therapeutic to be listened to, draw energy from one another, and seek reciprocity. In groups we contribute our time and energy to tasks that we would quickly tire of working alone. In fact, we have learned that one of the cruelest forms of punishment that can be inflicted on an individual is solitary confinement.

Cooperative humans realize that all of us together are more powerful, intellectually and physically, than any one individual. Probably the foremost disposition in postindustrial society is the heightened ability to think in concert with others; to find ourselves increasingly more interdependent and sensitive to the needs of others. Problem solving has become so complex that no one person can go it alone. No one has access to all the data needed to make critical decisions; no one person can consider as many alternatives as several people can.

Some students may not have learned to work in groups; they have underdeveloped social skills. They may feel isolated and prefer their solitude: "Leave me alone—I'll do it by myself." "They just don't like me." "I want to be alone." Some students seem unable to contribute to group work either by being a "job hog" or, conversely, letting others do all the work.

Working in groups requires the ability to justify ideas and to test the feasibility of solution strategies on others. It also requires the development of a willingness and openness to accept feedback from a critical friend. Through this interaction the group and the

Resources and References

individual continue to grow. Listening, consensus seeking, giving up an idea to work with someone else's, empathy, compassion, group leadership, knowing how to support group efforts, altruism—all are behaviors indicative of cooperative human beings.

16. Learning Continuously

> *Insanity is continuing to do the same thing over and over and expecting different results.*
> —Albert Einstein

Intelligent people are in a continuous learning mode. Their confidence, in combination with their inquisitiveness, allows them to constantly search for new and better ways. People with this Habit of Mind are always striving for improvement, always growing, always learning, always modifying and improving themselves. They seize problems, situations, tensions, conflicts, and circumstances as valuable opportunities to learn.

A great mystery about humans is that we confront learning opportunities with fear rather than mystery and wonder. We seem to feel better when we know rather than when we learn. We defend our biases, beliefs, and storehouses of knowledge rather than inviting the unknown, the creative, and the inspirational. Being certain and closed gives us comfort, while being doubtful and open gives us fear. From an early age, employing a curriculum of fragmentation, competition, and reactiveness, students are trained to believe that deep learning means figuring out the truth rather than developing capabilities for effective and thoughtful action. They are taught to value certainty rather than doubt, to give answers rather than to inquire, to know which choice is correct rather than to explore alternatives.

Our wish for our students is that they become creative people who are eager to learn. We include in that wish the humility of knowing that they don't know, which is the highest form of thinking we humans will ever learn. Paradoxically, unless we start off with humility we will never get anywhere, so as the first step we have to have what will eventually be the crowning glory of all learning: the humility to know—and admit—that we don't know, and then we must not be afraid to find out.

SUMMARY

Drawn from research on human effectiveness, descriptions of remarkable performers, and analyses of the characteristics of efficacious people, we have presented descriptions of 16 Habits of Mind. This list is not meant to be complete but to serve as a starting point for further elaboration and description.

These Habits of Mind may serve as mental disciplines. When confronted with problematic situations, students, parents, and teachers might habitually employ one or more of these Habits of Mind by asking themselves questions such as

- What is the most intelligent thing I can do right now?
- How can I learn from this? How can I draw on my past successes with problems like this? What do I already know about the problem? What resources do I have available or need to generate?
- How can I approach this problem flexibly? How might I look at the situation in another way? How can I draw upon my repertoire of problem-solving strategies? How can I look at this problem from a fresh perspective?
- How can I illuminate this problem to make it clearer, more precise? Do I need to check out my data sources? How might I break this problem down into its component parts and develop a strategy for understanding and accomplishing each step?
- What do I know or not know? What questions do I need to ask? What strategies are in my mind now? What am I aware of in terms of my own beliefs, values, and goals with this problem? What feelings or emotions am I aware of that might be blocking or enhancing my progress?

Interdependent thinkers might turn to others for help. They might ask: How can this problem affect others? How can we solve it together? What can I learn from others that would help me become a better problem solver?

Taking a reflective stance in the midst of active problem solving is often difficult. For that reason, all Habits of Mind are situational and transitory. There is no such thing as perfect realization of any of them. They are utopian states toward which we constantly aspire. Csikszentmihalyi (1993, p. 23) states, "Although every human brain is able to generate self-reflective consciousness, not everyone seems to use it equally."

Few people, notes Kegan (1994), ever fully reach the stage of cognitive complexity, and rarely before middle age.

These Habits of Mind transcend all subject matters commonly taught in school. They are characteristic of peak performers whether they be in homes or schools; on athletic fields; or in organizations, the military, governments, churches, or corporations. They are what make marriages successful, learning continual, workplaces productive, and democracies enduring.

The goal of education, therefore, should be to support others and ourselves in liberating, developing, and habituating these Habits of Mind fully. Taken together, they are a force directing us toward increasingly authentic, congruent, ethical behavior. They are the touchstones of integrity. They are the tools of disciplined choice making. They are the primary vehicles in the lifelong journey toward integration. They are the "right stuff" that makes human beings efficacious.

> *We are what we repeatedly do. Excellence, then, is not an act but a habit.*
>
> —Aristotle

REFERENCES

Briggs, T. W. (1999, Feb. 25). Passion for what they do keeps alumni on first team. *USA Today*, pp. 1A–2A.

Chiabetta, E. L. A. (1976). Review of Piagetian studies relevant to science instruction at the secondary and college levels. *Science Education, 60,* 253–261.

Costa, A. (1991). The search for intelligent life. In A. L. Costa (Ed.), *Developing minds: A resource book for teaching thinking* (pp. 100–106). Alexandria, VA: Association for Supervision and Curriculum Development.

Csikszentmihalyi, M. (1993). *The evolving self: A psychology for the third millennium.* New York: Harper Collins.

Covey, S. (1989). *The seven habits of highly effective people.* New York: Simon & Schuster.

DeBono, E. (1991). The Cort thinking program. In A. L. Costa (Ed.), *Developing minds: Programs for teaching thinking* (pp. 27–32). Alexandria, VA: Association for Supervision and Curriculum Development.

Dyer, J. (1997). Humor as process. In A. Costa & R. Liebmann (Eds.), *Envisioning process as content: Toward a Renaissance curriculum* (pp. 211–229). Thousand Oaks, CA: Corwin Press.

Ennis, R. (1991). Goals for a critical thinking curriculum. In A. L. Costa (Ed.), *Developing minds: A resource book for teaching thinking* (Rev. ed., Vol. 1, pp. 68–71). Alexandria, VA: Association for Supervision and Curriculum Development.

Feuerstein, R., Rand, Y. M., Hoffman, M. B., & Miller, R. (1980). *Instrumental enrichment: An intervention program for cognitive modifiability.* Baltimore: University Park Press.

Glatthorn, A., & Baron, J. (1985). The good thinker. In A. L. Costa (Ed.), *Developing minds: A resource book for teaching thinking*. Alexandria, VA: Association for Supervision and Curriculum Development.

Goleman, D. (1995). *Emotional intelligence: Why it can matter more than IQ*. New York: Bantam Books.

Kegan, R. (1994). *In over our heads: The mental complexity of modern life*. Cambridge, MA: Harvard University Press.

Perkins, D. (1985). What creative thinking is. In A. L. Costa (Ed.), *Developing minds: A resource book for teaching thinking* (pp. 85–88). Alexandria, VA: Association for Supervision and Curriculum Development.

Perkins, D. (1995). *Outsmarting IQ: The emerging science of learnable intelligence*. New York: The Free Press.

Senge, P., Ross, R., Smith, B., Roberts, C., & Kleiner, A. (1994). *The fifth discipline fieldbook: Strategies and tools for building a learning organization*. New York: Doubleday/Currency.

Sternberg, R., & Wagner, R. (1982). *Understanding intelligence: What's in it for education?* Paper submitted to the National Commission on Excellence in Education.

Sternberg, R. (1984). *Beyond IQ: A triarchic theory of human intelligence*. New York: Cambridge University Press.

Sternberg, R. (1983). *How can we teach intelligence?* Philadelphia, PA: Research for Better Schools.

Whimbey, A., & Whimbey L. S. (1975). *Intelligence can be taught*. New York: Lawrence Erlbaum Associates.

This article is adapted from Costa, A. & Kallick, B. (2000), *Habits of Mind: A Developmental Series*. Alexandria, VA: Association for Supervision and Curriculum Development.

Book I: *Discovering and exploring habits of mind*
Book II: *Activating and engaging habits of mind*
Book III: *Assessing and reporting growth in habits of mind*
Book IV: *Integrating and sustaining habits of mind*

Appendix B

TEMPLATES, EVALUATIONS, AND RUBRICS

Throughout this action tool, you will find a variety of assessment and planning resources specific to relevant content. This appendix provides additional resources. Included are generic planning tools and resource templates, such as a summary of the 16 Habits of Mind and a template for creating your own lesson plans. You will also find self-evaluation and teacher-evaluation tools, action plans, and checklists. In addition, a rubric for every Habit of Mind is available.

CONTENTS

Summary of 16 Habits of Mind

1. Persisting: *Stick to it.* Persevering in a task through to completion; remaining focused.	**2. Managing Impulsivity:** *Take your time.* Thinking before acting; remaining calm, thoughtful, and deliberative.
3. Listening with Understanding and Empathy: *Understand others.* Devoting mental energy to another person's thoughts and ideas; holding in one's own thoughts in order to perceive another's point of view and emotions.	**4. Thinking Flexibly:** *Look at it another way.* Being able to change perspectives, generate alternatives, and consider options.
5. Thinking About Thinking (Metacognition): *Know your knowing.* Being aware of one's own thoughts, strategies, feelings, and actions and their effects on others.	**6. Striving for Accuracy and Precision:** *Check it again.* A desire for exactness, fidelity, and craftsmanship.
7. Questioning and Posing Problems: *How do you know?* Having a questioning attitude; knowing what data are needed and developing questioning strategies to produce data; finding problems to solve.	**8. Applying Past Knowledge to New Situations:** *Use what you learn.* Accessing prior knowledge; transferring knowledge beyond the situation in which it was learned.
9. Thinking and Communicating with Clarity and Precision: *Be clear.* Striving for accurate communication in both written and oral form; avoiding over generalizations, distortions, and deletions.	**10. Gathering Data Through All Senses:** *Use your natural pathways.* Gathering data through all the sensory pathways: gustatory, olfactory, tactile, kinesthetic, auditory, and visual.
11. Creating, Imagining, and Innovating: *Try a different way.* Generating new and novel ideas, fluency, and originality.	**12. Responding with Wonderment and Awe:** *Have fun figuring it out.* Finding the world awesome and mysterious and being intrigued with phenomena and beauty.
13. Taking Responsible Risks: *Venture out.* Being adventuresome; living on the edge of one's competence.	**14. Finding Humor:** *Laugh a little.* Finding the whimsical, incongruous, and unexpected; being able to laugh at oneself.
15. Thinking Interdependently: *Work together.* Being able to work with and learn from others in reciprocal situations.	**16. Learning Continuously:** *Learn from experiences.* Having humility and pride when admitting one doesn't know; resisting complacency.

Lesson Plan Template

Lesson Title:

Lesson Overview:

Objectives	Materials Needed
•	•
•	•
•	•
•	•
Estimated Time Required	**Notes**

Suggested Sequence of Activities

- Motivational Activity:

- Core Activity:

- Reflection Activity:

- Synthesis Activity:

- Extension Activity:

Name _____ Class _____ Date _____

Y-Chart

You can use this chart to explore your thoughts about many different topics.

Topic:

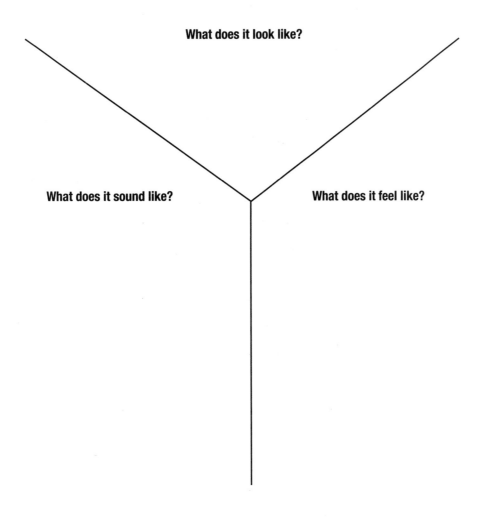

What does it look like?

What does it sound like?

What does it feel like?

Name _____ Class _____ Date _____

The C-A-F Model: Consider All Factors

Use the C-A-F model when you need to make a decision. To consider all the relevant factors, brainstorm a list of questions to ask yourself. The following will get you started. You can add more. When you are finished brainstorming, answer the questions to help you make a decision.

Key Questions:

What factors are involved?

Who is affected by my decision?

Have I thought of everything?

Do I have everything I need?

Name _____ Class _____ Date _____

The P-D-R Method:
Plan-Do-Review

Use the Plan-Do-Review method to think through a situation before attempting it.

> **Example:**
> Mission: Camp in the extreme wilderness for one month and live to tell about it.

Plan:

Do:

Review:

Name _____ Class _____ Date _____

K-W-L Chart

When you are about to start studying something new or are preparing for a test, complete this chart. Fill out the first two columns before you begin studying and fill out the last column after your studies.

What Do I Know Already?	What Do I Want to Learn?	What Have I Learned?

Name _____ Class _____ Date _____

Case Study _____

Ask a variety of questions, and then record your answers.

Questions	Answers
Who?	
Where?	
When?	
Why?	
What?	
How? (Which Habits of Mind?)	

Name _____ Class _____ Date _____

Key Research Questions

As you do your research, brainstorm questions you would like to get answered in order to learn more. The following are a few examples:

- Why was this person famous?
- Why did many people respect this person?
- What did this person achieve in his or her lifetime?
- What lessons does this person teach us?

Your Research Topic:

Questions:

Name _____ Class _____ Date _____

Obstacles on the Path

Complete the following tree map to show successes, failures, and obstacles that the subject of your research experienced on his or her path to success.

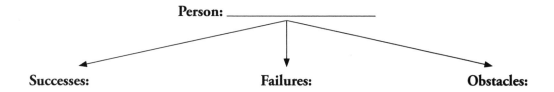

Person: _____

Successes: **Failures:**   **Obstacles:**

Which Habits of Mind helped this person overcome obstacles?	How did the Habits of Mind help this person?	What evidence supports your claim?

Name _____ Class _____ Date _____

Issue Analysis

The issue I am analyzing is: _____

Related Habits of Mind	Relevance of Habits of Mind	Consequences of Not Using Habits of Mind

Student Name _____ Class _____ Date _____

Teacher Evaluation of Student

This student is able to	Seldom	Sometimes	Usually	Consistently
Recognize increasingly diverse, complex, and novel situations in which to apply the Habits of Mind.				
Spontaneously use appropriate Habits of Mind when confronted with ambiguous and perplexing situations.				
Recognize a wide range of situations in which to apply the Habits of Mind.				
Recognize, without assistance, novel and complex situations in which to apply the Habits of Mind.				
Articulate the criteria upon which the decisions reflected in this review were made.				

Name _____ Class _____ Date _____

Student Self-Evaluation

Use this checklist to evaluate your progress in applying the Habits of Mind. Be honest with yourself! In the blank rows, include additional areas you would like to be aware of and improve.

I am able to	Seldom	Sometimes	Usually	Consistently
Recognize different and complex situations in which to use the Habits of Mind.				
Suggest which Habits of Mind are useful or relevant when looking at new situations.				
Recognize a wide range of situations in which to apply the Habits of Mind.				
Recognize, without assistance, new and complex situations in which to apply the Habits of Mind.				
Explain why I would use certain Habits of Mind in a situation.				

Teacher Self-Reflection Tool

Habit of Mind	I am a teacher who ...
Persisting	Perseveres with challenging students and ensures all students have a depth of understanding and skills as learners. *Rate yourself:* 1 2 3 4 5 6 7 8 9 10
Managing Impulsivity	Uses wait time and pausing, paraphrasing, and probing techniques; I demonstrate thoughtfulness. *Rate yourself:* 1 2 3 4 5 6 7 8 9 10
Listening with Understanding and Empathy	Actively listens to others. I make genuine attempts to understand where others are coming from and perceive their points of view. *Rate yourself:* 1 2 3 4 5 6 7 8 9 10
Thinking Flexibly	Is open to the points of view of others; changes plans and strategies when needed to better meet group needs; grasps the teachable moment to foster interest and achievement. *Rate yourself:* 1 2 3 4 5 6 7 8 9 10
Thinking About Thinking (Metacognition)	Is aware of my own thinking processes. I invest time in reflection; I model my thinking processes to those around me. *Rate yourself:* 1 2 3 4 5 6 7 8 9 10
Striving for Accuracy and Precision	Sets high standards in the things I do and in relations with others. I check for accuracy in written documents and communications. *Rate yourself:* 1 2 3 4 5 6 7 8 9 10
Questioning and Posing Problems	Is skilled in composing and asking complex questions. *Rate yourself:* 1 2 3 4 5 6 7 8 9 10
Applying Past Knowledge to New Situations	Uses past experiences, resources, and knowledge to ensure good practice. I offer wide knowledge to support student learning. *Rate yourself:* 1 2 3 4 5 6 7 8 9 10
Thinking and Communicating with Clarity and Precision	Strives to be accurate in all communications. I use thinking verbs when giving instructions. *Rate yourself:* 1 2 3 4 5 6 7 8 9 10
Gathering Data Through All Senses	Stays alert to people and situations by gathering data through my senses. *Rate yourself:* 1 2 3 4 5 6 7 8 9 10

Teacher Self-Reflection Tool

Habit of Mind	I am a teacher who ...
Creating, Imagining, and Innovating	Is creative and innovative in finding new ways and alternatives. *Rate yourself:* 1 2 3 4 5 6 7 8 9 10
Responding with Wonderment and Awe	Is enthusiastic about my teaching, my students' learning, and new discoveries. *Rate yourself:* 1 2 3 4 5 6 7 8 9 10
Taking Responsible Risks	Moves outside my comfort zone and becomes adventurous after thoughtful consideration. *Rate yourself:* 1 2 3 4 5 6 7 8 9 10
Finding Humor	Can laugh with others and at myself. I do not take myself too seriously. *Rate yourself:* 1 2 3 4 5 6 7 8 9 10
Thinking Interdependently	Works collaboratively with others. I can learn from those around me. *Rate yourself:* 1 2 3 4 5 6 7 8 9 10
Learning Continuously	Has the humility and pride to admit when I don't know something. I resist complacency. *Rate yourself:* 1 2 3 4 5 6 7 8 9 10

Student Self-Reflection Tool

Name _____ Class _____ Date _____

Habit of Mind	I am a student who ...
Persisting	Perseveres with my studies to gain a depth of understanding and skills as a learner. *Rate yourself: 1 2 3 4 5 6 7 8 9 10*
Managing Impulsivity	Controls impulses; stops and thinks before acting; demonstrates thoughtfulness. *Rate yourself: 1 2 3 4 5 6 7 8 9 10*
Listening with Understanding and Empathy	Actively listens to others; makes genuine attempts to understand where others are coming from and perceive their points of view. *Rate yourself: 1 2 3 4 5 6 7 8 9 10*
Thinking Flexibly	Is open to the points of view of others. I can change plans and strategies when needed to better meet group needs. *Rate yourself: 1 2 3 4 5 6 7 8 9 10*
Thinking About Thinking (Metacognition)	Is aware of my thinking processes and invests time in reflection. I can explain my thinking to others. *Rate yourself: 1 2 3 4 5 6 7 8 9 10*
Striving for Accuracy and Precision	Sets high standards in the things I do and in relations with others. I check for accuracy in written documents and communications. *Rate yourself: 1 2 3 4 5 6 7 8 9 10*
Questioning and Posing Problems	Is skilled in composing and asking complex questions. *Rate yourself: 1 2 3 4 5 6 7 8 9 10*
Applying Past Knowledge to New Situations	Uses past experiences, resources, and knowledge to ensure good practice. *Rate yourself: 1 2 3 4 5 6 7 8 9 10*
Thinking and Communicating with Clarity and Precision	Strives to be accurate in written and oral communication. *Rate yourself: 1 2 3 4 5 6 7 8 9 10*

Resources and References

Student Self-Reflection Tool

Habit of Mind	I am a student who …
Gathering Data Through All Senses	Stays alert to people and situations by gathering data through my senses. *Rate yourself: 1 2 3 4 5 6 7 8 9 10*
Creating, Imagining, and Innovating	Is creative and innovative in coming up with ideas and alternatives. *Rate yourself: 1 2 3 4 5 6 7 8 9 10*
Responding with Wonderment and Awe	Is enthusiastic about learning and new discoveries. *Rate yourself: 1 2 3 4 5 6 7 8 9 10*
Taking Responsible Risks	Can move outside my comfort zone and become adventurous after thoughtful consideration. *Rate yourself: 1 2 3 4 5 6 7 8 9 10*
Finding Humor	Can laugh with others and at myself. I do not take myself too seriously. *Rate yourself: 1 2 3 4 5 6 7 8 9 10*
Thinking Interdependently	Works collaboratively with others and can learn from those around me. *Rate yourself: 1 2 3 4 5 6 7 8 9 10*
Learning Continuously	Looks for opportunities to learn and improve; is open to growth and change. *Rate yourself: 1 2 3 4 5 6 7 8 9 10*

Resources and References

Name _____ Class _____ Date _____

Improving Habits

Select at least three Habits of Mind you need to improve. Explain why you think each is important. Then rank the habits in their order of importance.

Habits of Mind	How will this Habit of Mind help me?	Rank
Persisting		
Managing Impulsivity		
Listening with Understanding and Empathy		
Thinking Flexibly		
Thinking About Thinking (Metacognition)		
Striving for Accuracy and Precision		
Questioning and Posing Problems		
Applying Past Knowledge to New Situations		
Thinking and Communicating with Clarity and Precision		
Gathering Data Through All Senses		
Creating, Imagining, and Innovating		
Responding with Wonderment and Awe		
Taking Responsible Risks		
Finding Humor		
Thinking Interdependently		
Learning Continuously		

Name _____ Class _____ Date _____

Action Plan for Habits of Mind Development

Pick one Habit of Mind competency that you would like to improve. Then use this form to create an action plan for improvement.

The competency I would like to improve is _____

Action Plan to Improve This Competency in One Month

I will do these specific things:

I seek assistance from these sources:

I can monitor my improvement in these ways:

Name _____ Class _____ Date _____

Rubric for Persisting

Rating	Description
4 **EXPERT:** **Unconsciously** **Competent**	Does not give up no matter how difficult the solution is to find; has a repertoire of alternative strategies and will use them to find answers; evaluates the use of strategies, developing systematic methods for further use, including how to begin, steps to take, and relevant data to collect.
3 **PRACTITIONER:** **Consciously** **Competent**	Stays on task; develops a broad range of strategies and will use them when searching for an answer; does not give up until a solution is found or the assignment is finished.
2 **APPRENTICE:** **Consciously** **Incompetent**	Tries to complete tasks when answers are not readily available, but gives up easily if a task becomes difficult; fluctuates in staying focused for any length of time; uses few strategies to solve problems.
1 **NOVICE:** **Unconsciously** **Incompetent**	Does not complete any tasks; gives up easily; cannot think of or use strategies to solve problems.

Name _____ Class _____ Date _____

Rubric for Managing Impulsivity

Rating	Description
4 **EXPERT:** **Unconsciously** **Competent**	Carefully evaluates situations and seeks advice from other sources before taking appropriate action; is a thorough and careful researcher; effectively gathers important information; sets clear goals and describes each step taken to achieve goals; schedules and monitors progress.
3 **PRACTITIONER:** **Consciously** **Competent**	Thinks and searches for more information before taking action; evaluates a situation before taking appropriate action; has clear goals and can describe steps needed to achieve goals.
2 **APPRENTICE:** **Consciously** **Incompetent**	Searches for obvious information and then acts on impulse; will seek more information only if needed and easily available; is developing some steps to gather information to form decisions; is beginning to make goals and taking a few steps to achieve goals.
1 **NOVICE:** **Unconsciously** **Incompetent**	Acts before thinking; says the first answer that comes to his or her mind; rushes ahead with incomplete or inadequate information; shows little inclination to gather further data to form decisions; has random goals and is unclear about the steps needed to achieve goals.

Name _____ Class _____ Date _____

Rubric for Listening with Understanding and Empathy

Rating	Description
4 **EXPERT:** **Unconsciously Competent**	Is an attentive listener; demonstrates an understanding of other people's ideas via accurate paraphrasing, building upon statements, clarifying statements, or providing examples.
3 **PRACTITIONER:** **Consciously Competent**	Is an attentive listener; shows understanding and empathy for other people's ideas; is able to paraphrase and question to develop further understanding.
2 **APPRENTICE:** **Consciously Incompetent**	Is easily distracted and not a consistent listener; is able to repeat some parts of what has been said; has difficulty with other people, either because of a lack of comprehension or because of ridiculing, putting down, or mocking other people's ideas.
1 **NOVICE:** **Unconsciously Incompetent**	Is easily distracted from listening by outside and classroom noises; interrupts, daydreams; loses focus; can't paraphrase any part of spoken words.

Name _____ Class _____ Date _____

Rubric for Thinking Flexibly

Rating	Description
4 **EXPERT:** **Unconsciously Competent**	Looks at situations creatively and makes useful evaluations; values the opinions of other people and can incorporate or adjust thinking to accommodate new perspectives; consistently explores many alternatives when approaching tasks; illustrates diversity, originality, and effectiveness in ideas and solutions.
3 **PRACTITIONER:** **Consciously Competent**	Sees a variety of ways to view a situation and can make a supportive evaluation of each viewpoint; sees the points of view of other people; consistently generates alternative ways of approaching tasks and analyzes how those alternatives will affect tasks; shows some originality in approaching tasks.
2 **APPRENTICE:** **Consciously Incompetent**	Will occasionally view and describe different ways to see a situation; sees only his or her own perspective; sporadically generates alternative ways of approaching tasks with originality.
1 **NOVICE:** **Unconsciously Incompetent**	Looks at situations in only one way; doesn't generate alternative ideas and cannot see alternative ways of approaching tasks.

Name _____ Class _____ Date _____

Rubric for Thinking About Thinking (Metacognition)

Rating	Description
4 **EXPERT:** **Unconsciously Competent**	Describes steps of thinking in detail when solving problems or doing other mental tasks; explains in detail how and why metacognition helped improve work and learning; describes a plan before solving a problem; monitors steps and develops strategies while working; reflects on the efficiency of strategies and will improvise and develop further as needed.
3 **PRACTITIONER:** **Consciously Competent**	Describes thinking while problem solving, posing questions, making inferences, or reaching a conclusion; can explain how and why metacognition helped improve work or learning.
2 **APPRENTICE:** **Consciously Incompetent**	Includes sparse or incomplete information when describing thoughts on a topic; has difficulty coming to conclusions, formulating opinions, and recalling information in depth; is inconsistent when linking concepts, thinking sequentially, and solving problems.
1 **NOVICE:** **Unconsciously Incompetent**	Is confused about the relationship between thinking and problem solving; sees no link between thinking and learning; is unable to describe thinking when asked to reflect, recall, infer, provide an opinion, or suggest a solution; frequently answers, "I don't know."

Name _____ Class _____ Date _____

Rubric for Striving for Accuracy and Precision

Rating	Description
4 **EXPERT:** **Unconsciously Competent**	Always checks for accuracy and precision without being asked; always takes great care with a project, assignment, or assessment work; ensures all completed work is free of errors; sets a standard of excellence in all areas of his or her school life (academic, athletic, creative); strives to meet or exceed expectations in all areas.
3 **PRACTITIONER:** **Consciously Competent**	Checks work for accuracy; takes the time and care to check over work so that it is completely free of errors; sets high standards for accurate work and maintains those standards.
2 **APPRENTICE:** **Consciously Incompetent**	Is beginning to check work for errors and correct these errors when prompted; is showing some improvement in handing in work that shows some care has been taken to be more accurate and precise.
1 **NOVICE:** **Unconsciously Incompetent**	Does not and will not see errors in work; is doing incomplete, incorrect, and careless work; is settling for minimum effort rather than investing time and attention; will not take the time to revisit work to correct errors.

Name _____ Class _____ Date _____

Rubric for Questioning and Posing Problems

Rating	Description
4 **EXPERT:** **Unconsciously** **Competent**	Asks questions out of curiosity, intrigue, and interest; knows how to ask appropriate questions and has strategies in place to solve problems; uses questions to make causal connections and relationships; has a wide range and repertoire of question types.
3 **PRACTITIONER:** **Consciously** **Competent**	Asks appropriate questions and has strategies to solve problems; has a wide range of question types.
2 **APPRENTICE:** **Consciously** **Incompetent**	Is beginning to question and problem-solve; is developing strategies; is able to use a small range of question types.
1 **NOVICE:** **Unconsciously** **Incompetent**	Is oblivious to questions that arise in situations; cannot pose a simple problem or formulate a question; lacks strategies to search for or find a solution; is unaware of functions, types, or intentions in questions and questioning.

Name _____ Class _____ Date _____

Rubric for Applying Past Knowledge to New Situations

Rating	Description
4 **EXPERT:** **Unconsciously Competent**	Always builds a knowledge structure by revisiting previous information and drawing it forth; is able to use past knowledge and experiences as data to support, theories to explain, or processes to solve new challenges; transfers and applies information from past knowledge to new situations; modifies and develops new information from past knowledge, both inside and outside of school.
3 **PRACTITIONER:** **Consciously Competent**	Uses past knowledge as a framework to incorporate new information; uses prior knowledge to solve new challenges both in and out of school curriculum-based work.
2 **APPRENTICE:** **Consciously Incompetent**	Is recalling past information; will sometimes use prior knowledge to help solve simple challenges but becomes confused with more difficult situations; has difficulty transferring past knowledge across all areas of school life.
1 **NOVICE:** **Unconsciously Incompetent**	Is unsure of using past knowledge as a basis for learning new things; begins a new task as if it were being approached for the first time; cannot remember recent experiences; treats each event in life as separate, making no connections with what has come before and no relationship to what follows.

Name _____ Class _____ Date _____

Rubric for Thinking and Communicating with Clarity and Precision

Rating	Description
4 **EXPERT:** **Unconsciously Competent**	Always uses precise language; speaks and writes with precision in all subjects, elaborating on ideas and thoughts and using concise and descriptive language; is able to coherently state reasons for generalizations and provide data to support conclusions.
3 **PRACTITIONER:** **Consciously Competent**	Uses precise language in everyday speech; is able to clearly and effectively communicate thoughts using accurate language; is able to support statements with explanations, comparisons, and evidence.
2 **APPRENTICE:** **Consciously Incompetent**	Is beginning to use correct terms, labels, and names for ideas and objects; is broadening descriptive vocabulary such that similes and comparisons are used when prompted; is developing oral and written sentence structures.
1 **NOVICE:** **Unconsciously Incompetent**	Uses vague language to describe thoughts; speaks and writes in phrases rather than in complete sentences; punctuates communication with meaningless interjections such as "um," "er," and "uh" and names specific objects with nondescriptive words such as "stuff," "junk," and "things"; uses unqualified comparatives such as "I like lunch better."

Name _____ Class _____ Date _____

Rubric for Gathering Data Through All Senses

Rating	Description
4 **EXPERT:** **Unconsciously Competent**	Has strong powers of perception; efficiently and collectively engages and explores all the senses for observation and information gathering; has sensory pathways that are open, alert, and ready to absorb more information from the environment.
3 **PRACTITIONER:** **Consciously Competent**	Efficiently and collectively uses several senses to make observations and gather information.
2 **APPRENTICE:** **Consciously Incompetent**	Is beginning to use more than one sense to gather and present information; is beginning to notice and describe some textures, rhythms, and other sensory materials.
1 **NOVICE:** **Unconsciously Incompetent**	Has dull and sluggish senses; is oblivious to the textures, rhythms, patterns, sounds, and colors around him or her.

Resources and References

Name _____ Class _____ Date _____

Rubric for Creating, Imagining, and Innovating

Rating	Description
4 **EXPERT:** **Unconsciously** **Competent**	Thinks outside the box; has a variety of creative strategies to call upon; enjoys generating creative solutions; examines alternative possibilities from many angles; has an active imagination; strives to find new, inventive ways to work on a task; expands the possibility of creative insight by researching a topic in great detail; is eager to seek advice and use the ideas of others to find solutions; frequently reflects and uses metacognition; offers detailed feedback about whether ideas are acceptable; uses a variety of media to present ideas and projects.
3 **PRACTITIONER:** **Consciously** **Competent**	Generates new ideas to solve problems; develops and uses several strategies to complete tasks; is inventive; does detailed research; generates options and possibilities from attained knowledge; finishes the task no matter the length of time; shows well-developed reflection and metacognition skills.
2 **APPRENTICE:** **Consciously** **Incompetent**	Is beginning to volunteer one or two imaginative ideas; is increasingly developing strategies; needs encouragement to develop creative thinking; will stop persisting if answer is not gained after a short time; is developing metacognition with guidance.
1 **NOVICE:** **Unconsciously** **Incompetent**	Says things such as, "I was never good at art," "I can't draw," "I'm not creative," and "I can't." Has no strategies to call upon for new ideas; is afraid to be creative; will not seek alternative methods for solving new problems.

Name _____ Class _____ Date _____

Rubric for Responding with Wonderment and Awe

Rating	Description
4 **EXPERT:** **Unconsciously Competent**	Is actively aware of his or her surroundings and takes great care in protecting and conserving them; is very observant and derives pleasure from thinking and seeking answers to questions that stem from observations; has compassion and empathy for other life forms; is enraptured with awesome phenomena, intriguing situations, and jaw-dropping experiments.
3 **PRACTITIONER:** **Consciously Competent**	Is aware of his or her surroundings and understands the need to protect the environment; is developing an enthusiasm and passion about the physical world and will seek answers to inquiries with increasing independence; has respect and awe for other life forms.
2 **APPRENTICE:** **Consciously Incompetent**	Is making more detailed observations; has a developing curiosity and is asking questions about the immediate environment; is developing respect and empathy for other life forms.
1 **NOVICE:** **Unconsciously Incompetent**	Has no desire to learn about the world; does not search for knowledge; has limited observation skills and no eye for detail.

Name _____ Class _____ Date _____

Rubric for Taking Responsible Risks

Rating	Description
4 **EXPERT:** **Unconsciously** **Competent**	Always draws on past knowledge; applies considerable thought to consequences; has a well-trained sense of what is appropriate; knows the difference between taking a risk and taking a responsible risk; does not fear failure and will go beyond established limits to tackle challenging tasks, even when success is uncertain.
3 **PRACTITIONER:** **Consciously** **Competent**	Draws on past knowledge and thinks flexibly when considering risk factors; educates himself or herself about risks and curbs impulsiveness; accepts setbacks, confusion, and uncertainty as a natural part of a process that leads to a final outcome.
2 **APPRENTICE:** **Consciously** **Incompetent**	Begins to attempt some responsible risks but only if the correct outcome is within easy reach; is trapped by fear and mistrust; is reluctant to accept the challenge of a process in order to find an answer.
1 **NOVICE:** **Unconsciously** **Incompetent**	Will not take risks because the fear of failure is far greater than the desire for venture or adventure; will not play games, attempt new learning, or make new friendships because of a fear of losing, being wrong, or looking stupid.

Name _____ Class _____ Date _____

Rubric for Finding Humor

Rating	Description
4 **EXPERT:** **Unconsciously Competent**	Can see the humorous side of things and create a positive or productive outlook no matter how devastating a situation; is very quick-witted and uses humor to raise the spirits of self and others; is competent at generating funny stories, metaphors, and puns; is quick to laugh at herself or himself and with others.
3 **PRACTITIONER:** **Consciously Competent**	Knows the difference between clowning around and using humor to increase productivity; is able to diffuse situations by adding appropriate humor; tends to use humor; appreciates and understands the humor of others; laughs often at himself or herself and with others; doesn't use humor at inappropriate times.
2 **APPRENTICE:** **Consciously Incompetent**	Is beginning to find humor in some situations; is beginning to move away from offensive humor; is starting to not take himself or herself too seriously; is beginning to appreciate the humor of others without becoming defensive or offended; is learning to distinguish between appropriate and inappropriate humor.
1 **NOVICE:** **Unconsciously Incompetent**	Cannot laugh at self; distorts humor in cases of human differences, ineptitude, injurious behavior, vulgarity, violence, and profanity; uses humor at inappropriate times.

Name _____ Class _____ Date _____

Rubric for Thinking Interdependently

Rating	Description
4 **EXPERT:** **Unconsciously Competent**	Is always empathetic to others in the group; always devotes energy to enhancing group resourcefulness; is always working for the common cause, putting aside independence and ego for the betterment of the group; is all about "we" and "us," not "I" or "me"; is always a team player; focuses on analysis, synthesis, and the evaluation of tasks at hand.
3 **PRACTITIONER:** **Consciously Competent**	Is empathetic to others in the group; is an active participant and works for the common cause of the group; is increasingly more interdependent and sensitive to the needs of others.
2 **APPRENTICE:** **Consciously Incompetent**	Is beginning to contribute to the group; prefers to let others do most of the work; rarely contributes to discussions or participates in active tasks; will opt for working alone if group dynamics become difficult.
1 **NOVICE:** **Unconsciously Incompetent**	Lacks social skills; feels isolated and prefers solitude; says things like "Leave me alone; I'll do it myself," "They don't like me," or "I want to be alone."

Name _____ Class _____ Date _____

Rubric for Learning Continuously

Rating	Description
4 **EXPERT:** **Unconsciously Competent**	Is always open to continuous learning; is always inquisitive about the world and constantly searching for new and better methods and ideas; is always striving for improvement and is prepared to modify and change thinking when new evidence is substantiated; shows humility, commitment, and awe in learning.
3 **PRACTITIONER:** **Consciously Competent**	Is open to continuous learning; has a questioning mind and is eager and inquisitive to learn about the world; strives for improvement and is prepared to modify learning most of the time; is committed; finds opportunities to be amazed; is developing humility in learning.
2 **APPRENTICE:** **Consciously Incompetent**	Is developing an interest in the world; shows some continuous learning in areas of interest but is inclined to give up on expanding ideas if new information isn't readily available.
1 **NOVICE:** **Unconsciously Incompetent**	Does not like learning; shows no interest in independent learning; cannot correctly recall information; lacks questioning, researching, and curiosity skills.

References

Budd Rowe, M. (1986). Wait time: Slowing down may be a way of speeding up! *Journal of Teacher Education, 37,* 43–50.

Costa, A. (2007). *The school as a home for the mind: Creating mindful curriculum, instruction, and dialogue.* Thousand Oaks, CA: Corwin.

Costa, A., & Kallick, B. (Eds.). (2000). *Discovering and exploring habits of mind.* Alexandria, VA: Association for Supervision and Curriculum Development.

Costa, A., & Kallick, B. (Eds.). (2000). *Activating and engaging habits of mind.* Alexandria, VA: Association for Supervision and Curriculum Development.

Costa, A., & Kallick, B. (Eds.). (2000). *Assessing and reporting on habits of mind.* Alexandria, VA: Association for Supervision and Curriculum Development.

Costa, A., & Kallick, B. (Eds.). (2000). *Integrating and sustaining habits of mind.* Alexandria, VA: Association for Supervision and Curriculum Development.

Costa, A., & Kallick, B. (Eds.) (2008). *Learning and leading with habits of mind.* Alexandria, VA: Association for Supervision and Curriculum Development.

Costa, A., & Kallick, B. (Eds.). (2009). *Habits of mind across the curriculum.* Alexandria, VA: Association for Supervision and Curriculum Development.

de Bono, E. (1999). *Six thinking hats.* Boston: Back Bay Books.

Swartz, R., Costa, A., Beyer, B., Regan, R., & Kallick, B. (2007). *Thinking-based learning: Activating students' potential.* Norwood, MA: Christopher-Gordon.

Thiele, B., & Weiss, G. What a wonderful world [Recorded by Louis Armstrong, 1967, for ABC Records, New York].

Additional Resources

SUGGESTED CHILDREN'S LITERATURE FOR TEACHING HABITS OF MIND

Dahl, R. (1988). *James and the giant peach*. New York: Puffin-Scholastic.

Dahl, R (1975*). Danny the champion of the world*. New York: Penguin Books.

Eastman, P. D. (1960). *Are you my mother?* New York: Random House.

Frank, A. (1953). *The diary of a young girl*. New York: Simon & Schuster.

Galdon, P. (1985). *The little red hen*. New York: Houghton Mifflin.

Geisel, T. (Dr. Seuss). (1940). *Horton hatches the egg*. New York: Random House.

Kuo, L., & Kuo, Y. H. (1976). *Chinese folk tales*. Berkeley, CA: Celestial Arts.

Mahy, M. (1996). *The man whose mother was a pirate*. London: Puffin Books.

Mayer, M. (1992*). There's a nightmare in my closet*. New York: Puffin Books.

McNaughton, C. (2002). *Don't step on the crack*. New York: Picture Lions.

Pfister, M. (1999). *Rainbow fish and the big blue whale*. New York: North-South Books.

Piper, W. (1990). *The little engine that could*. New York: Grosset & Dunlap.

Rey, H. A. (2001). *The complete adventures* of *Curious George*. New York: Houghton Mifflin.

Rowling, J. K.(1998). *Harry Potter and the sorcerer's stone*. London: Scholastic Press.

Taylor, W. (2000). *Crash! The story of Poddy*. New York: Scholastic.

White, E. B. (1952). *Charlotte's web*. New York: Harper Collins.

About the Authors

Karen Boyes is described as Australasia's "Mrs. Education." An expert in effective teaching, learning, and living, she turns research into practical and simple-to-use techniques that create success. She is the founder of Spectrum Education, the New Zealand regional director of the Habits of Mind Institute, and New Zealand's 2001 Business Woman of the Year.

Boyes is the author of *Creating an Effective Learning Environment*, *Study Smart*, *Successful Woman*, and numerous DVDs. Her dynamic presentations provide information that participants can easily integrate. Thousands of teachers have gained renewed energy from her workshops and lectures around the world. In short, she not only educates but also inspires and motivates.

Graham Watts is one of the United Kingdom's leading experts in thinking skills. His knowledge has grown from developing thinking and learning programs in a diverse range of schools around the globe, making his lesson activities tried and tested. His appeal to teachers is his blending of theory with practical ideas that can be used in classrooms.

Watts has published teacher resources in the United Kingdom and the United States and works with teachers around the world in developing skillful thinkers and mindful schools. In addition to speaking at international conferences, he leads professional development days at schools across the United Kingdom and beyond. Recently named a regional director for the Institute for the Habits of Mind, Watts is leading Costa and Kallick's work across many British schools.